D1045559

"In place of today's fascination with wha̶t̶ ̶̶defined by sentimental anecdotes or near-d̶e̶a̶t̶h̶ ̶p̶e̶r̶s̶o̶n̶a̶l̶ ̶t̶e̶s̶t̶i̶m̶o̶-nials, Dan Barber and Robert Peterson have presented a highly readable yet thoroughly biblical exposition of the Christ-purchased and -promised eternal hope for every believer. In so doing, they also address the implications for the believer in the present state, and then outline the intermediate and final state, as described in Scripture. I highly commend this book, while even now planning to use it in my own ministry."

> —**Harry L. Reeder, III**, Senior Pastor, Briarwood Presby-
> terian Church, Birmingham, Alabama

"One of the remedies for a cynical and self-gratification culture is to have a hopeful and glorious view of eternal life with God. Robert and Dan help us to gain a view of heaven that is both hopeful and biblical. Heaven is about God. Read this book about heaven and you will learn more about the God who loves you and wants you to be with him forever."

> —**Darrin Patrick**, Lead Pastor, The Journey (an Acts 29
> church), St. Louis

"What makes this book so appealing and powerful is that it is grounded in a biblical view of heaven and the afterlife, rather than the personal speculations of those who claim to have gone there. The apostle Peter exhorts us to set our hope 'fully on the grace that will be brought' to us 'at the revelation of Jesus Christ' (1 Peter 1:13). This book will enable you to do precisely that. I highly recommend it."

> —**Sam Storms**, Senior Pastor, Bridgeway Church, Okla-
> homa City

"Dan Barber and Robert Peterson's *Life Everlasting* is clear, timely, and important. It is biblical, too, both in content and in structure, as it refrains from speculation and highlights the Bible's own key themes of heaven."

> —**Christopher Morgan**, Professor of Theology and Dean
> of the School of Christian Ministries, California Baptist
> University, Riverside

"What a delight to read Dan Barber and Robert Peterson's wonderful book, *Life Everlasting*! In a day and age when discussion of heaven is either purely speculative or mere sentimentality, this book carefully unfolds the biblical teaching on heaven in all its depth, breadth, and wonder. Following the Bible's own story line, and unfolding the story of heaven across the canon of Scripture, Barber and Peterson develop five beautiful pictures of our final state and what believers may look forward to in regard to life everlasting. Unpacking the Bible's own teaching on what heaven is—namely, the Christian dwelling in the glorious presence of our triune God in a new creation, enjoying our eternal Sabbath rest, ruling and reigning with Christ as subjects of God's kingdom, and enjoying the incredible presence of our holy, covenant God—this book leaves the reader with a breathtaking vision of our consummated state. Biblically faithful, theologically rich, and practically written for the church, this book is must reading if you want to think correctly about heaven. In addition, it will not only encourage you to greater love and adoration of our great Creator and Redeemer God, but also stir you anew to cry with the church in all ages, 'So come, Lord Jesus.'"

—**Stephen J. Wellum**, Professor of Christian Theology, The Southern Baptist Theological Seminary; Editor, *The Southern Baptist Journal of Theology*

"Sooner or later every theologian, pastor, and parent gets the question: Will my dog be in heaven? There is likely no subject more inquired about than that of heaven. And there's no shortage of answers and perspectives. Amid all the fog of careless speculation, we need a sure guide. This is the book. Peterson and Barber offer us a biblically grounded and hope-filled tour through the Bible's teaching on heaven. Skip the books on the forty-two seconds spent in heaven and the light at the end of the tunnel. This is the book you need."

—**Stephen J. Nichols**, Research Professor of Christianity and Culture, Lancaster Bible College, Lancaster, Pennsylvania

"Christians speak of going to heaven and of the blessings of heaven, but often have a very vague understanding of what the

Bible says about heaven and the final consummation of God's plan of salvation. Dan Barber and Robert Peterson's *Life Everlasting*, with clear and careful exegesis, presents what the Bible says about heaven. This is a valuable work for helping the believer to understand the future blessings that God has prepared for his people."

    —Van Lees, Pastor, Covenant of Grace Church, St. Charles, Missouri

Life Everlasting

Explorations in Biblical Theology

Anointed with the Spirit and Power: The Holy Spirit's Empowering Presence

The Elder: Today's Ministry Rooted in All of Scripture

Election and Free Will: God's Gracious Choice and Our Responsibility

Life Everlasting: The Unfolding Story of Heaven

The Nearness of God: His Presence with His People

Our Secure Salvation: Preservation and Apostasy

A Theology of James: Wisdom for God's People

A Theology of Mark: The Dynamic between Christology and Authentic Discipleship

Wisdom Christology: How Jesus Becomes God's Wisdom for Us

Robert A. Peterson, series editor

Life Everlasting

The Unfolding Story of Heaven

Dan C. Barber and
Robert A. Peterson

P&R PUBLISHING

P.O. BOX 817 • PHILLIPSBURG • NEW JERSEY 08865-0817

ISBN: 978-1-59638-165-0 (pbk)
ISBN: 978-1-59638-565-8 (ePub)
ISBN: 978-1-59638-566-5 (Mobi)

Compass image © istockphoto.com

Printed in the United States of America

Library of Congress Cataloging-in-Publication Data

Barber, Dan C., 1976-
  Life everlasting : the unfolding story of heaven / Dan C. Barber and Robert A. Peterson.
      p. cm. -- (Explorations in biblical theology)
  Includes bibliographical references and indexes.
  ISBN 978-1-59638-165-0 (pbk.)
 1. Heaven--Christianity. 2. Paradise--Christianity. 3. Future life--Christianity. 4. Creation--Biblical teaching. I. Peterson, Robert A., 1948- II. Title.
  BT846.3.B37 2012
  236'.24--dc23
                                        2012006209

We dedicate this volume to our precious wives:
April Barber and Mary Pat Peterson,
for their love, prayers, and unwavering support.

Contents

Series Introduction   ix

Acknowledgments   xi

Introduction   1

Part 1: Creation
1. Creation Marred   17
2. Creation Renewed   33

Part 2: Rest
3. Disturbed Rest   53
4. Perfect Rest   69

Part 3: Kingdom
5. The Kingdom at War   85
6. The Kingdom at Peace   103

Part 4: Presence
7. Banished from God's Presence   123
8. Blessed with God's Presence   137

Part 5: Glory
9. Exchange of Glory   157
10. Brilliance in Glory   169

CONTENTS

Conclusion   185

Frequently Asked Questions about Heaven   197

Questions for Study and Reflection   213

Select Resources on Heaven   219

Index of Scripture and Other Writings   221

Index of Subjects and Names   235

Series Introduction

BELIEVERS TODAY need high-quality literature that attracts them to good theology and builds them up in their faith. Currently, readers may find several sets of lengthy—and rather technical—books on Reformed theology, as well as some that are helpful and semipopular. Explorations in Biblical Theology takes a more midrange approach, seeking to offer readers the substantial content of the more lengthy books, on the one hand, while striving for the readability of the semipopular books, on the other.

The series includes two types of books: (1) some treating biblical themes and (2) others treating the theology of specific biblical books. The volumes dealing with biblical themes seek to cover the whole range of Christian theology, from the doctrine of God to last things. Representative early offerings in the series focus on the empowering of the Holy Spirit, justification, the presence of God, and preservation and apostasy. Examples of works dealing with the theology of specific biblical books include volumes on the theology of the Psalms and Isaiah in the Old Testament, and books on the theology of Mark and James in the New Testament.

Explorations in Biblical Theology is written for college seniors, seminarians, pastors, and thoughtful lay readers. These volumes are intended to be accessible and not obscured by excessive references to Hebrew, Greek, or theological jargon.

Each book seeks to be solidly Reformed in orientation, because the writers love the Reformed faith. The various theological themes and biblical books are treated from the perspective of biblical theology. Writers either trace doctrines through the Bible or open up the theology of the specific book they treat.

Writers desire not merely to dispense the Bible's good information, but also to apply that information to real needs today.

Explorations in Biblical Theology is committed to being warm and winsome, with a focus on applying God's truth to life. Authors aim to treat those with whom they disagree as they themselves would want to be treated. The motives for the rejection of error are not to fight, hurt, or wound, but to protect, help, and heal. The authors of this series are godly, capable scholars with a commitment to Reformed theology and a burden to minister that theology clearly to God's people.

Robert A. Peterson
Series Editor

Acknowledgments

WE HAVE MANY PEOPLE to thank for their help in the writing of this book.

- Bryce Craig, Marvin Padgett, and Ian Thompson of P&R Publishing, for believing in us.
- Friends who read the manuscript and shared comments: April Barber, Dan Herron, Van and Kathi Lees, Jake and Casi Neufeld, Catherine Noah, Mary Pat Peterson, and Pat Reynolds.
- Covenant Seminary's librarians, James Pakala and Steve Jamieson, for kind and expert help.
- Dr. Chris Morgan, for offering wise theological counsel. Dr. Jack Collins, for answering many questions.
- Bill White, Ben Porter, and Stephen Estock, for ongoing encouragement to Dan to write and providing many opportunities for him to teach on heaven.
- Karen Magnuson and Robert's TA, Elliott Pinegar, for carefully editing the entire manuscript.
- John J. Hughes, for serving as project manager.
- Rick Matt, for editing the Select Resources on Heaven.

Introduction

IT IS MY (DAN'S) FIRST MEMORY. My eyes fixed on her, watching her in her stillness. I was three years old but knew that something was very wrong with my four-day-old sister. I did not know her name. I never said a word to her, played with her, teased her, or fought with her. But I wish deeply that I had. I only stared as my mind filled with thoughts that remain with me so many years later. Who is she? What would she have been like? Maybe she would have been a gymnast, or an engineer. Would I have been good friends with her, would she have married a good man, with whom I would have become good friends? And would our daughters have played together, as cousins should? The thoughts bring tears again. I miss her so.

I was not able to articulate these thoughts then, of course. It would take years of soul-searching, much prayer and counsel to understand what I was feeling and thinking. Many new experiences brought back my pain and search for hope. At the age of eight I found myself with a similar image, looking at my grandmother lying still, knowing that something was very wrong about what I was seeing.

I (Robert) was confronted with death's stark reality in my first year of graduate-school teaching in St. Louis. A student and his wife asked me to perform the funeral for their two-year-old son, who had been born with many physical challenges. His death was no surprise, but it still shook us all. Jesus' words "I am the resurrection and the life" comforted us, but nothing immediately erased the pain of seeing that tiny body in a casket. Plainly, that was not the way the good Creator had designed the world. In Eden there was no death, no funerals, and no mourning. And those things will have no place in the new heavens and new earth. But in the meantime, ever since the fall of our first parents, we all struggle with pain, disappointment, failure, and death.

This book is about heaven—final salvation. It is a book about our looking forward to our resurrection and joyous participation in the new heavens and new earth. But before we explore those bright prospects, we need to answer an important question: Why do we need another book about heaven? We have four answers:

- People Seek Information about Heaven in the Wrong Places
- Writers Speculate about the End Times and Heaven
- The Bible's Teaching on Heaven Helps Us Now
- The Bible's Story about Heaven Offers Hope for the Future

People Seek Information about Heaven in the Wrong Places

The more we teach about heaven, the more we realize that people often get their conceptions of heaven from sources other than Scripture, such as Barbara Walters' television special *Heaven: Where Is It? How Do We Get There?*[1] Even though many have never seen these productions, their concepts become ingrained in popular culture:

- The better you live on earth, the higher "heaven" you will ascend to.
- The best people will live free from their bodily constraints among the stars.
- The primary activities of souls in heaven will be to sing to God and warn people on earth.

There are many other sources of misinformation. One such source is people who claim to have firsthand knowledge of heaven.

1. *Heaven: Where Is It? How Do We Get There?* DVD, directed by George Paul (Orland Park, IL: Mpi Home Video, 2006), information available at http://www.mpihomevideo.com/heaven_where_is_it_how_do_we_get_there/.

Online bookseller Amazon.com on July 14, 2011, revealed at least thirty-five books telling of such firsthand knowledge. The qualifications of the writers fall into various categories.

Some people claim to have received revelatory dreams of heaven, such as Rebecca Ruter Springer in *My Dream of Heaven*. Others say that they have had visions of heaven that they wish to share. These include Patti Miller Dunham in *I Saw Heaven* and Marietta Davis in *Nine Days in Heaven*, by Dennis Prince.

Many claim to have gone to heaven and come back to tell their stories, whether through near-death experiences or returning after actual death. Included among near-death experiences is the case of David Taylor. Although he claims to have taken many trips to heaven and hell, his book *Heaven: My Trip to Heaven, Face to Face with Jesus* tells of a special trip. Taylor claims that while he was asleep in 2000, Jesus came into his room and took his soul out of his body on a glorious trip to the third heaven, where he saw Jesus face-to-face and was given special messages for the world by the spirits of deceased pastors.

One woman claims to have spent more than a month in heaven in *40 Days in Heaven: The True Testimony of Seneca Sodi's Visitation to Paradise, the Holy City and the Glory of God's Throne*, by Elwood Scott. She says that while in heaven she discussed theology with Abraham, Moses, Isaiah, Daniel, and the apostle Paul.

Some claim to have actually died and to have returned to their bodies. Most famous is Pastor Don Piper's story—*90 Minutes in Heaven: A True Story of Death and Life*, which has sold 4 million copies. Another best seller is the story of four-year-old Colton Burpo's journey, recounted by his father, Todd, in *Heaven Is for Real: A Little Boy's Astounding Story of His Trip to Heaven and Back*.

Others are not as famous but are just as sure that they died and came back to life to share their experiences. Dannion Brinkley, in *Saved by the Light: The True Story of a Man Who Died Twice and the Profound Revelations He Received*, says that he was revived after dying on two occasions when struck by lightning. Brinkley claims to have been given 117 revelations of future events by thirteen angelic teachers.

We have read only a few of these books. We do not intend to read them all because they are seeking information about God and heaven in the wrong places. We do not question the sincerity of some of the writers of these books. And we do not claim the ability to evaluate accurately what happened in every case. But we are sure of this: the Word of God is our only reliable source of information about God and the afterlife.

Among the truths taught by the Reformers of the sixteenth century was *sola Scriptura* ("Scripture alone"). This does not mean that we reject all other sources of truth; we all appeal at times to experience, reason, and tradition. But *sola Scriptura* means that the Bible trumps all other sources. Scripture sits in judgment on every other authority in matters of what we believe and how we live.

It is obvious that the thirty-five books about heaven referred to above do not practice *sola Scriptura*. Almost all of them do not regard the Bible as the supreme court that rules over all other religious authorities. Instead, they too easily regard their experiences as the source of ultimate truth. This is especially disappointing in the case of Don Piper's *90 Minutes in Heaven*.[2] Mr. Piper is a Baptist minister and a sincere Christian. We do not doubt that he had an amazing experience. But we are sad that he (unintentionally?) puts his experience above Scripture:

> Now I can speak authoritatively about heaven from firsthand knowledge.[3]

> Without the slightest doubt, I know that heaven *is* real. It's more real than anything I've ever experienced in my life.[4]

We have never had a dream or vision of heaven, we have not journeyed there, and Jesus has not appeared to us. But, forgiven sinners that we are, we will speak authoritatively about heaven

---

2. Don Piper, *90 Minutes in Heaven: A True Story of Death and Life*, with Cecil Murphy (Grand Rapids: Revell, 2004).

3. Ibid., 129.

4. Ibid., 194 (italics in original).

in this book. As surely as Holy Scripture is the Word of God, it alone gives us reliable information on heaven (and all other matters spiritual). Furthermore, without a doubt, we know that heaven is real. Why? Because the Bible clearly and abundantly tells us so.

In fact, Jesus' words in the parable of the rich man and Lazarus are especially needed in light of these books' claims. The rich man, suffering in hell, cries out to father Abraham to send someone back from the dead to warn the rich man's five unrepentant brothers (Luke 16:27–28). Abraham, speaking for God, tells the rich man that his brothers should listen to "Moses and the Prophets" (v. 29). The rich man protests, "No, father Abraham, but if someone goes to them from the dead, they will repent" (v. 30). Jesus' last words in the parable ring in his hearers' ears and in ours: "If they do not hear Moses and the Prophets, neither will they be convinced if someone should rise from the dead" (v. 31). Our Lord and Savior's words should give pause to those who put greater stock in their experiences than in Scripture.

Writers Speculate about the End Times and Heaven

Repeatedly, teachers have made confident predictions of the date of Christ's return, the end of the world, and the coming of God's eternal kingdom. Although each prediction has proved false, this often does not deter the "prophets" from making additional sure predictions. Here are four examples.

1843–44: William Miller

William Miller, a converted deist, concluded from his study of the Bible that the second advent of Christ would occur between March 21, 1843, and March 21, 1844. He became a leader of what would become known as *Adventism*. Many people (estimates range from fifty thousand to a hundred thousand) accepted Miller's calculations and anticipated the coming of Christ. When Miller's prophecy failed, his follow-ers set a second date: October 22, 1844. When that date, too, passed without the coming of the great Day of Atonement, it became known instead as "the Great Disappointment" and led many to abandon the Christian faith.[5]

1874, 1925, and 1975: Jehovah's Witnesses

The Watchtower Society, the so-called Jehovah's Witnesses, claims to be God's only true prophet on earth today. According to the official *Watchtower* magazine, the prophet whom Jehovah promised to raise up in Deuteronomy 18:15–22 is "not an indi-vidual" but an organization. In fact, the Watchtower Society is God's "prophetlike organization."[6]

"However," as Ron Rhodes explains, "the Watchtower Soci-ety now admits that it was wrong in its prediction for 1874 (the second coming of Christ), 1925 (the coming of select Old Testament saints to earth), 1975 (the end of human history), and other times."[7]

The irony is that the very biblical passage that the Watchtower Society cites in claiming to be God's only true prophet today condemns the Watchtower Society:

> And if you say in your heart, "How may we know the word that the LORD has not spoken?"—when a prophet speaks in the name of the LORD, if the word does not come to pass or come true, that is a word that the LORD has not spoken; the prophet has spoken it presumptuously. (Deut. 18:21–22)

5. Craig D. Atwood, Frank S. Mead, and Samuel S. Hill, *Handbook of Denominations in the United States*, 13th ed. (Nashville: Abingdon Press, 2010), 231.

6. Ron Rhodes, *Reasoning from the Scriptures with the Jehovah's Witnesses* (Eugene, OR: Harvest House, 1993), 339. The claim was made in *Watchtower* (October 1, 1982): 27; *Watchtower* (October 1, 1964): 601.

7. Rhodes, *Reasoning from the Scriptures*, 340. Rhodes details these three Watchtower Society predictions on pages 343–51. The Watchtower Society accepts "responsibility for some of the disappointment a number felt concerning 1975" in *1980 Yearbook of Jehovah's Witnesses* (Brooklyn: Watchtower Bible and Tract Society, 1980), 30–31. For more concerning Jehovah's Witnesses' false predictions of Christ's return, see Robert M. Bowman Jr., *Jehovah's Witnesses*, Zondervan Guide to Cults and Religious Movements (Grand Rapids: Zondervan, 1995), 60–67.

September 11–13, 1988: Edward C. Whisenant

Edward Whisenant, a former NASA engineer and Bible student, penned *88 Reasons Why the Rapture Is in 1988*, claiming that the event would occur sometime from September 11 to 13. Ministers across America were sent three hundred thousand free copies, and bookstores sold another 4.5 million. Many individual Christians and even whole churches were caught up in the frenzy. As the days approached, the Trinity Broadcasting Network interrupted regular programming to give instructions on preparing for the rapture.[8] When the prophecy failed, Whisenant recalculated and wrote *89 Reasons Why the Rapture Is in 1989*. But this book did not sell nearly as well as its predecessor.

May 21 and October 21, 2011: Harold Camping

Harold Camping's third and fourth predictions of the end of the world and of the inauguration of the new creation failed in 2011. Though it was obvious that his teaching was misguided, that did not stop Camping. Instead, he reinterpreted May 21 as a spiritual return, a great judgment so that salvation would no longer be possible. When that prediction failed, he then predicted that the last day would occur on October 21, 2011, when the whole world would be judged and this age would come to an end. Again the prediction came to naught. Thus, Camping has twice more been shown to be a false prophet. But we would not be surprised if he checks his figures and tries a fifth time.

We Will Not Speculate

We refuse to set dates for the second coming and subsequent events because Scripture clearly prohibits us from doing so (Matt. 24:36–44; 25:13; Acts 1:7). And these prohibitions point to another reason why another book on heaven is needed—because there are so many harmful voices shouting out, vying for people's assent to their views. *We need to recover a biblical perspective on heaven.*

---

8. Wikipedia, http://en.wikipedia.org/wiki/Edgar_C._Whisenant.

And that involves heeding the important distinction made in Deuteronomy 29:29: "The secret things belong to the LORD our God, but the things that are revealed belong to us and to our children forever." There are things revealed to us about heaven, and these are appropriate to discuss, and there are things that are not revealed about heaven, and these are not worthy of discussion.

We are confident, in the words of the apostle Peter, that God has told us in Scripture everything necessary for "life and godliness" (2 Peter 1:3). He has not told us everything there is to know about heaven, nor is he in the business of revealing to individuals today previously unknown things about heaven. His written revelation is complete, and everything we need to know about heaven is made known in two critical areas. First, God has told us all we need to know in order to go to heaven. Second, God has told us all we need to know to live a God-honoring life in the meantime.

The Bible's Teaching on Heaven Helps Us Now

Our first two reasons for writing this book are admittedly negative—to stop people from looking for information about heaven in the wrong places and to discourage speculation. Now we share two positive reasons to read the book. Both of them deal with encouragements to be found in the Bible's story about heaven. God tells us about heaven to affect us deeply now and to increase our joy and anticipation of Christ's future return.

We have all heard the common criticism that some Christians are too heavenly minded to be of much earthly good. We beg to differ. We do not know a single person who fits that description. Indeed, most of us are far too earthly minded to be of much heavenly good! One reason to study God's message about heaven is that he wants to use that message to change our lives for good now. Do you honestly know of anyone who fits Izaak Walton's description of his contemporary Richard Sibbes?

Of that blessed man,
Let this just praise be given:

That heaven was in him
Before he was in heaven.[9]

Consider: Why did God tell us about our final salvation ahead of time? He wants to whet our appetites for heaven now, even in the midst of struggles: "For I consider that the sufferings of this present time are not worth comparing with the glory that is to be revealed to us" (Rom. 8:18). He desires that our hope of heaven transform our present earthly existence. For this reason Scripture exhorts us in the midst of this life to lift up our eyes to the next one: "If then you have been raised with Christ, seek the things that are above, where Christ is, seated at the right hand of God. Set your minds on things that are above, not on things that are on earth" (Col. 3:1–2).

Too often, however, our vision rises no higher than the things of this earth. Sadly, we sometimes spiritually resemble the pathetic figure described by John Stott in one of his famous Inter-Varsity Mission Convention messages at Urbana, Illinois, in 1976:

> Lift up your eyes! You are certainly a creature of time, but you are also a child of eternity. You are a citizen of heaven, and an alien and exile on earth, a pilgrim travelling to the celestial city. I read some years ago of a young man who found a five-dollar bill on the street and who "from that time on never lifted his eyes when walking. In the course of years he accumulated 29,516 buttons, 54,172 pins, 12 cents, a bent back and a miserly disposition." But think what he lost. He couldn't see the radiance of the sunlight, and sheen of the stars, the smile on the face of his friends, or the blossoms of springtime, for his eyes were in the gutter. There are too many Christians like that. We have important duties on earth, but we must never allow them to preoccupy us in such a way that we forget who we are or where we are going.[10]

9. Quoted in K. Scott Oliphint and Sinclair B. Ferguson, *If I Should Die before I Wake: Help for Those Who Hope for Heaven* (Grand Rapids: Baker, 1995), 99.

10. Quoted in Alister E. McGrath, *A Brief History of Heaven* (Malden, MA: Blackwell Publishing, 2003), 174–75.

We want to take Stott's wise words to heart and pray that this book would both inform and transform.

The Bible's Story about Heaven Offers Hope for the Future

Scripture Speaks about Heaven in Three Ways

One of the difficulties in discussing heaven is the word *heaven* itself. The Bible speaks about heaven in three different ways.

The Sky. "In the beginning, God created the heavens and the earth" (Gen. 1:1). Genesis then enlarges on these two spheres, the *heavens* in verses 6–8 and the *earth* in verses 9–10. Moses writes, "And God made the expanse and separated the waters that were under the expanse from the waters that were above the expanse. And it was so. And God called the expanse Heaven" (1:7–8). That is, God called the sky, in which is set the "waters above" (clouds that produce rain), *heaven.*

The Abode of the Stars. But biblical authors also call the abode of the stars—what we would call outer space—*heaven.* When God declares his covenant promise to Abraham for the third time, he says, "I will surely bless you, and I will surely multiply your offspring as the *stars of heaven* and as the sand that is on the seashore" (Gen. 22:17). Both of these meanings of the word *heaven*—the sky and the abode of the stars—are phenomenological expressions. They express phenomena as human beings perceive them. We are familiar with this. Does the sun really set or rise? No, we use *sunset* and *sunrise* to refer to the phenomena resulting from the earth's rotation on its axis as it appears to us. The majority of the references to *heaven* in the Bible relate to the sky or the stars. Note that they both refer to the space above the earth on which humankind dwells.

The Unseen Spiritual Realm Where God Dwells. But there is a third meaning, the one that we typically associate with the word *heaven* today—the unseen spiritual realm where God dwells. Paul explains, "For by him all things were created, in heaven and on earth, visible and invisible, whether thrones or dominions or rulers or authorities—all things were created through him and for him" (Col. 1:16). Notice that Paul contrasts "in heaven" with "on earth" and contrasts "visible" with "invisible." The things on earth are visible; the things in heaven are invisible. Paul here gives us the key characteristic of this third meaning of *heaven* as the dwelling place of God. It is the invisible realm. It is not located above or below or in any other direction in the sense that you can travel to it. So when Paul says in 2 Corinthians 12:2 that he was "caught up to the third heaven," he does not mean that he was floating in the sky but that he had a personal encounter with the invisible dwelling place of God.

Scripture tells us about this third sense of *heaven* to increase our hope for the future. I (Robert) remember God's gracious dealings with Sammy. He lived in a nursing home near Hope Presbyterian Church in Collinsville, Illinois, where I served as interim pastor. Some of my students ministered in the church and on numerous occasions shared the gospel with Sammy. He confided in the students that he did not trust Christ for salvation. Then one Sunday morning when it came time for praise and prayer, Sammy rose to speak. Every eye was trained on him, for this was unusual. He shared publicly that he had come to believe in Jesus because of the love and witness of the students. I will not soon forget his next words: "I know now where I am going, and if I die next week, I know I will be in heaven." Well, he did die the next week, and a spirit of awe and of gratefulness to God for his amazing grace fell upon the congregation. Sammy had wasted most of his life, but for a week he enjoyed a living hope in salvation (1 Peter 1:3). Do we?

Scripture Distinguishes between the Present, Intermediate, and Final States

Another question that sometimes perplexes people is *when* is heaven? Is it now, when we die, or when Christ returns? The Bible's answer is yes; it is all three.

The Present State. We refer to life in the body now as the present state to distinguish it from the intermediate state, which consists of life after death and before the resurrection of the dead, and from the final state, which refers to life after the resurrection. Is there a sense in which heaven as the presence of God refers to the present state? The answer is yes, as long as we acknowledge that heaven is not only present, but also future. John contrasts the present states of the saved and lost: "Whoever believes in him [the Son of God] is not condemned, but whoever does not believe is condemned already, because he has not believed in the name of the only Son of God" (John 3:18). Later in the same chapter, John makes the same stark contrast: "Whoever believes in the Son has eternal life; whoever does not obey the Son shall not see life, but the wrath of God remains on him" (v. 36). Our purpose at present is not to speak of unbelievers' fate. It is rather to show that there is a sense that Christians enjoy heaven and eternal life—knowing the Father and the Son (17:3)—now.

The Intermediate State. When most people refer to heaven, they speak of the intermediate state—that which follows death and precedes resurrection. Jesus promises the repentant thief on the cross, "Truly, I say to you, today you will be with me in Paradise" (Luke 23:43). Paul wanted to remain alive to keep serving his beloved Philippians but admitted, "My desire is to depart and be with Christ, for that is far better" (Phil. 1:23). And in what might be the most familiar passage on the intermediate state, the apostle expresses his hope: "we would rather be away from the body and at home with the Lord" (2 Cor. 5:8). People are not mistaken when they say the Bible teaches that believers' spirits survive death and immediately enjoy Christ's presence in heaven. But they make a big mistake if they regard this as exhausting our Christian hope.

The Final State. It is not wrong to speak of heaven in regard to the present and intermediate states. But neither of these is the greatest hope of believers. That distinction belongs to the final state. The final state involves our resurrection from the dead and being equipped with bodies that are immortal, imperishable, powerful, glorious, and spiritual (ruled by the Holy Spirit) (1 Cor. 15:42–49, 51–56; Phil. 3:20–21). It involves God's renewal of heaven and earth (Isa. 65:17; 66:22–23; Rom. 8:18–23; 2 Peter 3:7, 10–13; Rev. 21–22). This grand prospect is our chief hope according to the biblical story. So when we refer to *heaven* in this book, we speak of heaven in the final state. Though we do address a few questions regarding the intermediate state (see Frequently Asked Questions about Heaven near the end of this book), we will not focus on it. Rather, our focus will be on the resurrection, as was Paul's when he wrote to encourage the Thessalonians, "The dead in Christ will rise first. Then we who are alive . . . will be caught up together with them in the clouds to meet the Lord in the air, and so we will always be with the Lord" (1 Thess. 4:16–17).

A Road Map to This Book

We will treat five major biblical pictures or themes that portray heaven's final state. Why did we choose these themes from among the many in Scripture? Because we find them compelling and encompassing of some of the others. We will trace each picture from Genesis to Revelation and will devote ten chapters to this task. We will allot two chapters apiece to each of the pictures: creation, rest, kingdom, presence, and glory. The first chapter devoted to each picture will describe it in terms of creation, fall, and redemption. And the following chapter will describe that same picture in terms of the restoration.

Part 1: Creation
1. Creation Marred
2. Creation Renewed

Part 2: Rest
3. Disturbed Rest
4. Perfect Rest

Part 3: Kingdom
5. The Kingdom at War
6. The Kingdom at Peace

Part 4: Presence
7. Banished from God's Presence
8. Blessed with God's Presence

Part 5: Glory
9. Exchange of Glory
10. Brilliance in Glory

The odd-numbered chapters will each contain three parts. Each odd-numbered chapter will begin with a discussion of *creation*: we will view that picture as original and undefiled. Second, we will explore how that picture was marred in the *fall* by the sin of Adam and Eve and ruined for us all in the process. Third, we will examine the process of *redemption* that began directly after the fall and that culminates in Christ's death and resurrection. These three stages in the odd-numbered chapters lay a foundation for us to examine heaven as *restoration* in the corresponding even-numbered chapters. These chapters will be devoted to studying the renewal of believers and of heaven and earth. Each even-numbered chapter will conclude with implications for life here on this present earth, since God intends his revelation concerning heaven to produce *transformation* in us: "So then let us not sleep [that is, live as though heaven were not a present and a future reality], as others do, but let us keep awake and be sober" (1 Thess. 5:6).

We have both been impacted by the Word of God's message about heaven and long for you to have the same experience. Listen to the apostle John's words:

> Beloved, we are God's children now, and what we will be has not yet appeared; but we know that when he appears we shall be like him, because we shall see him as he is. And everyone who thus hopes in him purifies himself as he is pure. (1 John 3:2–3)

Part 1

Creation

Creation Marred

IT WAS THE DAWN OF A NEW ERA. In 1961, Yuri Gagarin became the first man to orbit the earth in outer space. The globe was abuzz with space talk: interstellar travel, lodging, tourist flights, even space warfare. But what impacted Yuri the most? He was taken aback by the sheer beauty of the world. In a signed Russian document after his historic flight, he pleaded, "Orbiting earth in the spaceship, I saw how beautiful our planet is. People, let us preserve and increase this beauty, not destroy it!"[1]

What it must be like to see the planet from space! We have seen hundreds of pictures of the earth from space. But we have never seen it directly. The first civilian to do so was Russian Konstantin Petrovich Feoktistov, the first non-Communist cosmonaut to orbit the earth. Noting that an artist or poet would be better suited to offer a description, he nevertheless tried to describe the ineffable:

> From the height of four hundred kilometers our earth is really very beautiful. The air crown around the earth is wonderful. There is an amazing gamut of colors in the outer space landscape. Against the background of the dark, completely dark sky, the . . . constellations shine brightly, like diamonds. And the sun? If all the people on the earth could see it rise and set the way we did, how they would love the heavenly body! The sun

1. L. A. Lebedev, Boris Lyk´yanov, and A. Romanov, *Sons of the Blue Planet*, trans. Prema Pande, 3rd ed. (New Delhi: Amerind Publishing, 1981), 13.

would appear from behind the horizon very suddenly, at first as a bright reddish line. . . . It would grow in front of our eyes instantaneously. At first we saw a greatly stretched oval figure and then the sun became a huge, round disk and it would dazzle the eyes in such a way that it was impossible to look at it.[2]

Now imagine God's perspective. The universe is his good creation. He has created it in every color, shape, and size. The world, his creation, must appear very beautiful to him, its Maker. But the universe has been blighted by sin, the beautiful canvas smeared with all manner of evil. And this is why renewal is central to the biblical story. Renewed creation is anticipated from Genesis 3 onward. Something went very wrong, and it needs to be rectified for creation to be restored and humankind to live as God intends. The Bible tells the grand story of this new creation in four movements:

- Creation: Heaven and Earth Made
- Fall: Heaven and Earth Marred
- Redemption: Heaven and Earth Waiting
- Restoration: Heaven and Earth Repaired

We will examine the first three movements in this chapter and the restoration of heaven and earth in the next one.

Creation: Heaven and Earth Made

Debates today on Genesis 1–3 center on the historicity of Adam and Eve and the interpretation of the seven creation days.[3] But three thousand years ago, the Israelites in the wilderness of Sinai had different concerns. Egypt was a culture

2. L. A. Lebedev, Boris Lyk´yanov, and A. Romanov, *Sons of the Blue Planet*, trans. Prema Pande (New Delhi: Amerind Publishing, 1973), 85–86.

3. On the historicity of Adam and Eve, see C. John Collins, *Did Adam and Eve Really Exist? Who They Were and Why You Should Care* (Wheaton, IL: Crossway, 2011). For a synopsis of the creation-days debate, see Sandra L. Richter, *The Epic of Eden: A Christian Entry into the Old Testament* (Grand Rapids: InterVarsity Press, 2008), 92–103.

with a radically different worldview from Israel, including its many deities. And Israel had been enslaved there four hundred years (Gen. 15:13).

So when Yahweh brings Moses to the king of Egypt and delivers his people, the question arises: Who is this God whom Israel worships who just plundered the most powerful empire at the time? The first chapters of Genesis serve, in large part, to answer that question. And their answer is that the God of Israel, its Redeemer, is also the Creator of the world—everything and everyone in it.[4]

The World Is Created

Jay Leno has a well-known bit on his show called "Jaywalking," when he asks the public a series of simple questions that anyone should be able to answer. One segment asked people to complete famous phrases:

- "Ask not what your country can do for you but . . ." (John F. Kennedy)
- "One small step for man . . ." (Neil Armstrong)
- "In the beginning . . ." (the Bible)

Interestingly, most people could not finish the quotations, except for Genesis 1:1. That's how well known the Bible's claim that God created heaven and earth is today. But in Moses' day, such a claim was not so easily understood by the average Israelite. Remember that when Genesis was written, Israel was a wandering people. They were not yet a nation like Egypt and lacked their own land. In Genesis 1–11 God sets the record straight, beginning with creation.

The Redeemer Is the Creator. The Egyptians, like the ancient Greeks and many other cultures, believed in a pantheon of deities, each with its own realm. Anubis watched over the dead as they

---

4. Gordon J. Wenham, *Genesis 1–15*, Word Biblical Commentary (Waco, TX: Word, 1987), xlv.

were embalmed and delivered them up safely to Osiris, judge of the underworld. Osiris was married to Isis, goddess of motherhood and fertility. Ra (or Amun-Ra) was the sun god and co-creator of the universe along with Atum, Ptah, and others. Nut, depicted as a cow, was the goddess of the sky and the heavens and kept the stars in their course.

"In the beginning, God created the heavens and the earth" (Gen. 1:1). Against the backdrop of the Redeemer's delivering the Israelites from Egyptian bondage, these words are pregnant with meaning. When Moses writes that God created "the heavens and the earth," he means that God—this one God, Yahweh—created everything. It was not a collective of individual deities but a single God, one who also defeated the gods of Egypt through ten public displays (the plagues) of his awesome power over creation and all that is in it. The God of Israel is the God of the universe.

The Creation Reflects the Creator. Every creation bears the imprint of its creator. Picasso's works bear his surname, usually in the lower left-hand corner. Leonardo da Vinci not only signed his works, like the famous Vitruvian Man, but wrote most of his work with inverted writing; you can read it only if you look at its reflection in a mirror. E. E. Cummings wrote much of his poetry in all lowercase with little if any punctuation.

All creations in some way reflect their maker, including the work of the Great Artist, as both Testaments affirm:

> The heavens declare the glory of God,
> and the sky above proclaims his handiwork. (Ps. 19:1)

> For his invisible attributes, namely, his eternal power and divine nature, have been clearly perceived, ever since the creation of the world, in the things that have been made. (Rom. 1:20)

> By faith we understand that the universe was created by the word of God, so that what is seen was not made out of things that are visible. (Heb. 11:3)

These passages reveal that the Creator displays his unique signature on his creation. The invisible God created from nothing all things seen and unseen. And the fact that he is Creator, as Paul says, is obvious in his creation—not just in people, who are made in his image, but in everything.[5] And everything, though it does not speak with words, shouts "Glory to God!" because it was made to glorify him.

The Worshipers in the Garden

Humankind is not the result of random biological processes. Rather, "the LORD God formed the man of dust from the ground and breathed into his nostrils the breath of life, and the man became a living creature" (Gen. 2:7).

Unique Bodies. When we read the creation account, we cannot help but notice the last statement of each day: "And it was so." But for the days on which God creates some sort of organism, another phrase directly precedes: "bearing fruit . . . each according to its kind" (Gen. 1:11–12, 21, 25). Humankind was created male and female and likewise told to "be fruitful and multiply" (v. 28)—the same command given to the creatures of the sea (v. 22), along with a similar pronouncement of blessing.

Reproduction, however, is a curious thing. No two plants or no two fish are the same. They are similar in general appearance, structure, and composite molecules, but are individually unique. Similarly, human beings do not reproduce clones but unique individuals. With each new day, each reproductive cycle, the diversity and majesty of creation increases.

> There is the most profuse diversity and yet, in that diversity, there is also a superlative kind of unity. The foundation of both diversity and unity is in God. . . . Here is a unity that does not destroy but rather maintains diversity, and a diversity

5. This concept is not some form of pantheism, in which "everything is god." True, God is ever-present (Ps. 139:7–12). But trees are not God. It is a grave mistake to confuse "the glory of the immortal God" with "images resembling mortal man and birds and animals and creeping things" (Rom. 1:23). That kind of confusion leads to idolatry (v. 25).

that does not come at the expense of unity, but rather unfolds it in its riches.[6]

The doctrine of creation teaches us that we each individually matter to God, that he loves us uniquely and specially in the way a father loves his sons and daughters.

The Image of God. We note that humanity alone is created in God's image. Of what does this image consist? It is not simply "the breath of life" (Gen. 2:7), since animals also have that (7:15, 22). The image includes humankind's task to rule over the earth and to care for it on behalf of the Creator.

The image of God is not solely spiritual in nature, since man and woman are not just spiritual beings. We are a unity of body and soul, whole persons. You are you because of your body, not just your mental and emotional faculties. In Eden, body and spirit operate as one to the glory of God.

Both male and female are created in God's image. Neither is better than the other. Genesis 1 radically unites all human creatures in equal dignity and honor: "It is . . . significant that whereas in the rest of the Ancient Near East the image of God was limited to the king, in Israel it was regarded as characteristic of mankind generally, without distinction between king and commoner, man and woman, or Israelite and non-Israelite."[7]

True Beauty. Certainly creation was a sight to behold. Eden is referred to as a *paradise*, a word for "park" or "garden," precisely because of its beautiful landscape. Moses describes it as being bounded on one side by the river Pishon, "the one that flowed around the whole land of Havilah, where there is gold. And the gold of that land is good; bdellium and onyx stone are there" (Gen. 2:11–12). This is a beauty that permeates God's good creation.

This beauty extends to the bodies of Adam and Eve, who were created naked. "The body has been consistently depreciated in Christian theology, under the influence of Platonic, Aristote-

6. Herman Bavinck, *Reformed Dogmatics*, ed. John Bolt, trans. John Vriend (Grand Rapids: Baker, 2004), 2:435–36.
7. David J. A. Clines, "The Image of God in Man," *Tyndale Bulletin* 19 (1968): 94.

lian, and Stoic conceptions of man as primarily *nous*, 'mind' or 'reason.' . . . In biblical thought a far higher value is set upon the body."[8] The human body, male and female, is a thing of exquisite beauty, a good creation by God, and it should be treated as such.

The Creation of the Family. God declares something "good" many times in Genesis 1, and he tells us what is "not good" in Genesis 2: "It is not good that the man should be alone" (v. 18). Next follows the so-called parade of animals before Adam, when he names each one. When no suitable helper is found among the animals, God forms one out of Adam's rib. We can almost imagine Adam's thought process:

> "No, this one isn't like me . . . I will call it 'Bull.'"
> "This one isn't like me, either . . . I will call it 'Horse.'"
> "This one certainly isn't like me . . . I will call it 'Dog.'"
> "This at last is bone of my bones . . . ; she shall be called 'Woman.'" (Gen. 2:23)

The parade functions to help Adam understand who exactly his helper is supposed to be—Eve. And so our first parents become "one flesh" (v. 24), uniting to accomplish the work set before them in the garden.

The Work to Be Done

Adam and Eve are to "work it [or serve it] and keep it" (Gen. 2:15)—language of the worship of God to the Israelite ear. They were to worship God by the caretaking of creation and creatively expressing whatever their hearts desired, resulting in the ongoing praise of his glory. There were no express limitations for their task, save one: do not eat of the tree of the knowledge of good and evil (v. 17). Imagine the creative possibilities! Sandra Richter summarizes: "In essence, Adam and Eve are free to do anything except decide for themselves what is good and evil."[9]

8. Ibid., 86.
9. Richter, *The Epic of Eden*, 104.

This was the good creation of God, the crown of his glory made manifest as the *world* filled with his *worshipers* doing his *work*. Richter articulates it well:

> This was Adam and Eve's perfect world. Not just fruit and fig leaves, but an entire race of people stretching their cognitive and creative powers to the limit to build a society of balance and justice and joy. Here the sons of Adam and the daughters of Eve would learn life at the feet of the Father, build their city in the shadow of the almighty, create and design and expand within the protective confines of his kingdom. The blessing of this gift? A civilization without greed, malice or envy; progress without pollution, expansion without extinction. Can you imagine it?[10]

Fall: Heaven and Earth Marred

Unfortunately, the perfection enjoyed by Adam and Eve did not last. When the devil tempted them, they did indeed decide to choose for themselves what was right and wrong, and in so doing irreparably damaged the peace and beauty of God's good creation. The blessings of creation are now tainted by the curses of the fall.

The World Is Cursed

It is said often, but believed too little: sin affects everything. It never "affects only me." And the classic example of this truth is the first pronouncement of curse for Adam's sin: "cursed is the ground because of you" (Gen. 3:17). The ground as created was to bring forth plentiful vegetation for the food of humans and animals alike. Now, because of Adam's sin, the ground is subjected to an alien unfruitfulness. The animals have done nothing wrong, yet their food source is damaged because of Adam. And the earth's vegetation is also damaged. As Paul explains, "the creation was subjected to futility, not willingly" (Rom. 8:20). All

10. Ibid.

24

that was good and beautiful—the harmony of human beings, beasts, and ground—is disrupted by the pollution of Adam's sin.

The Worshipers Are Cursed

The most glaring reversal of blessing befalls Eve. The blessing of male and female to "multiply" (Gen. 1:28) now turns to curse: "I will surely multiply your pain in childbearing; in pain you shall bring forth children" (3:16). The pain is not just limited to the actual moment of birth. Nor is it limited to the gestational period, though that is also painful. The pain of childbearing extends to miscarriage, to birth defects, to diseases, even to the untimely death of children. None of these was part of Eden before the fall; they follow the sin of our first parents.

The second reversal strikes the marriage relationship itself. Eve's desire is changed from one of helping her husband to helping herself (Gen. 3:16),[11] just as she "helped herself" to the fruit of the tree of the knowledge of good and evil. She saw that the tree was good for food, that it was beautiful, and that it was desirable to make her wise, so she ate. She did not help Adam to keep God's command; she helped him to violate it along with her. For both husband and wife, the curse introduces opposition and self-centeredness into the marriage covenant where there once was mutuality and self-sacrifice. Both Adam and Eve are responsible for the results of sin on the marriage relationship, which God had intended to reflect his very image.

The Work Is Cursed

Completing the reversal, the curse now spreads to the work. Humankind's charge to work and keep the garden is no longer easy because of sin. Now, instead of cooperating with Adam in perfect harmony, the ground only grudgingly produces "thorns

11. This is a modification of the interpretation that the woman's desire is to "domineer" over the man. See Susan T. Foh, "What Is the Woman's Desire?" *Westminster Theological Journal* 37, 3 (1975): 376–83; Robert I. Vasholz, "'He (?) Will Rule Over You': A Thought on Genesis 3:16," *Presbyterion* 20 (1994): 51–52.

and thistles" (Gen. 3:18), with the result that Adam (and Eve) would live only "by the sweat of" their faces (v. 19). The work that was previously enjoyable is now laborious. It is slow because the fruitfulness of the ground and of our labor has been hindered by sin. Now we must exert more effort while we accomplish less.

In short, the creational blessing "be fruitful and multiply" has degenerated into blighted productivity and painful accomplishment. Samuel Medley captures our lament:

> Weary of earth, myself, and sin,
> Dear Jesus, set me free.[12]

Redemption: Heaven and Earth Waiting

Since that dreadful day, every human being has longed for a return to perfection. But how can something that is polluted become pure again? No matter how many times you distill water, pass it through carbon filters, diamond filters, and chemical filters, it still contains trace amounts of pollutants. It is never truly pure again. Purity must be introduced from an outside source. And that source is the incarnation. "Since therefore the children share in flesh and blood, he himself likewise partook of the same things, that through death he might destroy the one who has the power of death, that is, the devil, and deliver all those who through fear of death were subject to lifelong slavery" (Heb. 2:14–15). The solution to the pollution of human sin is the human embodiment of the only remaining perfection, God himself.

The World Groans

Tsunamis in Japan, Thailand, and Indonesia. Earthquakes in Haiti and Chile. Fierce tornadoes in Alabama and Missouri. We call them *natural disasters*. But in point of fact, there is nothing natural about their destructive effects on humankind. Those

12. Samuel Medley, "Weary of Earth, Myself, and Sin," in William Gadsby, *A Selection of Hymns for Public Worship: In Four Parts*, 10th ed. (London: Paternoster, 1844), no. 386.

effects are unnatural, a result of the brokenness of this world.[13] Therefore, Paul writes:

> For the creation waits with eager longing for the revealing of the sons of God. For the creation was subjected to futility, not willingly, but because of him who subjected it. . . . For we know that the whole creation has been groaning together in the pains of childbirth until now. (Rom. 8:19–20, 22)

With the first advent of Jesus Christ, the decisive blow against the devil has been struck. But the weeds have not yet been pulled from among the wheat (Matt. 13:24–30), and the world has not yet been purified of the corruption of the works of the devil. So it waits. It eagerly longs for justice. It awaits the final day when it, along with humankind, will be made right forever.

The Gospels give us a glimpse of this restoration in one of Jesus' miracles. In Mark 4, Jesus is asleep on a boat crossing the Sea of Galilee and a great storm arises, striking fear into his disciples, seasoned seafarers. Jesus commands the storm, "Peace! Be still!" (v. 39). And the storm obeys: "And the wind ceased, and there was a great calm." Certainly the main point of the narrative is the disciples' weak faith in their moment of struggle.

But there is also here a description of what creation looks like under the perfect, righteous rule of the Creator. When Jesus speaks, "Peace!" he is in effect saying, "Silence!" There is no indication in the passage that the storm subsides by natural causes—quite the opposite, in fact. The experienced fishermen marvel and are filled with "great fear" (Mark 4:41), seeing that the winds and sea instantly obey Jesus' command. The picture is that of a command issued by one in authority. The sea is in a state of chaos, disturbing the peace of the boat and its passengers. The Creator-King commands; peace is restored. Similarly, creation

---

13. In the Bible, *disasters* may at times be the result of individual or collective sin, but we know that only because God's Word reveals it to us (e.g., Ex. 2–12; Num. 16:30). Thus, there is no way to know whether any event today is directly related to any particular sin(s) or is part of the general brokenness of creation. In fact, Jesus instructs us not to assume that a tragedy is necessarily the direct result of sin (Luke 13:1–5; John 9:1–7).

eagerly awaits the last day when the Creator will once again issue his command, this time to all of heaven and earth, rebuke all that rages, and cause all chaos to cease.

The Worshipers Struggle

The description of the current state of affairs in creation continues in Romans 8:23, shifting to human brokenness: "And not only the creation, but we ourselves, who have the firstfruits of the Spirit, groan inwardly as we wait eagerly for adoption as sons, the redemption of our bodies."

We all know that our bodies are weak and frail. And all of life centers on the harsh reality of our mortality. We scramble for everything we can get: the best opportunities for our kids for elementary school so that they can get into a good high school, attend a better college, land that perfect job, marry an equally well-off spouse, and save enough to retire comfortably and put their children and their children's children on the same path before they die. Did we leave anything out? It is like a rat race, all driven by the ticking clock, because we know that we will not be on this earth forever.

And so we struggle. We struggle to be faithful in every area to which God has called us. More deeply, we struggle, as Paul says, not "against flesh and blood, but against the rulers, against the authorities, against the cosmic powers over this present darkness, against the spiritual forces of evil in the heavenly places" (Eph. 6:12). These things are a result of the brokenness of the world introduced by sin and under the influence of Satan. We struggle against our own sinful tendencies (e.g., Rom. 6:12–19; Col. 3:5–17). We struggle against a world that is hostile to the things of God (e.g., Ps. 34:21; John 16:33). And we struggle against the schemes that Satan himself has set up in opposition to the risen Savior (e.g., 2 Cor. 10:3–6; Rev. 12–14).

Yet even in our struggles, we see much of what is to come. The power of sin has been broken. And we have put on the new self, which even now "is being renewed in knowledge after the image of its creator" (Col. 3:10). This is just one way that the Bible describes the ongoing process of becoming more like Jesus Christ. To grow in holiness is to be increasingly transformed into the kind of people we were created to be until at last, either by death or by Christ's appearing, we burst into the full brilliance of our heavenly perfection. And so, Paul says, we "toil, struggling with all his energy that he powerfully works within" us (Col. 1:29).

The Work Progresses

Is the work of Christ progressing? In terms of the overall mission of God, we must answer yes, since more people worship Christ than ever before.

The Works of Common Grace. Christians use the term *common grace* to refer to the grace that God as Creator gives to all people, regardless of their acknowledgment of him. For example, Jesus teaches us that the Father "makes his sun rise on the evil and on the good, and sends rain on the just and on the unjust" (Matt. 5:45). People have not ceased to be human because of the fall; they still bear the image of God (James 3:9). And by the manifold grace of God that extends to everyone, people everywhere are engaged in making culture: building buildings, establishing customs, preserving justice, and providing for those in need. It is important to remember that God's call to "fill the earth and subdue it and have dominion" (Gen. 1:28) and to "work it and keep it" (2:15) is not something exclusively done by Christians. True, we should be doing it. And it is a great tragedy that non-Christians, even atheists, by means of God's common grace sometimes fulfill the task of creation-caretaking and culture-making better than God's children do. But as we will see, this work of common grace is an integral part of the renewed creation, even as it is now.

The Works of Special Grace. In even greater degree, God's work of special grace is abounding in Christ and in his church. Special grace is the work of God that draws people to himself by faith in Jesus Christ (e.g., John 6:44, 65). And most typically associated with the work of God's special grace is the conversion of the lost. The gospel is going forth into more new places and back into places such as the Middle East, where Christianity was once the stalwart religion. Most estimates today place the number of Christians worldwide, including nominal ones, at around 2 billion. And that is just a snapshot at this point in time; historically, who knows how many have become heirs of eternal life?

Also included in the work of God's special grace is the performance of miracles. When Jesus begins his public ministry, he starts by reading in the synagogue from the Isaiah scroll: "The Spirit of the Lord is upon me, because he has anointed me to proclaim good news to the poor. He has sent me to proclaim liberty to the captives and recovering of sight to the blind, to set at liberty those who are oppressed, to proclaim the year of the Lord's favor" (Luke 4:18–19, quoting Isa. 61:1–2). This new turn in redemptive history (Luke 11:20) is marked by the advent of Jesus Christ, who has brought the kingdom of heaven with him. Luke links Jesus' performing miracles with the Holy Spirit's special work.

Consider the healing of the man with leprosy whom Jesus encounters: "And when he saw Jesus, he fell on his face and begged him, 'Lord, if you will, you can make me clean.' And Jesus stretched out his hand and touched him, saying, 'I will; be clean.' And immediately the leprosy left him" (Luke 5:12–13).

This is no sleight of hand. Luke goes out of his way to describe the man as being full of leprosy. Nor was it a "natural" cure; no cure was that immediate. What occurs is the reconstitution of this man to full health, and this is a picture of the renewal that is to come in the new creation. Graham Twelftree explains:

> The biblical theology of [miracles] is dominated by Jesus. . . .
> His ministry is best understood in the light of [Old Testament] conceptions of God's continuous creativity, in which some events reveal his nature and saving power more clearly than others. . . . [They] carry the signature of the one who

30

performed them; God himself is revealed and is eschatologically at work in Jesus.[14]

In other words, the incarnation of Jesus also brought the power of the kingdom of heaven. Jesus' miracles provide pictures of the renewal that is to come to creation and humanity. In them God gives a foretaste of the future now. And what a future it will be for the citizens of heaven!

In the meantime, believers who make up the church, the creation itself, and even the Holy Spirit groan for final redemption:

> The whole creation has been groaning together in the pains of childbirth until now. And not only the creation, but we ourselves . . . groan inwardly as we wait eagerly for adoption as sons, the redemption of our bodies. . . . The Spirit himself intercedes for us with groanings too deep for words. (Rom. 8:22–23, 26)

We rejoice that God's work in Christ is progressing through the life and mission of the church. This is the special locus of God's presence in the world and is for the sake of the world. The church joins in the groaning of the creation and the Spirit most especially when it recognizes its role in God's mission and in this way actively waits for the coming kingdom. This longed-for final redemption is the focus of the next chapter.

---

14. G. H. Twelftree, "Signs and Wonders," in *New Dictionary of Biblical Theology: Exploring the Unity & Diversity of Scripture*, ed. T. Desmond Alexander et al. (Downers Grove, IL: IVP Academic, 2000), 886.

Creation Renewed

WHEN REFERRING TO final salvation, "Christians often talk about living with God 'in heaven' forever. But in fact the biblical teaching is richer than that: it tells us that there will be new heavens *and a new earth*—an entirely renewed creation—and we will live with God there."[1] Wayne Grudem is correct. In the previous chapter, we viewed creation as made, marred, and waiting for final restoration. In this one, we concentrate on that restoration.

- The World Is Renewed in Righteousness
- The Worshipers Are Resurrected in Righteousness
- The Work Is Completed in Righteousness
- Transformation

The World Is Renewed in Righteousness

The New Heavens and Earth Predicted in the Old Testament

Although the roots of the new heavens and new earth sink deep into Old Testament soil (to God's land-promise to Abraham in Gen. 17:8), the terms first appear in Isaiah 65 and 66:

1. Wayne Grudem, *Systematic Theology: An Introduction to Biblical Doctrine* (Grand Rapids: Zondervan, 1994), 1158 (italics in original).

For behold, I create new heavens
    and a new earth,
and the former things shall not be remembered
    or come into mind. (Isa. 65:17)

For as the new heavens and the new earth
    that I make
shall remain before me, says the LORD,
    so shall your offspring and your name remain.
From new moon to new moon,
    and from Sabbath to Sabbath,
all flesh shall come to worship before me,
declares the LORD. (Isa. 66:22–23)

The prophet Isaiah foresees a future life that is new (65:17), joyous (v. 19), secure (vv. 20–23), peaceful (vv. 24–25), unending, universal, and worshipful (66:23).[2] Many of these themes are picked up in Revelation 21 and 22.

The New Heavens and Earth Promised by Jesus

In reply to Peter's question, "See, we have left everything and followed you. What then will we have?" (Matt. 19:27), Jesus teaches about the new earth:

> Truly, I say to you, in the new world, when the Son of Man will sit on his glorious throne, you who have followed me will also sit on twelve thrones, judging the twelve tribes of Israel. And everyone who has left houses or brothers or sisters or father or mother or children or lands, for my name's sake, will receive a hundredfold and will inherit eternal life. (19:28–29)

Jesus predicts a world characterized by newness, the renewal of all things. The word he uses occurs only here and in Titus 3:5, where it speaks of the "regeneration" of human beings. This

2. For more detail, see J. Alec Motyer, *The Prophecy of Isaiah* (Downers Grove, IL: InterVarsity Press, 1993), 529–31.

new world is characterized by believers' exercising dominion under Christ (Matt. 19:28), as God intended from the beginning (Gen. 1:26). It is also described by abundance, rich fellowship, and eternal life (Matt. 19:29)—both a quantity of life, lasting forever (Matt. 25:46), and a quality of life, one that involves knowing God (John 17:3).

The New Heavens and Earth Hoped for by Paul

Paul, too, has things to say about the new creation:

> For the creation waits with eager longing for the revealing of the sons of God. For the creation was subjected to futility, not willingly, but because of him who subjected it, in hope that the creation itself will be set free from its bondage to corruption and obtain the freedom of the glory of the children of God. For we know that the whole creation has been groaning together in the pains of childbirth until now. And not only the creation, but we ourselves, who have the firstfruits of the Spirit, groan inwardly as we wait eagerly for adoption as sons, the redemption of our bodies. (Rom. 8:19–23)

The apostle speaks of the redemption both of believers and of creation. In fact, the former is a microcosm of the latter. By God's grace, we will be completely redeemed. We will have great glory (Rom. 8:18, 21; 2 Cor. 4:17) and will be free from sin (Rom. 8:21) and the groaning caused by our struggles with sin (v. 23). We will enjoy our final adoption, "the redemption of our bodies" (v. 23), even resurrection from the dead.

Contemplating our resurrection helps us to understand Paul's words concerning the redemption of the cosmos. Our resurrection will involve a complete renewal of our present persons—body and soul. Our bodies will not be totally destroyed and re-created, but God will raise our bodies and unite them with our spirits, which were not annihilated at death but went to be with the Lord (Luke 23:43; 2 Cor. 5:8; Phil. 1:20–23). In the resurrection, God "who raised Christ Jesus from the dead will also give life to" our "mortal bodies through his Spirit who dwells in" us (Rom. 8:11). The body of Christ, who is "the firstfruits" of the resurrection (1 Cor. 15:20), was not annihilated and re-created, but his own body was raised from the dead (John 2:19–22; 10:17–18).

Just as we will not be destroyed but renewed, so it is with God's creation. We are a microcosm of the creation. Even as we long for final salvation, the creation personified as an expectant mother does the same. The creation is eager to "be set free from its bondage to corruption and obtain the freedom of the glory of the children of God" (Rom. 8:21). The creation longs, so to speak, for removal of the curse (vv. 20–22). This is not destruction and re-creation but great renovation of the present cosmos. Paul's teaching helps us to understand Peter's.[3]

The New Heavens and Earth Looked for by Peter

The apostle Peter contributes to our study of the new heavens and earth:

> The heavens and earth that now exist are stored up for fire, being kept until the day of judgment and destruction of the ungodly. . . . But the day of the Lord will come like a thief, and then the heavens will pass away with a roar, and the heavenly bodies will be burned up and dissolved, and the earth and the works that are done on it will be exposed.
>
> Since all these things are thus to be dissolved, what sort of people ought you to be in lives of holiness and godliness, waiting for and hastening the coming of the day of God, because of which the heavens will be set on fire and dissolved, and the heavenly bodies will melt as they burn! But according to his promise we are waiting for new heavens and a new earth in which righteousness dwells. (2 Peter 3:7, 10–13)

Peter accentuates the difference between the present creation and the new one (2 Peter 3:10–12). His words have led some to

---

3. For more, see Douglas J. Moo, *The Epistle to the Romans*, New International Commentary on the New Testament (Grand Rapids: Eerdmans, 1996), 513–21.

argue for the extinction of the present cosmos and the creation of a totally new cosmos:

> The heavens and earth that now exist are stored up for fire. (3:7)

> The heavens will pass away with a roar, and the heavenly bodies will be burned up and dissolved. (3:10)

> The heavens will be set on fire and dissolved, and the heavenly bodies will melt as they burn! (3:12)

Do not these words seem to teach destruction and re-creation? Yes. Do they actually teach this? We answer no for five reasons. First, such an interpretation makes Peter contradict Paul in Romans 8:20–21 and John in Revelation 22:3, both of whom speak of the removal of the curse, not the extinction and re-creation of God's world.

Second, Romans 8:22–23 presents human beings and the creation as microcosm and macrocosm, respectively. Even as God will not annihilate and re-create us, but will cleanse and transform us, so he will do for his world. He will cleanse and transform it.

Third, in the preceding verse, Peter says: "The world that then existed was deluged with water and perished" (2 Peter 3:6). *Perished* here does not speak of a literal destruction of the world but of its cleansing through the judgment of unbelievers in the flood. Similarly, when Peter speaks of the heavens and earth as being "burned up and dissolved," the result is not the world's destruction but that "the earth and the works that are done on it will be exposed" under the glare of divine judgment (vv. 7, 10). The language of burning does entail obliteration but is figurative of a deep cleansing of the earth, as in Noah's day. Gale Heide is right: "Just as purifying water once covered the world, so fire will once again expose and destroy all unrighteousness."[4]

4. Gale Z. Heide, "What Is New about the New Heaven and the New Earth? A Theology of Creation from Revelation 21 and 2 Peter 3," *Journal of the Evangelical Theological Society* 40, 1 (March 1997): 51.

Fourth, Peter compares the fate of the earth and of unbe-lievers: "The heavens and earth that now exist are stored up for fire, being kept until the day of judgment and destruction of the ungodly" (2 Peter 3:7). The "destruction of the ungodly" does not mean their annihilation. Rather, it is figurative language for the loss of all that is worthwhile in human life and means eternal, con-scious punishment (Matt. 25:41, 46; 2 Thess. 1:5–9; Rev. 20:10–15).

Fifth, all of this is in keeping with Peter's description of the new heavens and earth: "we are waiting for new heavens and a new earth in which righteousness dwells" (2 Peter 3:13). His con-cern is with a cleansing of the creation of sinners, resulting in righteousness rather than in an obliteration of the earth. Heide is apt: "When he [Peter] describes the new heavens and new earth, it is not a place with new physical substances or new elements of creation. He describes it as a place where 'righteousness dwells.'"[5]

For Peter, then, the governing paradigm for the new cre-ation is the all-pervasive perfection of the cosmos, for redemption must reach as far as the damage of sin. Furthermore, Peter, the pastor, applies his message to his hearers and to us. We should live as those who will give an account to God (2 Peter 3:10), who therefore strive for godliness (v. 12), and above all who yearn for Jesus' return (vv. 12–13).

The New Heavens and Earth Seen by John

The previous passages all point to this final one:

> Then I saw a new heaven and a new earth, for the first heaven and the first earth had passed away, and the sea was no more. . . .
> And he who was seated on the throne said, "Behold, I am making all things new." (Rev. 21:1, 5)

In a vision John sees the new heavens and earth replace the first heavens and earth. Does the language here and in Revela-tion 20:11 indicate the annihilation of the present heavens and

5. Ibid., 54.

earth? Although at first glance this appears to be so, it is not if we understand John's apocalyptic vision.

Revelation 21:1 must be understood in light of 20:11, which speaks of "earth and sky" fleeing away from the presence of the awesome Judge, so that "no place was found for them." We see that this does not indicate the destruction of the creation, if we place 20:11 alongside of 6:15–16, where sinners are described as trying to hide from "the wrath of the Lamb." In 20:11 the whole created order is personified as defiled by human sin and fleeing from God's holy presence. This fleeing is symbolic of the comprehensiveness of the final judgment. "The point of the earth and heaven not finding a 'place' symbolizes the fact that no one and nothing can hide from this judgment."[6]

But what about Revelation 21:1? What does it mean to say that "the first earth had passed away, and the sea was no more"? John means that the first heavens and earth had departed from his sight. "He is using symbolic language familiar to his audience to emphasize the fact that the final judgment is over."[7] Similar to 2 Peter 3, John symbolically communicates that a comprehensive purging of sin has taken place. But what about the disappearance of the sea? Similar to the heavens and earth, the sea has also disappeared in John's vision. Heide cautions: "Let us not be too hasty in equating this sea with the Pacific, Atlantic, Mediterranean, or any other. We need only turn back a few chapters to Revelation 13 to discover a rather symbolic representation of the sea."[8] Dennis Johnson agrees:

> The "sea" that no longer exists symbolizes the realm from which chaos and rebellion have emerged to ravage the first earth. . . . It was from the sea that John saw the beast emerge to receive the dragon's devilish power and wage his devilish war against the saints (Rev. 13:1). The sea in heaven is calm and clear as glass (15:2), but the earthly sea that gave rise to the beast stormed with restless, threatening rebellion.

6. Ibid., 41–42.
7. Ibid., 43.
8. Ibid., 39.

Its absence from the new earth further dramatizes the new home's peace and purity.[9]

Therefore, when God speaks in Revelation 21:5, he does not say that he is making all things *anew*, but: "Behold, I am making all things new."

Summary: Renewal, Not Re-Creation

Anthony Hoekema summarizes our conclusion:

> In his redemptive activity, God does not destroy the works of his hands, but cleanses them from sin and perfects them, so that they may finally reach the goal for which he created them. . . . This principle means that the new earth to which we look forward will not be totally different from the present one, but will be a renewal and glorification of the earth on which we now live.[10]

The Worshipers Are Resurrected in Righteousness

If the earth itself will be renewed, what about us as resurrected human beings? Three key texts address this question:

> So is it with the resurrection of the dead. What is sown is perishable; what is raised is imperishable. It is sown in dishonor; it is raised in glory. It is sown in weakness; it is raised in power. It is sown a natural body; it is raised a spiritual body. (1 Cor. 15:42–44)

> For the trumpet will sound, and the dead will be raised imperishable, and we shall be changed. For this perishable body must put on the imperishable, and this mortal body must put on immortality. (1 Cor. 15:52–53)

9. Dennis E. Johnson, *Triumph of the Lamb: A Commentary on Revelation* (Phillipsburg, NJ: P&R Publishing, 2001), 303–4.
10. Anthony A. Hoekema, *The Bible and the Future* (Grand Rapids: Eerdmans, 1979), 73.

But our citizenship is in heaven, and from it we await a Savior, the Lord Jesus Christ, who will transform our lowly body to be like his glorious body, by the power that enables him even to subject all things to himself. (Phil. 3:20–21)

Resurrected Bodies

What will our resurrected bodies be like? The Corinthians ask Paul that very question, and he responds with an agricultural analogy. He says that the planter does not plant "the body that is to be," but the seed (1 Cor. 15:37). The seed bears little resemblance to the plant it becomes. God knows what the resurrection body will be like, and he purposely "sows" the seeds (our current bodies) in death with the intention of growing them up into mature plants (our resurrected bodies).

No one possesses his or her "mature" body before death. That is, both infants and the elderly possess immature (that is, earthly) bodies; whether a person dies at a young or old age is somewhat irrelevant, since all life on earth exists in the immature seed state. So the question of what age we will be in heaven is not the right question, since it intends to inquire about physical development and appearance. John bridles our curiosity: "Beloved, we are God's children now, and what we will be has not yet appeared" (1 John 3:2).

So, then, what are the signature characteristics of our resurrected bodies? First, they will be imperishable and immortal (1 Cor. 15:42, 53–54), not perishable or mortal as our current bodies are. They will not be able to get sick, decay, or otherwise succumb to loss. Our bodies will be raised with all the effects of the fall overcome. Forever we will be who we were created to be, in fullness, without defect.

Second, they will be glorious (1 Cor. 15:43). Our present bodies are "sown in dishonor." What a tragedy for a creature made in God's image to be put into a grave! But thank God, our bodies will be "raised in glory" (v. 43). Our "Savior, the Lord Jesus Christ, . . . will transform our lowly body to be like his glorious body" by his almighty power (Phil. 3:20–21).

Third, resurrected bodies will be powerful (1 Cor. 15:43). They are "sown in weakness" but "raised in power" (v. 43). Unlike in this life, when the very young and the very old are weak, in the next life we will not grow tired or lack energy to do God's will. No longer will it be said: "The spirit indeed is willing, but the flesh is weak" (Mark 14:38). Rather, the perfected soul (Heb. 12:23) will receive an equally perfect body empowered to live for eternity. Body and spirit will be one, equally willing and equipped to serve God on the new earth.

Fourth, they will be spiritual bodies (1 Cor. 15:44). In a chapter emphasizing Jesus' resurrection and ours, the apostle does not mean "nonphysical" when he calls our bodies "spiritual." Instead, he means that our new bodies will be controlled by the Holy Spirit. Gordon Fee deserves quotation: "The transformed body, therefore, is not composed of 'spirit'; it is a *body* adapted to the eschatological [future] existence that is under the ultimate domination of the Spirit."[11]

Will our bodies grow old and age? For that matter, what age will we be? To the best of our knowledge, Scripture does not answer these questions.

Resurrected Thinking

We enjoy the television show *The Mentalist*, which features the character Patrick Jane, a keenly observant man—so much so that people think he is telepathic. But actually, he is just someone who has trained his thinking abilities to a greater extent than most. We like to think of Patrick Jane as exemplifying what resurrected thinking might be like. Now our knowledge is clouded by imperfection. But when perfection comes, our minds will apprehend God, ourselves, and our friends with perfect clarity. All our thoughts will finally make perfect sense!

Imperfect thinking is a result of the fall. Sin has diminished our powers of observation, reasoning, and memory. It has spoiled

11. Gordon D. Fee, *The First Epistle to the Corinthians*, New International Commentary on the New Testament (Grand Rapids: Eerdmans, 1987), 786 (italics in original).

some of our emotions, such as fear, and has shrunk others, such as love. But these will all be liberated from the corruption of sin in the resurrection.

Resurrected Beauty

The adage "Beauty is in the eye of the beholder" rings true for the new creation, with one key qualification: every beholder's sight will be perfect! In heaven, we will see ourselves and others as God sees us, as his perfect, beautiful creatures—each one unique and exquisitely decorated as a bride for her husband. C. S. Lewis brightens our hearts:

> I am considering not how, but why, He makes each soul unique. If He had no use for all these differences, I do not see why He should have created more souls than one. Be sure that the ins and outs of your individuality are no mystery to him; and one day they will no longer be a mystery to you.[12]

Lewis further explains that our individuality seems strange because we don't exactly know how it fits in God's grand plan. It is like seeing a key without ever having seen any lock. We are tempted to think that we are worthless because we do not see how God can use us now, let alone in the new creation. But the truth is that God has created each of us for a singular purpose, and when the perfect comes, as Paul says, we will finally understand what that purpose is and finally realize the true beauty for which we were created.

Resurrected Family

Another frequently asked question, one dear to our hearts, is: "How will I relate to my spouse in heaven?" We saw in chapter 1 that God created the institution of the family before the fall and that the family was essential for the fulfillment of humankind's task to fill the earth, rule over it, care for it, and worship God in it.

12. C. S. Lewis, *Made for Heaven: And Why on Earth It Matters* (San Francisco: Harper, 2005), 21–22.

But Paul regards marriage as a picture of the greater, more intimate reality of our union with Christ (Eph. 5:31–32). In this way, the earthly family is a kind of shadow of Christ and the church (our heavenly family). Scripture affirms that the temporal shadows of eternal things will be done away with when the full realities are manifested (Col. 2:17; Heb. 8:5; 10:1). N. T. Wright, who describes such things as signposts, puts it aptly: "When the reality is [in front of you], the signpost is no longer necessary."[13]

Jesus affirms this truth: "In the resurrection they neither marry nor are given in marriage, but are like angels in heaven" (Matt. 22:30). Jesus does not say that we will become angels or be like them in every way—common misconceptions that press the analogy too far. Stanley Hauerwas explains: "We will, with the angels, have a life with God and with each other where there is no aloneness to overcome."[14] The problem of humankind's aloneness is finally resolved by the heavenly family in the New Jerusalem. This means that our relationships with our spouses will be enhanced on the new earth.

The Bible teaches that the marriage covenant dissolves upon death (Rom. 7:1–2; 1 Cor. 7:39). But this is not only a New Testament teaching; it was the understanding of marriage in the Old Testament, too. In Israel, if a husband died, his brother was supposed to marry the widow so that the children and property would remain with the family (see Deut. 25:5–6). This was called *Levirate marriage*. What makes it possible without being adulterous is the death of the spouse, which breaks the covenant of marriage.

With the marriage covenant dissolved, what will our relationships be? We are all united to Christ. We are his brothers and sisters (Luke 8:19–21; Heb. 2:11–12), coheirs with him in the family of God. Surely this does not mean that our relationships with our spouses will be diminished. Instead, we will enjoy greater union

13. N. T. Wright, *Surprised by Hope: Rethinking Heaven, the Resurrection, and the Mission of the Church* (New York: HarperOne, 2008), 105.
14. Stanley Hauerwas, *Matthew*, Brazos Theological Commentary on the Bible (Grand Rapids: Brazos Press, 2007), 191.

with one another because of the renewal of our heads and hearts. We will meet new brothers and sisters in Christ. And because of the absence of sin, we will know them better than the persons we know best now. How much better will we know our spouses, our friends, our loved ones, considering that we already know them well!

There is a corollary of this question: Will there be sex in heaven? By now, it is obvious that the answer is no. But more explanation is in order. First, God created us male and female, in his image, and both that image and our genders will continue in the world to come. So males will still be males and females will be females. Although there will be no need for sexual relations, we will enjoy gendered relations even as we do now, only better because sin will be a thing of the past.

Second, will the lack of sex cause us to be less than satisfied in the new creation? The answer is a clear no because we will be enthralled by our relationship with the living God and other saints, which will be the culmination of our best relationships, including sexual, on earth. In terms of intimacy, sex only fosters and approximates the kind of intimacy that we will experience in the new creation. C. S. Lewis helps us to understand that there is pleasure that is more enjoyable than sex and an intimacy deeper than the union of husband and wife:

> Our present outlook might be like that of a small boy who, on being told that the sexual act was the highest bodily pleasure[,] should immediately ask whether you ate chocolates at the same time. On receiving the answer "No," he might regard absence of chocolates as the chief characteristic of sexuality. In vain would you tell him that the reason lovers in their carnal raptures don't bother about chocolates is that they have something better to think of. The boy knows chocolate: he does not know the positive thing that excludes it. We are in the same position. We know the sexual life; we do not know, except in glimpses, the other thing which, in Heaven, will leave no room for it.[15]

15. C. S. Lewis, *Miracles* (New York: HarperOne, 2001), 261–62.

In sum, while the marriage bond and sexual relations are dissolved at death, in the resurrection the most important aspects of marriage will continue and even be enhanced—joint fellowship with God and one another and deep, caring friendship. We will love our spouses more and enjoy their fellowship forever.

The Work Is Completed in Righteousness

Our Work Is Finished

In John's final vision, he hears the words of the One seated on the throne: "It is done! I am the Alpha and the Omega, the beginning and the end" (Rev. 21:6). There is nothing left to be fulfilled; all has been accomplished by Jesus. Paul tells how everything will be put in subjection to King Jesus, who then will offer up the kingdom to the Father (1 Cor. 15:24–28). There will be no further growth in terms of the number of citizens in the heavenly city (Matt. 22:30). Furthermore, "the earth will be filled with the knowledge of the glory of the LORD as the waters cover the sea" (Hab. 2:14; see also Isa. 11:9).

Our Work Is Only Just Beginning

At the same time, our work is only just beginning. We previously saw that work itself is not a curse—toilsome labor is. In fact, the satisfaction of an honest, hard day's work is a gift from God (Eccl. 3:13). So it will be in the new creation. We will love our work.

Jesus' parable of the talents conveys this idea. Three servants are stewards of various amounts of money while the master is away. This corresponds to the things that Jesus has given every human being while he is "away" in heaven. The return of the master corresponds to Jesus' second coming, when all things will be called into account. The servant who showed by his negligence that he was unsaved was cast into hell. The servants who were faithful and multiplied their money, however, received Jesus' accolade: "Well done, good and faithful servant. You have been faithful over a little; I will set you over much. Enter into the joy of your master" (Matt. 25:23). The reward for good stewardship on earth is greater service on the new earth and great joy.[16]

In the new creation, "no longer will there be anything accursed, but the throne of God and of the Lamb will be in it, and his servants will worship [or serve] him" (Rev. 22:3). This verse does not mean that all we will do is sit around and play harps. First, we are servants of the King. And servants attend to their king. Who would not want to attend to Jesus' presence in the resurrection! But it is even more. To be servants is to obey the master in addition to their own pursuits. Second, all of life is worship (Rom. 12:1–2). Sometimes people think that heaven will be boring because they have a narrow view of worship. Corporate public worship is what we attend on Sundays with others in the body of Christ. But worship is not supposed to stop when we leave the church building. We are to worship Jesus with our every breath.

So in the new creation, we will be his servants, doing Jesus' will. He is the supreme commander, and with our renewed bodies and minds our thoughts and actions will be perfect. Therefore, what the Lord commands we will do without fear of doing it wrong. As it was in the garden of Eden before the fall, there will be no wrong choices. God will tell us what to do, and we will do it with freedom and perfection. Jesus' saying will be manifested everywhere: "if the Son sets you free, you will be free indeed" (John 8:36). And there will be plenty to do. Eden was not in a stagnant state. It was growing and changing. And the new earth will be the same and even better.

What Will Remain of the Works on This Earth?

The earth will not be re-created as a blank slate. Neither will human culture start over as a reversion to ancient times. Paul concludes his treatise on resurrection: "Therefore, my beloved

16. The parable of the ten servants in Luke 19:11–27 conveys a similar message.

brothers, be steadfast, immovable, always abounding in the work of the Lord, knowing that in the Lord your labor is not in vain" (1 Cor. 15:58). It is not in vain because it will carry over to the new creation.

Further, by virtue of God's grace, the redeemed will enjoy the earth, utilizing every good thing for God's glory. "The kings of the earth will bring their glory into [the city]" (Rev. 21:24). The "glory" here is the purified products of human culture (1 Cor. 3:13–15). John is actually citing ideas from Isaiah 60 regarding the new creation. There, as Richard Mouw explains, Isaiah pictures "the Holy City as a center of commerce, a place that receives the vessels, goods and currency of commercial activity. . . . Animal, vegetable, mineral—they are all brought into the renewed Jerusalem."[17]

Of course, there is nothing wrong with cultural artifacts in themselves. The Internet is a gift from God; it connects millions of Christians around the world in ways never before possible. Is it used for evil? Sadly, much of the time. But according to a wise theological saying, "the abuse of a thing does not negate its proper use." Anything that is good will be preserved and purified into an instrument of perfect righteousness. But all that is harmful to creation or human flourishing will not be preserved. In this way Jesus' third beatitude will be most fully realized: "Blessed are the meek, for they shall inherit the earth" (Matt. 5:5).

Transformation

Scriptural teaching on resurrection and renewal has far more implications than we can list here. Every aspect of life will be affected.

Caring for Our Environment

Today it is trendy to "go green." Everyone is doing it. Tech companies, health care, even NASCAR auto racing! But the future

17. Richard J. Mouw, *When the Kings Come Marching In: Isaiah and the New Jerusalem*, rev. ed. (Grand Rapids: Eerdmans, 2002), 20.

of the earth teaches us that properly caring for and stewarding the earth is not a trend. It is what we were created to do.

The renewal of the earth makes us think about what will be preserved for eternity. Certainly landscapes, animals, and such. If this is true, then how should we care for them today? If in the new earth we will rightly relate to the earth and its creatures, should we not seek to do so now? The answer is yes, but we can only approximate the life to come; we cannot make it reality before Christ's return.

Christians more than anyone else, therefore, should be concerned for the environment. We know what a high value God places on it, since Jesus died to redeem it! Our churches and homes should be places that are environmentally friendly, as far as possible. Sadly, often non-Christians are better at caring for God's world and creatures than we are.

Caring for Our Physical Bodies

Paul says that "bodily training is of some value" (1 Tim. 4:8). And the resurrection also gives us a goal for which to strive. We see in the resurrection the way that our bodies were meant to be. We see the things that we were meant to do with our bodies and how useful they can be for God's service. We should strive, then, to conform our bodies to the picture of the resurrection. Matthew Lee Anderson is correct: "Creation care is human care, and human care is creation care. Because our bodies connect us to others and the world, the resurrection of the body is inextricably linked to the restoration of the cosmos."[18]

Carrying Out the Mission of God

Sometimes Christians work as though nothing we do today will affect our life in the world to come. We just do what we have to do to "get by." We work hard now so that we will not have to

---

18. Matthew Lee Anderson, *Earthen Vessels: Why Our Bodies Matter to Our Faith* (Bloomington, MN: Bethany House, 2011), 82.

work in heaven. Christians mistakenly believe that this world will be obliterated and God will start over. This has led to a devaluation of work and a lack of concern for the environment and for justice issues. And well-meaning Christians sometimes point to Scripture to justify their ideas: "For what does it profit a man to gain the whole world and forfeit his soul?" (Mark 8:36). Thus the thinking goes: Only two things are eternal, the Word of God and the souls of men. As for the rest, well, "you can't take it with you." But as we have seen, the plan of God involves nothing less than the renewal of all things. If God will work to renew the ground, the trees, the planet, the animals, as well as human institutions and humanity itself, we must be concerned with such things.

The renewal of creation, including our resurrection, is the most important way that Scripture presents our final salvation. But it is not the only one. Scripture paints at least twenty stunning pictures of heaven. We have selected five major pictures for close examination and proceed to consider the second of these—heaven as everlasting rest for God's people.

Part 2

Rest

3

Disturbed Rest

ALTHOUGH DR. EDWARD HALLOWELL'S vacation was supposed to be restful, he found himself growing increasingly irritated. Why? His cottage, lacking any modern cellular service, provided communication with the outside world only via a solitary old black rotary phone. The longer he sat there and tried to dial, the more aggravated he became. "I could have entered the entire number on a touchtone phone in the time it took me to dial just one number on this obsolete contraption!" he complained.[1]

The irony is that Dr. Hallowell is the director of the Hallowell Center for Cognitive and Emotional Health. He shares this story in his book *CrazyBusy: Overstretched, Overbooked, and About to Snap!* as an illustration of a modern paradox. Technology such as the cell phone makes communication quicker and easier and is supposed to leave more time for other things. But in reality, it often results in increased busyness and greater disconnectedness. And worst of all, most of us are so used to this frenetic pace that we hardly know how important rest is to being human, let alone to reflecting the character of the Creator.

Thankfully, ancient hymn writers call us back to a biblical theme that has fallen out of favor—that of rest. Historically, believers who have lived less busy lives than we do have drawn

---

1. Edward M. Hallowell, *CrazyBusy: Overstretched, Overbooked, and About to Snap! Strategies for Handling Your Fast-Paced Life* (New York: Ballantine Books, 2007), 3–4.

great comfort from the prospect of everlasting rest. How much more do Christians today need the Bible's promise and practice of rest! Consider the beautiful words of Peter Abelard, a twelfth-century theologian:

> How mighty are the Sabbaths,
>   How mighty and how deep,
> That the high courts of heaven
>   To everlasting keep.
> What peace unto the weary,
>   What pride unto the strong,
> When God in Whom are all things
>   Shall be all things to men.
>
> But of the courts of heaven
>   And Him who is the King,
> The rest and the refreshing,
>   The joy that is therein,
> Let those that know it answer .
>   Who in that bliss have part,
> If any word can utter
>   The fullness of the heart.
>
> There, all vexation ended,
>   And from all grieving free,
> We sing the song of Zion
>   In deep security.
> And everlasting praises
>   For all Thy gifts of grace
> Rise from Thy happy people,
>   Lord of our blessedness.
>
> There Sabbath unto Sabbath
>   Succeeds eternally,
> The joy that has no ending
>   Of souls in holiday.
> And never shall the rapture
>   Beyond all mortal ken

> Cease from the eternal chorus
>> That angels sing with men.[2]

Scripture presents our final hope as the eternal Sabbath rest for the people of God. Let us trace this neglected theme through the Bible in four stages:

- Creation: Divine Rest
- Fall: Disturbed Rest
- Redemption: Promised Rest
- Restoration: Perfect Rest

We will look at the first three stages in this chapter and at the fourth stage in the next one.

Creation: Divine Rest

Rest is described in a variety of ways in Scripture, including human beings' experience of rest. And as is true of many other themes in the biblical story, the roots of this teaching lie in the person of God himself.

God's Sabbath Rest

After describing the creation of animals, plants, fields, and creatures of the air and sea, Moses closes the creation narrative: "And on the seventh day God finished his work that he had done, and he *rested* on the seventh day from all his work that he had done. So God blessed the seventh day and made it holy, because on it God *rested* from all his work that he had done in creation" (Gen. 2:2–3). The word *rested* in Genesis 2 is the Hebrew *shabat*, from which the concept of the Sabbath was later developed. The Israelites were likely already familiar with this concept when they read Genesis in the Sinai wilderness. By linking Israelite

2. Helen Waddell, *Mediaeval Latin Lyrics* (London: Constable & Co, 1933), 163–65.

practice with the activity—or here inactivity—of their Creator, Moses paints a picture in stark contrast to other ancient cultures. The observance of special days was by no means unique to Israel; nearly every culture recognized special days. What makes Israel's practice unique is its character. Gordon Wenham explains:

> In Mesopotamia the 7th, 14th, 19th, 21st and 28th days of each month were regarded by some as unlucky. It seems likely that the Israelite Sabbath was introduced as a deliberate counter-blast to this lunar regulated cycle. The Sabbath was quite independent from the phases of the moon, and far from being unlucky, was blessed and sanctified by the creator.[3]

Far from the superstitions of the surrounding nations, Israel's Sabbath day was exalted above the other days as a day of great joy. The Sabbath was to be a celebration of God, for it was God's own celebration of completing all his creative work. By observing the Sabbath and keeping it holy, the people of Israel declared God to be their God and proclaimed his name among the nations, even as they enjoyed fellowship with him in worship and fellowship with one another (Ex. 31:14, 16; Lev. 25:2; Deut. 5:12, 15). This is why it is included in the Ten Commandments in Exodus 20, because to observe the Sabbath is to commune with God and his people and to proclaim him to a watching world.

Why does God rest? These words echo the questions of many a child in Sunday school. Was God tired? Certainly such a notion cannot be true, given the descriptions of God elsewhere:

> Behold, he who keeps Israel
>   will neither slumber nor sleep. (Ps. 121:4)

> Have you not known? Have you not heard?
> The LORD is the everlasting God,
>   the Creator of the ends of the earth.
> He does not faint or grow weary. (Isa. 40:28)

3. Gordon J. Wenham, *Genesis 1–15*, Word Biblical Commentary (Waco, TX: Word, 1987), 35.

The best explanation is simply that God ceased from his creative activity; his work was finished, and there was no more creation to make. This harmonizes well with the explanation of the fourth commandment:

> Remember the Sabbath day, to keep it holy. Six days you shall labor, and do all your work, but the seventh day is a Sabbath to the LORD your God. On it you shall not do any work, you, or your son, or your daughter, your male servant, or your female servant, or your livestock, or the sojourner who is within your gates. For in six days the LORD made heaven and earth, the sea, and all that is in them, and rested on the seventh day. (Ex. 20:8–11)

The Sabbath is primarily about the cessation of particular works, not about recovery of strength, which is what most modern Christians think. Put another way, the Sabbath was intended to be a day *of* rest, but it was not intended to be a day *for* rest. That is, the Sabbath is primarily about God, not about us. It is about us only insofar as we are called to reflect or image him in all that we do, or in this case, in all that we stop doing. Do we receive rest via the proper observance of the Lord's Day? Of course we do, by God's gracious design. But this is only a by-product and not the goal.

God's Resting Place

When reading through the first two chapters of Genesis, the English reader is unable to pick up on many nuances in the Hebrew, which is one reason why many pastors learn to study the Bible in its original languages. One point that would be missed in English alone is found in Genesis 2:8, "And the LORD God planted a garden in Eden, in the east, and there he put the man whom he had formed." This seems repeated in verse 15, with a little more detail as to why Adam was put in the garden: "The LORD God took the man and put him in the garden of Eden to work it and keep it." But something else stands out in Hebrew:

And the LORD God . . . put [*sim*] the man whom he had formed. (2:8)

The LORD God . . . put [*nuah*] him in the garden. (2:15)

Why does Moses choose different words in these two similar sentences? One answer may be that he did it simply for variety, and this is plausible. But while it is important not to overemphasize the importance of a single word, the presence of *nuah* (meaning "rest") here seems to be more than stylistic variation for at least these reasons:

- Genesis 2:15 provides the basis to make parallels between service in the garden with service in the temple, the latter being God's "resting place" with his people (2 Chron. 6:41; Ps. 132:8, 14).
- The Lord's promise to Israel is that "my presence will go with you, and I will give you rest" (Ex. 33:14). The presence of the Lord God is directly linked to the rest that his people experience.
- Exodus 20:8–11 explains the command to keep the Sabbath. There Moses parallels the Sabbath (*shabbat*) and rest (*nuah*). The original readers, already observing the Sabbath, would likely have noticed in Genesis 2:15 connections to *both* Genesis 2:2–3 and 2:8.

It seems that Moses links *rest* and *garden*—the garden of Eden was a place of rest because God dwelled there.[4] And if it was, in fact, God's first dwelling place, then Genesis 2:15 hints at what is later made explicit: God's presence brings rest. To be in God's presence is to enjoy his rest, to be under his care. Therefore, Adam and Eve enjoyed rest because they lived in Eden, God's very own resting place.

Our Resting Place with God

If Eden was God's place of divine rest, then it is significant that God placed Adam within that same resting place. God created

---

4. For more on the topic of Eden as God's first dwelling place, and the garden's connections with the tabernacle and temple, see chapter 7.

us with the intent to participate fully in his own perfect rest. This does not mean that Adam was lying around all day with nothing to do. We wonder how long the naming of all the animals of the earth took! Victor Hamilton is correct: "Physical labor is not a consequence of sin. Work enters the picture before sin does, and if man had never sinned he would still be working."[5] Thus, a major thrust of this section of Genesis 2 is the origin of work, answering negatively the question: "Is work a result of the fall?" Moses explains in Genesis 2:15 that work is a gift and blessing from God, and God is not, contrary to much of ancient religious thought, uninterested in what his creatures do. Adam's work was "restful" because it was done in perfect holiness. His work originally was not toilsome, but work became arduous when his sin disturbed the rest of Eden. And the fall is also the reason why everyone from then onward was born not into a state of rest but into a state of sin and misery.

Fall: Disturbed Rest

If God's presence is the source of rest in every way, then sin disrupts the rest experienced in Eden because it disrupts communion with God. Adam and Eve instantly know this, hiding themselves from God's presence as he walks through the garden (Gen. 3:8).

Wearisome Warring

The first disruption comes in the curse of the woman. The Lord God pronounces, "I will put enmity between you [the serpent] and the woman, and between your offspring and her offspring; he shall bruise your head, and you shall bruise his heel" (Gen. 3:15). Sin introduces a grand conflict, one from which all other conflicts arise.[6] The promise here is explicit, though general:

5. Victor P. Hamilton, *The Book of Genesis*, New International Commentary on the Old Testament (Grand Rapids: Eerdmans, 1990), 171.
6. For more on the theme of spiritual warfare in the kingdom, see chapter 5.

there will be a great conflict, but in the end God's people will be victorious. The battle will not be without great difficulty, for even though God's people will win, the serpent will still bruise the heel. Though God will ultimately rescue his people and be victorious over sin, the flesh, and the devil, God's people are not left unscathed by the consequences of their sin.

Wearisome Working

Sin's consequences multiply the disruption of rest in Eden when God turns to Adam. He pronounces his righteous judgment on the man: "Cursed is the ground because of you; in pain you shall eat of it all the days of your life; thorns and thistles it shall bring forth for you; and you shall eat the plants of the field. By the sweat of your face you shall eat bread, till you return to the ground" (Gen. 3:17–19).

Nowhere is the difficulty of work better pictured than in farming. Those who live in cities would do well to take a lesson from agrarian life. Farmers work hard, pure and simple. They work hard because the work itself is hard, and it is hard because of the curse of sin. No one knew this better than Lamech, Noah's father: "When Lamech had lived 182 years, he fathered a son and called his name Noah, saying, 'Out of the ground that the LORD has cursed this one shall bring us relief from our work and from the painful toil of our hands'" (Gen. 5:28–29). The English Standard Version of the Bible notes in the margin for verse 29, "*Noah* sounds like the Hebrew for *rest*." Moses makes the subtle point that Lamech's "painful toil" (5:29, the same word as in 3:17) was so great that he hoped Noah (*noach*) would bring him rest (*nuah*).

Adam's work in the garden was a great joy, a joy that we have never known because we have always lived on this side of the fall. We all, like Lamech, know only the toilsome pain of work. But even in these early pages of Genesis, in the naming of Noah there is an implied promise of a coming rest from the toil of our work brought about by sin.

Wearisome Wandering

Not having a place to call "home" is one of the most difficult problems in human experience. What child ever said, "When I grow up, I want to be homeless, a wanderer, going from place to place for the rest of my life"? No one! But that's exactly what happened to Adam and Eve as a result of their sin.

After pronouncing the curses on the serpent, the woman, the man, and the ground, "the LORD God sent [Adam] out from the garden of Eden to work the ground from which he was taken. He drove out the man, and at the east of the garden of Eden he placed the cherubim and a flaming sword that turned every way to guard the way to the tree of life" (Gen. 3:23–24). Eden had been their home. Now Adam and Eve were banished from it.

Again Scripture paints a picture of the weariness that sin creates and the rest it disturbs. Genesis 4 reminds us of the devastating effects of sin. Cain rises up and slays his brother Abel. For that, the Lord pronounces this punishment: "You shall be a fugitive and a wanderer on the earth" (Gen. 4:12). Cain knows the pain that this will bring into his life, the weariness that it will create, for he cries to the Lord, "My punishment is greater than I can bear" (v. 13). When humans were driven out of Eden because of rebellion against their Maker, they lost not only their perfect righteousness but also their perfect home.

Redemption: Promised Rest

Not long thereafter, God begins to unpack the promise of rest in Genesis 3:15. Gradually he gives details and illumines the promise to his people. Walter Kaiser sums it up: "God's rest is the gracious gift of the land promised to the patriarchs with its attendant blessings such as the cessation of all hostile enemy action. It is also the place where the presence of the Lord dwells."[7] The land of Canaan was to be a place of rest for all generations,

7. Walter C. Kaiser, "Promise Theme and the Theology of Rest," *Bibliotheca Sacra* 130, 518 (1973): 140.

where God would dwell and his people would dwell in security with him (Deut. 12:10), and where the promise of rest would be realized (Ex. 33:14).

Promised Rest in Canaan

The land is so close that the people can smell it. They can see it and taste the honey on their lips. Joshua has taken Moses' place, and the people are eager to obey the Lord and take possession of the Promised Land. Joshua enjoins them at the outset, "Remember the word that Moses the servant of the LORD commanded you, saying, 'The LORD your God is providing you a place of rest and will give you this land'" (Josh. 1:13). The tribes are to act as one people; even though their portion of the land might be conquered, the men are not allowed to remain behind "until the LORD gives rest to your brothers as he has to you, and they also take possession of the land that the LORD your God is giving them" (v. 15).

As they cross over into the land of their rest, God gives them an opportunity to reflect and remember that he fulfilled his word to bring an end to their wandering and give them rest. Joshua 4 recounts the first corporate act of the people of God in the Promised Land—worship. The Lord commands Joshua, "Take twelve stones from here out of the midst of the Jordan, from the very place where the priests' feet stood firmly, and bring them over with you and lay them down [*nuah*] in the place where you lodge tonight" (Josh. 4:3). Again, one must ask why the author uses this particular word instead of any of several others. It seems that here God wants to create a reminder for the people; it was to be a sign for them (vv. 6–7). A sign of what? That the Lord had opened up the Jordan and allowed them to cross into Canaan on dry land. But what is so special about that? Had he not done the very same thing in Egypt?

The answer lies in the significance of crossing into *this* land. Egypt was merely a stopover; Canaan was the goal. Joshua set up the stones as a memorial commemorating the people's reception of God's gift of the land (Josh. 4:19–24). In Canaan they were to find the rest that had eluded them for so long and dwell in safety with their God. Not only that, but the people were to find rest from their enemies (11:23; 14:15).[8] And since Canaan is the "land flowing with milk and honey" (Ex. 3:8; Deut. 6:3), God's people would enjoy prosperity in all that they did (Deut. 29:9), so that even their work would be a sort of rest. Joshua sums up the promise of the land of Canaan for Israel: "And the LORD gave them rest on every side just as he had sworn to their fathers. Not one of all their enemies had withstood them, for the LORD had given all their enemies into their hands" (Josh. 21:44).

But the rest of redemption did not last long. God's people failed to be completely obedient to the Lord in the land. The book of Judges exemplifies the cycle of rebellion, which in some ways reflects the pattern of our lives today: Israel's downward spiral begins with *sin*, which then leads to *subjugation* (oppression), which draws the people back to God through *supplication*, after which God provides *salvation* by raising up a judge to rescue them. In between these sin-subjugation-supplication-salvation cycles, readers encounter the words "and the land had rest" (Judg. 3:11, 30; 5:31; 8:28)—words that began to appear during the conquest of Canaan (Josh. 11:23; 14:15). But again Kaiser instructs us: "[The] repeated notices of 'rest' in Judges . . . reflect [periods] which were not the permanent rest promised," but rather were "a temporary lull in the continuous surge of the restless sea, Isaiah 57:20, a 'respite' from days of trouble, Psalm 94:13. This type of rest must be separated from what God calls 'My Rest.'"[9]

Why were they temporary? Because sin was still present in the hearts and lives of the people, who were unable to fulfill completely all the Lord's commands. They needed someone better, a king, to bring permanent rest.

8. For discussion of the moral questions surrounding the conquest of Canaan, see C. S. Cowles et al., *Show Them No Mercy: 4 Views on God and Canaanite Genocide*, ed. Stanley N. Gundry, Counterpoints (Grand Rapids: Zondervan, 2003); Christopher J. H. Wright, *The God I Don't Understand: Reflections on Tough Questions of Faith* (Grand Rapids: Zondervan, 2008), 76–108.

9. Kaiser, "Promise Theme and the Theology of Rest," 139.

Promised Rest in Israel

The kingship of David and Solomon brings the first real experience of rest for several generations. God gives David "rest on every side" (2 Sam. 7:1 NASB), and Israel enjoys a time of prosperity and blessing, for as it goes with the king, so it goes with the people. David, relishing the blessing of the Lord, desires to honor him by building a more magnificent dwelling for his King. In the longest monologue since the Lord spoke to Moses, Nathan the prophet delivers the Lord's answer to David:

> Thus says the LORD of hosts, I took you from the pasture, from following the sheep, that you should be prince over my people Israel. And I have been with you wherever you went and have cut off all your enemies from before you. And I will make for you a great name, like the name of the great ones of the earth. And I will appoint a place for my people Israel and will plant them, so that they may dwell in their own place and be disturbed no more. And violent men shall afflict them no more, as formerly, from the time that I appointed judges over my people Israel. *And I will give you rest* from all your enemies. Moreover, the LORD declares to you that the LORD will make you a house. When your days are fulfilled and you lie down with your fathers, I will raise up your offspring after you, who shall come from your body, and I will establish his kingdom. He shall build a house for my name, and I will establish the throne of his kingdom forever. I will be to him a father, and he shall be to me a son. When he commits iniquity, I will discipline him with the rod of men, with the stripes of the sons of men, but my steadfast love will not depart from him, as I took it from Saul, whom I put away from before you. And your house and your kingdom shall be made sure forever before me. Your throne shall be established forever. (2 Sam. 7:8–16)

David's rest was a real, God-given rest, but it was not the final rest. It was but a token of the rest that was yet to come, the rest that will come from his "offspring after" him, whose throne will "be established forever." Why was David's rest insufficient? Because it could not last, for David was not a perfect king. Neither was Solomon. Although they were great kings who enjoyed much prosperity and blessing from the Lord, the only means to attain the perfect rest of the Lord is through the perfect kingship of the One whom God will call "my Son." The disruption of rest (*shalom*) must be repaired.

Promised Rest Fulfilled in Jesus

By the time Jesus is born into the world, the people of Israel have lost all traces of rest. Their kings had failed them. Their nation had imploded, and almost six hundred years before Jesus' birth they had been carried off to captivity yet again because of their unfaithfulness to the Lord. While they have returned and rebuilt the holy place in Jerusalem, things are simply not the same. The former glory of Israel is shrouded in Roman control. Where is the rest that was promised so long ago by the Lord?

Jesus answers this very question. After John the Baptist is imprisoned by Herod, John sends his disciples to Jesus to ask, "Are you the one who is to come, or shall we look for another?" (Matt. 11:3). Jesus replies that he is the Anointed One, the Messiah, who will bring complete rest, and he alludes to several promises of restoration found in the Old Testament Prophets (vv. 4–6). Jesus explains that the world does not recognize this, just as it did not recognize that John the Baptist was preparing the way for the Messiah. But that does not change the reality—the King has come (vv. 8–10).

Then Jesus reveals himself to be the Davidic King, the heir of God's promise to David, an ancient but not forgotten promise:

> Come to me, all who are weary and heavy-laden, and I will give you rest. Take My yoke upon you and learn from Me, for I am gentle and humble in heart, and you will find rest for your souls. For My yoke is easy and My burden is light. (Matt. 11:28–30 NASB)

In the space of these three verses, Jesus claims to be the answer— the answer to the endless warring of God's people against their enemies, the answer to the weariness of their labor, and the place for which wandering souls have been searching since the fall.

Jesus Gives Rest from War. Compare Jesus' words with the Lord's words to David concerning the everlasting kingship that would be established, beginning with David himself:

> And violent men shall afflict them no more, as formerly, from the time that I appointed judges over my people Israel. And I will give you rest from all your enemies. (2 Sam. 7:10–11)

Jesus' words are astounding! Yes he is the King, and by quoting these particular words he essentially says, "And I myself am also the Lord who will give you the promised rest." In other words, Jesus is both Lord and King. He is the Giver of everlasting rest and the One who will administer that rest forever. He is the One who defeats all of Israel's enemies once and for all, establishing his throne forever. This rest, promised in 2 Samuel 7, is that to which Jesus freely invites all: "Come to me, all who are weary and heavy-laden, and I will give you rest."

Jesus Gives Rest from Working. The references to the hardships of life in a broken world are obvious on the surface with terms such as *weary* and *heavy-laden*. But the solution that Jesus presents is not so easy. Jesus says to the weary, "Take my yoke upon you, and learn from me, for I am gentle and lowly in heart, and you will find rest for your souls" (Matt. 11:29). How is it that the tired should find rest by taking on another burden? It is a paradox.

The way to understand the paradox comes in the final verse: "For my yoke is easy, and my burden is light" (Matt. 11:30). Because of the sin of Adam and Eve, no one has been able to keep himself wholly faithful to the Lord. It is, as Peter says later concerning the Jews, "a yoke on the neck . . . that neither our fathers nor we have been able to bear" (Acts 15:10). Jesus offers another yoke, a different yoke. It is a yoke that is easy and light. But how can that be? Because Jesus has done all the heavy lifting for us. Make no mistake—when you step into the yoke with Jesus, you are not propping him up; he is propping you up, upheld by his work of the cross and resurrection. He has borne the burden that no one else can bear, and because he has done so, we can enter his rest.

This is in accord with the message of Hebrews, as summarized by Grant Osborne: it is "rest from all the labors of life . . . the eschatological rest promised for the kingdom age . . . closely aligned with the 'rest' theme of Heb 3:7–4:16. . . . The rest is both present and future, both the present relationship with God and the eternal rest in heaven. In coming to Jesus, the disciple enters the rest of God."[10]

Jesus Gives Rest from Wandering. When Jesus concludes Matthew 11:29, he quotes from the prophet Jeremiah, changing a single word. Jeremiah 6:16 is a call to repentance, for Israel has strayed from the path, a straying symbolized by the people's captivity. They have quite literally lost their place in the world. Jeremiah calls the people back to faithfulness: "Thus says the LORD: 'Stand by the roads, and look, and ask for the ancient paths, where the good way is; and walk in it, and find rest for your souls'" (6:16). Applying this verse to himself, Jesus declares that rest is not to be found in a piece of land or in a comfortable home or in a prosperous lifestyle—as the people thought—but in relationship with him, in covenant faithfulness to him. Matthew writes in the same spirit as Jesus' words recorded by the apostle John: "I am the way, and the truth, and the life" (John 14:6); that is, Jesus is both the path and the place of rest for the human soul.

Here we have seen Scripture's theme of the Sabbath rest for the people of God in terms of creation (divine rest), the fall (disturbed rest), and redemption (promised rest). It remains for us in the next chapter to see Sabbath rest as perfect and never-ending in the restoration.

---

10. Grant R. Osborne, *Matthew*, Zondervan Exegetical Commentary on the New Testament (Grand Rapids: Zondervan, 2010), 442.

Perfect Rest

IN THE PREVIOUS CHAPTER, we considered the Sabbath rest for God's people as divine rest at creation, as disturbed rest in the fall, and as promised rest in redemption. Here we consider perfect rest in God's restoration of all things.

- A Sabbath's Rest from Work
- A Kingdom's Rest from War
- A People's Rest from Wandering
- Transformation

Through his perfect life and atoning death, Jesus has opened the door for us to participate in God's perfect rest in a way unavailable since the garden of Eden. Walter Kaiser explains:

> It is not that the Sabbath is a type of the eschaton or of heaven, but it was the commencement of the divine rest which the Creator entered into after his six days of creative work. He had intended that man should also share this sabbath with Him, but then there was the Fall. Now the way . . . is made available in promise form and finally in the actual inheritance of all that was promised.[1]

And it is a better rest. It is better not because the divine rest has somehow changed, for Jesus is the same yesterday, today, and

1. Walter C. Kaiser, "Promise Theme and the Theology of Rest," *Bibliotheca Sacra* 130, 518 (1973): 147.

forever (Heb. 13:8). Nor is it better because it is a return to a better time before the fall. Rather, the rest that Jesus brings is a conquering of the effects of the fall—evil itself. As King and Conqueror, he is now restoring rest to his whole kingdom—a kingdom into which he freely invites all.

A Sabbath's Rest from Work

Perhaps the first thought that comes to mind when one thinks about the coming rest in the new creation is rest from labor. Our theology can be dramatically affected by the American "working for the weekend" mentality. Work itself is not to be enjoyed, and in fact the absence of work is far better. But as we saw in chapter 3, this is a problem with our theology of work, not with work itself. Work is from God and therefore is good, both intrinsically and practically. But many Christians today misunderstand what Scripture means when it says that they will "rest from their labors" (Rev. 14:13).

We Will Have Rest from Our Work because of Our Faith

In a famous passage, the author of Hebrews outlines a brief theology of rest. Reflecting on the Old Testament, he explains that if Canaan had been the final rest promised by God, then he would never have spoken to David in Psalm 95 about another rest yet to be obtained. "So then, there remains a Sabbath rest for the people of God, for whoever has entered God's rest has also rested from his works as God did from his" (Heb. 4:9–10). The comparison is this: God did all his work—not just the work of creation, but of ordaining everything that would happen for all time in his creation (Ps. 33:11; Isa. 14:24; Acts 2:23)—and then rested from all his work on the seventh day. Similarly, Christians, having completed all that the Lord ordained for them to do (Eph. 2:10), will cease from all their activities in this life and enter into God's creational rest, that is, the completion of all their labor.

Now, this rest is obtained only by faith: "For good news came to us just as to them [the unbelieving Israelites in the wilderness], but the message they heard did not benefit them, because they were not united by faith with those who listened. For we who have believed enter that rest" (Heb. 4:2–3). For Israel, the promise of God was the land of Canaan. For us, it is the promised rest based on the finished work of our Great High Priest, "who has passed through the heavens, Jesus, the Son of God" (4:14). By faith in that finished work, we are united to God and enter into his rest. The author of Hebrews makes a compelling analogy: just as Israel journeyed through the wilderness to the Promised Land, so we, too, will journey through this life into the life to come. Both destinations contained the promise of rest, but the only enduring rest is the rest that comes from eternal life with the Father, Son, and Holy Spirit. That is why "there remains a Sabbath rest for the people of God" (4:9). Thus the exhortation to all believers from the same preacher: "we desire each one of you to show the same earnestness to have the full assurance of hope until the end, so that you may not be sluggish, but imitators of those who through faith and patience inherit the promises" (6:11–12).

We Will Have Rest from Our Work Because Our Works Endure

A second reason for rest is threaded throughout Hebrews: we will have rest because of the justice of God:

> For God is not unjust so as to overlook your work and the love that you have shown for his name in serving the saints, as you still do. (Heb. 6:10)

> Therefore do not throw away your confidence, which has a great reward. For you have need of endurance, so that when you have done the will of God you may receive what is promised. (10:35–36)

> And without faith it is impossible to please him, for whoever would draw near to God must believe that he exists and that he rewards those who seek him. (11:6)

These all died in faith, not having received the things promised, but having seen them and greeted them from afar. . . . But as it is, they desire a better country, that is, a heavenly one. Therefore God is not ashamed to be called their God, for he has prepared for them a city. (11:13, 16)

When speaking of God's justice, Christians often focus on punishment. "We want justice!" we cry at the wrongs perpetrated against us, against those whom we love, and against those who are weak and helpless. But just as God's justice in eternal punishment is shown against those who rebel against him, so also God's justice in eternal reward is shown toward those who love and obey him. Both demonstrations of his justice are necessary, for "he cannot deny himself" (2 Tim. 2:13; see also Col. 3:24–25).

This is what the apostle John means: "And I heard a voice from heaven saying, 'Write this: Blessed are the dead who die in the Lord from now on.' 'Blessed indeed,' says the Spirit, 'that they may rest from their labors, *for their deeds follow them!'*" (Rev. 14:13). The idea of "their deeds" following them is another way of saying that Christians will be justly rewarded for their faith,[2] for genuine faith shows itself in deeds (James 2:14–26). These are encouraging words of God's Spirit!

Of course, our works in and of themselves never earn God's favor. For in fact, our righteous deeds are possible only by the ongoing work of the Father, "who works in you, both to will and to work for his good pleasure" (Phil. 2:13). They are produced only in those who abide in the vine Jesus, without whom we can do nothing (John 15:5). They are the fruit of the Holy Spirit (Gal. 5:22–23). Our good works, then, find their source and power in the Holy Trinity.

If this is the case, then, in the words of Stuart Townend, "Why should I gain from His reward?"[3] A good question, indeed. The answer is simple, and yet in a sense unfathomable: God has

2. Robert H. Mounce, *The Book of Revelation*, rev. ed. (Grand Rapids: Eerdmans, 1998), 276.
3. Stuart Townend, "How Deep the Father's Love for Us" (1995).

given to us all the full obedience of Jesus Christ: "For our sake he made him to be sin who knew no sin, so that in him we might become the righteousness of God" (2 Cor. 5:21). Christ gives us his perfect life and sacrifice (Rom. 5:19), so in effect when God looks at us he sees not our misdeeds and disobedience—which Christ paid for on the cross—but holy persons who have kept every commandment. And in so doing, God has qualified us to share in the inheritance of Jesus Christ: "The Spirit himself bears witness with our spirit that we are children of God, and if children, then heirs—heirs of God and fellow heirs with Christ" (Rom. 8:16–17; cf. Gal. 4:7).

The question naturally follows: What is the relationship, if any, between the "inheritance" of Christ and the "rewards" of faith? First, we have already established that all of this is from the Trinity, and we should never forget this, that God might be glorified. Second, both concepts envision the life to come in terms of our present lives in words that we can understand. We have been willed an inheritance that can never be rescinded or corrupted (1 Peter 1:4–5). In addition, we are awaiting a reward for our struggles to remain faithful in spite of opposition from the world that opposes a godly life (1 John 2:15–17). How do we correlate free inheritance and earned reward?

Fortunately, Paul does this for us. Apart from Jesus, Paul uses the language of *reward* and *inheritance* more than anyone else in the New Testament. The key verse in understanding the relationship between the two is Colossians 3:24, here set in the context of its preceding and following verses:

> Whatever you do, work heartily, as for the Lord and not for men, knowing that from the Lord you will receive the inheritance *as* your reward. You are serving the Lord Christ. For the wrongdoer will be paid back for the wrong he has done, and there is no partiality. (Col. 3:23–25)

Translated stiffly, Paul says that "you will receive the reward of the inheritance." Commentators generally agree that the reward "consists of the inheritance."[4] So it is not a question of either reward or inheritance, but both: the reward *is* the inheritance, and the inheritance *is* the reward. Thus, when the biblical authors want to affirm that the blessings of the life to come are guaranteed to all of the Father's true children, they use the language of *inheritance*. And when they want to show the necessity of human obedience for the life to come, they use the language of *reward*. The two perspectives are different sides of the same coin. So while we may not have any reward or inheritance in this world to look forward to, we can anticipate a far better and lasting one in the life to come, "one that [we] will share on precisely equal terms with all other Christians."[5] This is the true rest from all our labors that John envisions (Rev. 14:13), in which we reap the rewards of godliness, which "is of value in every way, as it holds promise for the present life and also for the life to come" (1 Tim. 4:8).

We Will Have Rest from Our Work Because the Curse Is Lifted

Remember the beginning of the story. All of life—all activity, all thoughts, all feelings, everything—was in a state of perfect harmony. Creation was at rest. And remember what disturbed that rest: our sin. The remedy for our restlessness is therefore the same as the remedy for sin. And since Jesus Christ became a curse for us in his death (Gal. 3:13), he redeemed us from the curse by canceling it on the cross (Col. 2:14).

We now await the full realization of Christ's conquering the curse. In a sense, sin has been arrested, indicted, tried, pronounced guilty, and sentenced—but is currently out on bail under a suspended sentence. But the hope for rest in the new creation is the full carrying out of that sentence once and for all. John writes:

And I heard a loud voice from the throne saying, "Behold, the dwelling place of God is with man. He will dwell with them,

4. For example, see Peter T. O'Brien, *Colossians, Philemon*, Word Biblical Commentary (Waco, TX: Word, 1982), 229.
5. Douglas J. Moo, *The Letters to the Colossians and to Philemon*, Pillar New Testament Commentary (Grand Rapids: Eerdmans, 2008), 313.

and they will be his people, and God himself will be with them as their God. He will wipe away every tear from their eyes, and death shall be no more, neither shall there be mourning, nor crying, nor pain anymore, for the former things have passed away." (Rev. 21:3–4)

No longer will there be anything accursed, but the throne of God and of the Lamb will be in it, and his servants will worship him. (22:3)

All the things that steal our rest from us today—want, unfruitfulness, disease, death, or, in short, all the effects of the fall—will be eliminated when the curse is removed. No longer will there be anything accursed in all of God's good creation. All will be reknit and sanctified until the dross is completely removed and all that remains is pure gold, like transparent glass. Then we will truly be at rest with God, with creation, and with ourselves.

A Kingdom's Rest from War[6]

The ways in which our rest is disturbed in the West are minor compared to the suffering of many of our brothers and sisters in Christ in persecuted lands. Many believers in North Korea, Indonesia, China, and South Sudan know disturbance of rest in ways that, Lord willing, we never will. Some are denied educational opportunities for their faith, persecuted, imprisoned, and even killed. They can understand more easily than we Peter's stern warning: "Be sober-minded; be watchful. Your adversary the devil prowls around like a roaring lion, seeking someone to devour" (1 Peter 5:8). Right now, regardless of where we live on earth, all Christians are at war: with our flesh, the world, and the devil.

But God's kingdom will not always be so. Jesus, in his concluding remarks to John and in his last recorded canonical words, says: "I, Jesus, have sent my angel to testify to you about these

6. The next two chapters discuss this concept in greater depth.

things for the churches. I am the root and the descendant of David, the bright morning star. . . . Surely I am coming soon" (Rev. 22:16, 20). Why does Jesus choose to conclude his revealed words with a reference to David? Because he wants us to know that he is the end that the story has envisioned from the beginning. The promise was given to David and his heir: "violent men shall afflict them no more, as formerly. . . . And I will give you rest from all your enemies" (2 Sam. 7:10–11). The book of Revelation dedicates at least a third of its content to describing the defeat of all the enemies of Jesus Christ and his people. Therefore, it is fitting that Jesus refers to himself as the Davidic heir, since he is the One who fulfills the promise, the heir who is established upon the throne of God's kingdom forever, the One to whom God grants perfect rest from all adversaries.

What is it that makes this rest so lasting? The finality of judgment. Just before the promise of rest is given in Revelation 14:13, there is a vision of final judgment: anyone who refuses to worship God and instead worships other things "will drink the wine of God's wrath, poured full strength into the cup of his anger, and he will be tormented with fire and sulfur in the presence of the holy angels and in the presence of the Lamb. And the smoke of their torment goes up forever and ever, and they have no rest, day or night" (vv. 10–11). Like the parable of the rich man and Lazarus in Luke 16, there is a contrast here between life now and the life to come. The wicked seemingly have ease in this life because they do not face the struggles of living a godly life in a hostile world. Ironically, however, in the next life, the tables will be turned. Those who struggled for righteousness here will enjoy rest, while those who refused to bow their hearts to Jesus Christ will suffer utter unrest. Every enemy will be systematically and thoroughly vanquished, never to arise again. Rest from our enemies in the consummated kingdom of God is as certain as Christ's death and resurrection. Because Christ's saving work is finished, our eternal rest is assured. But in the meantime, unfortunately, many Christians worldwide do not enjoy rest.

A People's Rest from Wandering

Displacement. That is what we call it when people are forced to relocate as a result of political or ethnic unrest. We also call it *ugly*. Human beings were never meant to wander the face of the earth like nomads. Today, very few Americans are displaced because of their faith. But not so for believers in the majority world. According to International Christian Concern, an organization that advocates for persecuted Christians, about one hundred five thousand Christians are martyred annually. Their families and friends, if not killed along with them, are often displaced. It is difficult to estimate how many Christians are displaced annually, but the number is much higher. American Christians need to care more and pray more for these fellow believers.

It is no wonder, then, that the biblical authors describe us as strangers and aliens in this world (Eph. 2:19; Heb. 11:13). Because of the original sin of Adam and Eve and our actual sins, we have all been displaced from our proper place in Eden. But Jesus' coming puts an end to our wandering.

Anticipation of Our Eternal Home with God

In a famous Bible passage, David writes, "You prepare a table before me in the presence of my enemies; you anoint my head with oil; my cup overflows. Surely goodness and mercy shall follow me all the days of my life, and I shall dwell in the house of the LORD forever" (Ps. 23:5–6). These words prompt a question: How can one eat in the presence of one's enemies? The most common answer is that the enemies have been conquered and are now effectively prisoners of war. And this is the answer that David envisions. A time will come when all his enemies are defeated and he himself enjoys a meal with the Lord God, at rest within God's house.

Jesus expands this theme of dwelling in God's house. In a misunderstood passage, he sets forth Christians' expectation for a permanent home with him and the Father:

77

Let not your hearts be troubled. Believe in God; believe also in me. In my Father's house are many rooms. If it were not so, would I have told you that I go to prepare a place for you? And if I go and prepare a place for you, I will come again and will take you to myself, that where I am you may be also. (John 14:1–3)

Misunderstanding arises from the King James Version of the text: "In my Father's house are many mansions" (v. 2). That is an unfortunate translation that has been corrected in some modern versions. Jesus does not describe the physical characteristics of individual dwellings in the new creation. He has just told his disciples that he will leave them shortly. And he has just told Peter that Peter will deny him three times. The disciples don't understand. They are terrified. Are they going to miss out on Jesus' kingdom?

The answer, of course, is no. Jesus' words here are a pastoral encouragement to friends and disciples who believe they are about to be displaced, to lose their home, which is Jesus. They have left their actual physical homes to follow him, and he is now their home. And he is going away. But he is going away to prepare their permanent home, a home not built with human hands but one built by God himself, as Paul says (2 Cor. 5:1–9). Jesus says that there are many rooms in this home. The point? There is enough room in the Father's house for all who desire to dwell there with him. The point is that David is not the only one who can look forward to dwelling in the house of the Lord always, that anyone who loves him and keeps his Word will also be loved by the Father, "and we will come to him and make our home with him" (John 14:23). Jonathan Edwards masterfully summarizes Jesus' words:

There is room in heaven for a vast multitude. Yea, room enough for all mankind that are or ever shall be. . . . It is not with the heavenly temple as it often is with houses of public worship in this world that they fill up and become too small and scanty for those that would meet in them so that there is not convenient room for all. There is room enough in our heavenly Father's house.[7]

The hope of the gospel is the hope of an everlasting home with Jesus Christ in the Father's house, where we will never be disturbed or displaced again.

Realization of Our Eternal Home with God

The promise of dwelling with God is most clearly portrayed in the vision of the New Jerusalem:

> Then I saw a new heaven and a new earth, for the first heaven and the first earth had passed away, and the sea was no more. And I saw the holy city, the new Jerusalem, coming down out of heaven from God, prepared as a bride adorned for her husband. And I heard a loud voice from the throne saying, "Behold, the dwelling place of God is with man. He will dwell with them, and they will be his people, and God himself will be with them as their God." (Rev. 21:1–3)

This is an echo of Leviticus 26, where God lays out the blessings of covenant faithfulness to the people of Israel as inheritors of the Promised Land:

> I will turn to you and make you fruitful and multiply you and will confirm my covenant with you. You shall eat old store long kept, and you shall clear out the old to make way for the new. I will make my dwelling among you, and my soul shall not abhor you. And I will walk among you and will be your God, and you shall be my people. (26:9–12)

God has promised once again to walk among us, as he did in Eden (Gen. 3:8). Now John sees a picture of this very thing in the New Jerusalem. The promise of God given to Israel in

7. Jonathan Edwards, *Selected Sermons of Jonathan Edwards*, ed. H. Norman Gardiner (New York: Macmillan, 1904), 68.

Leviticus and the promise of Jesus given to the disciples in John come to fruition in the new creation. God's home is now our home. Our home is his home. We live together. There is no temple, there are no walls we cannot cross, there are no ceremonies we must perform before we speak together. There is just uninhibited fellowship. We are finally at home the way we were meant to be.

And this is possible only because we are not merely guests enjoying the hospitality of an unrelated host. Rather, we are children of the Father. In a passage following the one above, John hears an explanation of what he has just seen:

> And he who was seated on the throne said, "Behold, I am making all things new." Also he said, "Write this down, for these words are trustworthy and true." And he said to me, "It is done! I am the Alpha and the Omega, the beginning and the end. To the thirsty I will give from the spring of the water of life without payment. The one who conquers will have this heritage, and I will be his God and he will be my son." (Rev. 21:5–7)

Rest from our homeless wandering in this life is bound up with the finalizing of our adoption as God's sons and daughters (Rom. 8:20–23). Adoption is the undoing of displacement; it is the homecoming of those who were once strangers and aliens. Those who have lost loved ones, houses, jobs, and respect because of their faith, who have "left everything" to follow Jesus, have a home, eternal in the new creation, prepared for them.

Transformation

Most Americans do not value rest. The number of hours worked per year has grown dramatically in the last hundred years and shows little signs of decrease or plateau. For many, to live in America is to value busyness over rest, and that puts Christians seeking rest in conflict with the culture around them.

Rest Is Not Found Automatically

Do not mistakenly think that rest will find you; you must seek it out. Put yourself in the shoes of non-Christians. Many of Christianity's practices make little sense from the outside. Tithing, for example, is ridiculous. Abstaining from normal activities on the Lord's Day in order to worship is ridiculous. Both of these practices will cost you a lot of money over the course of a lifetime.

But the truth is that such practices bring us a glimpse of the heavenly rest to come. Many spiritual disciplines are designed to do just that, to practice the life to come and so to enjoy its benefits now in part. Tithing, for example, gives us rest from the daily worries of financial provision and teaches us to hold loosely the material things that we have from God. It gives us rest from a materialistic world. Observing the Lord's Day gives us rest from our careers, competition, and the hustle and bustle of life. It teaches us that we have a heavenly family, a heavenly home, which will not take so much "work" to enjoy. These practices free us up to focus on the most important thing: a good relationship with Jesus Christ and his people.

We sometimes mistakenly think that rest from temptation means the absence of it. Actually, rest is found in resisting temptation, as Peter reminds us:

> Resist him [the devil], firm in your faith, knowing that the same kinds of suffering are being experienced by your brotherhood throughout the world. And after you have suffered a little while, the God of all grace, who has called you to his eternal glory in Christ, will himself restore, confirm, strengthen, and establish you. (1 Peter 5:9–10)

Likewise, James exhorts us, "Resist the devil, and he will flee from you" (James 4:7). Fighting hard to resist sin is actually the pathway to obtaining rest from temptation.

Christians desiring a lifestyle characterized by godly practices of rest will not find such a lifestyle by accident. If they do not intentionally order their lives and their family's lives to preserve this lifestyle, it will be overcome by the cares of the world. A tragedy in the American church today is our lack of restfulness because we are too busy, and as a result we hurt our witness to the watching world.

Rest Is Found in Righteousness

The psalmist got it right many years ago: "Be still, and know that I am God" (Ps. 46:10). But we are sometimes slow to learn. Rest will not be found in escape—in food, video games, alcohol, work, sex, or sports. There is nothing wrong with any of these things in and of themselves. And something resembling rest can be found in them. But true lasting rest can be found only in submission and obedience to God. And in spending time alone in his presence and together with other believers on the Lord's Day.

Too often we live as though we did not believe this. Often we struggle with believing that fighting for obedience in the moment will produce greater rest than giving in to sin. And when we do obey, we sometimes tell ourselves to abstain from wrong things, but not to indulge in the right things. In short, we focus on eliminating bad desires instead of increasing good ones. Imagine if Jesus in the wilderness had said to himself, "Just don't think about bread. You're not really hungry." We need to return to our first love and listen to the actual words of our Savior, who summarized the Old Testament ethic: "You shall love the Lord your God with all your heart and with all your soul and with all your mind" (Matt. 22:37, quoting Deut. 6:5). Jesus pointed us to the source of true rest now—loving the Lord with all that we have and living accordingly.

Imagine, then, the rest that we will experience in the new creation, having been made perfect (Heb. 12:23). No more fighting temptation. No more oppression from the devil and his angels. No more hostility from the world and pressure to conform to it and not make enemies. No more self-loathing. No more struggling. Oh, come quickly, Lord Jesus!

Having surveyed two biblical themes of final salvation— creation and rest—in the next two chapters we move to a third theme: the kingdom of God.

Part 3

Kingdom

The Kingdom at War

WHEN HE COMES AGAIN, King Jesus will tell his people, "Come, you who are blessed by my Father, inherit the kingdom prepared for you from the foundation of the world" (Matt. 25:34). Because we live in a Western democracy, it is sometimes difficult for us to wrap our minds around the concept of the kingdom of God and what it means to reign with Christ.

Richard Baxter (1615–91), however, understood these things very well. Baxter, an English Puritan theologian and pastor, ministered during tumultuous times in the English monarchy. Though written long ago, his exposition of Matthew 25:34 still helps us today to understand the wonderful expectation of participating with Christ in the final kingdom of God:

> And with this solemn and blessed proclamation shall he enthrone them; "Come, ye blessed of my father, inherit the kingdom prepared for you from the foundation of the world." Every word is full of life and joy. . . . No longer bondmen, nor servants only, nor children under age, who differ not in possession, but only in the title from servants: but now, we are "heirs of the kingdom, coheirs with Christ." . . . No less than the kingdom! Indeed to be King of kings, and Lord of lords, is our Lord's own title: but to be kings and reign with him, is ours: the fruition of this kingdom, is as the fruition of the light of the sun, each hath the whole, and the rest never the less. . . . He prepared the kingdom for us, and then prepared us for the kingdom. . . . Not for believers

only in general, but for you in particular. . . . Not only from the promise after Adam's fall, but from eternity.[1]

It is helpful to track the kingdom of God through various stages in Scripture to gain a better understanding of the whole and especially of the final stage of the kingdom.

- Creation: The Kingdom Inaugurated
- Fall: The Kingdom at War
- Redemption: The Kingdom Victorious
- Restoration: The Kingdom at Peace

We will view the stages of the kingdom corresponding to creation, fall, and redemption in this chapter and those pertaining to restoration and transformation in the next.

Creation: The Kingdom Inaugurated

As twenty-first-century US citizens, we tend to read Genesis 1 as an account in which God creates the material universe: the stars and planets, seas and dry land, birds, fish, beasts, and finally humankind. And while the Israelites, to whom the book was written, would have understood this, they would likely have recognized something more: Genesis 1 is the account of God's establishment of his created kingdom and his vice-regents who rule on his behalf over his creation.

The Lord Creates His Visible Kingdom

The Creator Is the King of the Universe. Genesis 1 portrays the picture of a king sitting on his throne, issuing forth his sovereign decrees:

1. Richard Baxter, *The Saints Everlasting Rest: Or, A Treatise of the Blessed State of the Saints, in Their Enjoyment of God in Glory*, ed. John Wesley (New York: Joshua Soule and Thomas Mason, for the Methodist Episcopal Church in the United States, 1817), 32–33, available at http://books.google.com /books?id=_ZEQAAAAIAAJ&pg=PA1#v=onepage.

- "And God said, 'Let there be light,' and there was light" (v. 3).
- "And God said, 'Let there be an expanse. . . .' And it was so" (vv. 6–7).
- "And God said, 'Let . . . the dry land appear.' And it was so" (v. 9).
- "And God said, 'Let the earth sprout vegetation. . . .' And it was so" (v. 11).
- "And God said, 'Let there be lights in the expanse. . . .' And it was so" (vv. 14–15).
- "And God said, 'Let the earth bring forth living creatures. . . .' And it was so" (v. 24).

Only a king could issue such commands and have them carried out immediately, a fact that the psalmist recognizes when reflecting on God's creative acts: "And he established [the stars, heavens] forever and ever; he gave a decree, and it shall not pass away" (Ps. 148:6). Genesis 1 makes it clear that the Creator of all things is the reigning King. It is he who sets the stars in their courses and appoints day and night. He alone is King; there is no other.

The Creator Is the Lord of the Covenant. Not only is the central figure in Genesis 1 the King of the universe, but he is also Israel's covenant God. This is a crucial link for Israel and the reason the account is written as it is. Genesis 1 is not the only record of a creation story; there are similar accounts throughout the ancient world.[2] When reading Genesis 1, modern Christians tend to focus on the fact that everything was created out of nothing (and this is important: Rom. 4:17; Heb. 11:3). But to Israelites—as with other ancient peoples—the focus of the creation account is not as much on *how* but *why* things came into being. Who is this Creator-King? What effect does he have on our lives? These are some of the questions that Israelites would ask. For God's people, reading this for the first time somewhere in the Sinai wilderness,

2. For examples, see Gordon J. Wenham, *Genesis 1–15*, Word Biblical Commentary (Waco, TX: Word, 1987), xlvi–l.

Genesis 1 is not just an explanation of how things came into being. It is also a "narrative recounting how God initially establishes his kingdom and thereby justifies his kingly claim to possess and dispose of whatever *is*, and correspondingly, why the land [of Canaan] rightfully belongs to Israel as [the Lord's] people"[3] (Gen. 15:18; Deut. 31:16–20).

The Lord Appoints His Royal Rulers

Humankind Is Created in the Image of the Lord. Having established that the God of Israel is also the King of the universe, the text declares that humankind—both male and female—is created in his image:

> Then God said, "Let us make man in our image, after our likeness. And let them have dominion over the fish of the sea and over the birds of the heavens and over the livestock and over all the earth and over every creeping thing that creeps on the earth."
> So God created man in his own image,
>   in the image of God he created him;
>   male and female he created them.
> And God blessed them. And God said to them, "Be fruitful and multiply and fill the earth and subdue it and have dominion over the fish of the sea and over the birds of the heavens and over every living thing that moves on the earth." (Gen. 1:26–28)

In ancient Israelite culture, the notion of being made in the image of a god was not a revolutionary concept in and of itself. But David Clines points out two radical departures in Genesis 1 from the typical ancient conceptions of image-bearing. First, the idea that women are created equal with men in dignity, value, and relation to God was virtually unheard of. Second, divine images were limited to kings (or statues of kings), who ruled on behalf of the gods. Thus, in Israel's world the statement of Genesis 1:27 radically globalized the concept of the image of God: it was to

---

3. Bruce R. Reichenbach, "Genesis 1 as a Theological-Political Narrative of Kingdom Establishment," *Bulletin for Biblical Research* 13, 1 (2003): 56 (italics in original).

be "regarded as characteristic of mankind generally, without distinction between king and commoner, man and woman, or Israelite and non-Israelite."[4]

Humankind's Functions Are Described in Kingly Language. When reading Genesis 1:26–28, readers cannot help but notice the royal terms *have dominion* and *subdue*. This is the language of kingship. For example, 1 Kings 4:24 notes that King Solomon "*had dominion* over all the region west of the Euphrates from Tiphsah to Gaza." Second Samuel likewise recounts how King David dedicated to God the spoils "from all the nations he *subdued*, from Edom, Moab, the Ammonites, the Philistines, Amalek . . ." (2 Sam. 8:11–12).

The most striking parallel is found in Psalm 8. There David reflects on God's creation, and on humanity in particular:

> Yet you have made him a little lower than the heavenly beings
>   and crowned him with glory and honor.
> You have given him dominion over the works of your hands;
>   you have put all things under his feet. (Ps. 8:5–6)

David, marveling at God's awesome creation, asks the simple question, "Who are we, O King of the universe, that you care about us?" His answer recalls Genesis 1. The metaphorical language of crowning pictures kingship. The things with which humankind is crowned—glory and honor—seem to affirm such a conclusion. Furthermore, the picture of putting "all things under his feet" is shorthand for granting royal authority. When Solomon sent a letter to Hiram, king of Tyre, to ask for materials for the construction of God's temple, he wrote, "You know that David my father could not build a house for the name of the LORD his God because of the warfare with which his enemies surrounded him, until the LORD put them under the soles of his feet" (1 Kings 5:3). The image of being "under foot" indicates subjugation, and the one whose feet you are under is your ruler. In Psalm 8 David

4. David J. A. Clines, "The Image of God in Man," *Tyndale Bulletin* 19 (1968): 94.

describes all of creation as being under the feet of humankind, thereby affirming our kingship over creation.

Humankind Is Endowed with Royal Rule on God's Behalf. As a result of being God's image-bearers, humankind is empowered as royal rulers in God's place. We are servant-kings. But the rule of humankind is derivative and dependent. Men and women have authority only insofar as they are enacting the will of the Creator-King. Gordon Wenham explains:

> Ancient oriental kings were expected to be devoted to the welfare of their subjects, especially the poorest and weakest members of society (Ps 72:12–14). By upholding divine principles of law and justice, rulers promoted peace and prosperity for all their subjects. Similarly, mankind is here commissioned to rule nature as a benevolent king, acting as God's representative over them and therefore treating them in the same way as God who created them.[5]

God is not absent. The invisible King is made visible in the members of humankind, manifested in their faithful governance of his creation.

Fall: The Kingdom at War

For a while, God's kingdom enjoyed perfect peace, what the Hebrews called *shalom*. Harmony abounded. All was joy and worship. But then the unthinkable occurred: Adam and Eve rebelled against their Creator. Genesis 3 records the first assault on the kingdom of God and the resulting mutiny against the King of the universe—and it would not be the last.

Satanic Rebellion Attacks God's Kingdom

The first attack on God's kingdom comes from an unusual place: his own creation. Genesis 3:1 introduces a new character

5. Wenham, *Genesis 1–15*, 33.

in the creation story, the serpent, who was "more crafty than any other beast of the field *that the LORD God had made*." Little detail is given about the origins of the serpent, but there is no doubt that he is the antagonist of the story. Genesis 3 portrays the serpent as an enemy acting against the kingdom of God, somehow in cahoots with an as-yet-unknown evil power—a power aligned against God. This power, "though undisclosed in Genesis . . . is later revealed to be Satan,"[6] depicted by the apostle John as "that ancient serpent, who is called the devil and Satan" (Rev. 12:9; 20:2). Likewise, Jesus describes Satan as a murderer and a liar from the very beginning (John 8:44), a reference to the garden of Eden.

In Genesis 3, Satan directly opposes the King's decree of Genesis 2:17 in a twofold assault against our first parents, using deception and seduction. He launches his attack in verses 4 and 5, where he says to Eve: "You will not surely die. For God knows that when you eat of it your eyes will be opened, and you will be like God, knowing good and evil." The first assault is against the truth of God's command: Satan denies it! Using brazen deception, he calls into question the motivation and character of the King. Second, he reinforces his attack with an enticement: "Eve, you can be like God." Satan seduces her with the lures of self-exaltation and instant gratification. Deception and seduction are the two primary weapons that Satan's forces will wield against God's kingdom throughout the biblical story.

Human Rebellion Attacks God's Kingdom

How does the text present Adam and Eve in all of this? The bottom line is that God's vice-regents fail miserably to execute their kingly duties. This is evident both from the shame they suddenly feel and from the subsequent story in Genesis 4, where Cain murders his brother Abel. The human condition degrades further and further until the flood, when "the LORD saw that the

6. G. K. Beale, *The Book of Revelation: A Commentary on the Greek Text*, New International Greek Testament Commentary (Grand Rapids: Eerdmans, 1999), 655–56.

wickedness of man was great in the earth, and that every intention of the thoughts of his heart was only evil continually" (6:5). Even after God cleanses the earth, preserving only Noah and his family, the sin of Adam and Eve continues to manifest itself. Scripture portrays the insatiable quest of men and women to become kings and queens unto themselves, to rule on their own behalf instead of their Creator's.

God's Kingdom Remains Intact despite Rebellion

From the very first attempted coup, the Scriptures affirm the ongoing sovereignty of God. In Genesis 3, the Lord commands the presence of Adam and Eve, and even the serpent (vv. 9–13), pronounces judgment against all parties (vv. 14–19), and banishes Adam and Eve from the garden (vv. 22–24)—all of which demonstrate his continued rule. Although God's mission for humanity to be faithful stewards over all creation has been negatively affected, the Lord's kingship remains firmly intact, as the psalmist notes, "The LORD has established his throne in the heavens, and his kingdom rules over all" (Ps. 103:19; see also 93:1–2). Even the mightiest earthly kings, such as Nebuchadnezzar, salute God's ongoing kingship over all, for "he does according to his will among the host of heaven and among the inhabitants of the earth; and none can stay his hand" (Dan. 4:35).

Redemption: The Kingdom Victorious

Without leaving Genesis 3, humanity hears the first hint of victory over the enemies of the kingdom of God when God curses the serpent: "I will put enmity between you and the woman, and between your offspring and her offspring; he shall bruise your head, and you shall bruise his heel" (v. 15). God explains that a war has now begun, and it will be hard-fought. God's people will experience injury in the conflict as they battle evil opposition, but ultimately the serpent will be crushed underfoot, indicating a kingly conquest of evil in the future.

True to God's word, the Bible subsequently records many conflicts between God's kingdom and the evil prince of this world (and his servants) after the events of Genesis 3. These stories are not isolated events but campaigns in the ongoing war that began in the garden. Additionally, each scene highlights aspects of God's warrior-leaders to help his people later recognize the work of Jesus Christ, *the* Victor. We will examine three such battle scenes from the Old Testament and show how each is a lens through which to view Christ's victory.

Battle Scene 1: Abraham the Mighty Rescues Lot

The Lord instructs Abraham: "Lift up your eyes . . . , for all the land that you see I will give to you and to your offspring forever. . . . Arise, walk through the length and the breadth of the land, for I will give it to you" (Gen. 13:14–17). While Abraham is sojourning there, five Canaanite kings join forces and come down from the north to conquer the land. They are eventually met in battle by four kings who form an alliance to repel the aggressors. The battle rages from one end of the Promised Land to the other, and when the four defending kings are defeated and scattered during the ensuing skirmishes, Abraham's nephew Lot is captured as a prisoner of war. When Abraham learns of this, he gathers his allies and his fighting forces and pursues the attackers, risking his own life. He overtakes them and overpowers them, rescuing Lot and returning with great plunder. This victory shows just how mighty God has made Abraham: he and ordinary men defeat the powerful alliance of the five kings and their professional armies.

After the victory, the kings of Sodom and Salem come out to meet Abraham returning from his conquest (Gen. 14:17–24). At this point, most of the attention is focused—both in the text itself and in commentaries—on the response of Melchizedek, the king of Salem and priest of the Most High God, and rightfully so. There is, however, a second and subtler point made in the contrasting response of the king of Sodom (v. 21). He recognizes the might of

Abraham and fears him, and in an attempt to placate him suggests that Abraham take the plunder, not the people. Why does the king of Sodom fear Abraham? Because in the ancient world, "he who carries the biggest stick wins." And as the narrative unfolds, it seems a natural progression that Abraham, the mighty victor, would become a significant ruler in this part of Canaan. Such a development would set up his descendants to inherit the Promised Land as God had promised.

Then why does Abraham not take possession of part of the land? Surely he could have made some sort of arrangement with the two kings. But Abraham refuses rule and instead demonstrates his reliance on the Lord in his answer to the king of Sodom: "I have lifted my hand to the Lord, God Most High, Possessor of heaven and earth, that I would not take a thread or a sandal strap or anything that is yours" (Gen. 14:22–23). Abraham knows that God's plan will not be accomplished by sheer military might. In fact, all of Abraham's strength is by the grace of his covenant Lord. Thus, the story of Genesis 14 reveals that God provides the strength to rescue his people from their oppressors, even from enemies stronger than they.

Battle Scene 2: Moses the Deliverer and the Exodus

God then explains that his promise to make Abraham into a mighty kingdom will not come without much conflict: "Then the Lord said to Abram, 'Know for certain that your offspring will be sojourners in a land that is not theirs and will be servants there, and they will be afflicted for four hundred years. But I will bring judgment on the nation that they serve, and afterward they shall come out with great possessions'" (Gen. 15:13–14). As part of the ongoing war, God's people will become prisoner-slaves of another kingdom. This comes to fruition through Joseph, the great-grandson of Abraham, who, though his brothers sold him into slavery, eventually rose to be second-in-command to Pharaoh in Egypt. In this way, Joseph was able to provide for Israel during a great famine in the land that drove Israel down to Egypt. "Thus Israel settled in the land of Egypt, in the land of Goshen. And they gained possessions in it, and were fruitful and multiplied greatly" (Gen. 47:27).

But then a pharaoh came to power who did not know Joseph, and feeling threatened by the wealth and power of Israel in Egypt, he enslaved all the Israelites and attempted to control them by killing all their newborn males (Ex. 1). God delivered Moses, who fled to Midian. Exodus 3 recounts Moses' being called by God to return to Egypt to deliver God's people from Pharaoh's hand. But God explained that powerful Pharaoh would not easily relinquish his slave labor: "I know that the king of Egypt will not let you go unless compelled by a mighty hand" (v. 19). Pharaoh confirmed the Lord's word, for it was only after a devastating series of ten plagues, aimed at Pharaoh and the gods of Egypt, that the Israelites were finally liberated (12:33–36). Even after that, Pharaoh regretted his decision and tried to recapture the Hebrews, only to fail and lose his own life in the process (chapter 14).

The story of the exodus from Egypt is the battle between two great powers: Pharaoh, "the greatest potentate on earth" at the time,[7] and the true Creator-God. But the outcome of the battle is never in question. Moses, Miriam, and the people of Israel sing about the victory of the Lord as they journey to Sinai, including the refrain: "I will sing to the LORD, for he has triumphed gloriously" (Ex. 15:1, 21). The Lord's victory in the battle of the exodus shows his commitment to the covenant, to deliver his people from their foes, to bring them into their inheritance, the Promised Land, and to constitute them as his kingdom. All of this is so that they may worship him as he intended from the very start (19:1–6). Indeed, at Mount Sinai, before God gives his people the law, he comforts them:

You yourselves have seen what I did to the Egyptians, and how I bore you on eagles' wings and brought you to myself. Now therefore, if you will indeed obey my voice and keep my covenant,

7. Douglas K. Stuart, *Exodus*, New American Commentary (Nashville: Broadman & Holman, 2006), 118.

you shall be my treasured possession among all peoples, for all the earth is mine; and you shall be to me a kingdom of priests and a holy nation. (19:4–6)

Note the kingdom emphasis in the Lord's words to his people. Because of God's lordship over all the earth, Israel will be "a kingdom of priests and a holy nation" (v. 6). If only the Israelites had obeyed the Lord and entered fully into this glorious promise!

Battle Scene 3: David the Shepherd Faces Goliath

After Israel takes possession of the Promised Land, God's people are incorporated into a theocracy, a single nation under the direct kingship of the Lord God. Eventually they ask for an earthly king "like all the nations" (1 Sam. 8:5, 20). God grants their request and establishes a king in Israel from among them to be his representative. The king's job is to protect his people from evil, to provide for their material needs, and to lead them into right worship of their Creator-King. In short, the job of the king is to lead the people into covenant faithfulness by exemplifying covenant faithfulness himself (Deut. 17:18–20). Saul is chosen as the first king over Israel, but because of his disobedience to the Lord, his kingdom is taken from him (1 Samuel 15).

First Samuel 17 picks up Israel's history shortly thereafter. The Philistines have come against the Israelites to conquer them and their land. Employing a wily tactic, they present a champion, their greatest warrior, Goliath of Gath. He challenges Israel to send out its greatest warrior, winner take all. Saul should have been the one to respond to the challenge, not only because he was Israel's most powerful warrior, standing taller than other soldiers (9:2), but because he was the king of Israel, charged with protecting Israel under God. But instead he cowers at the rear of the encampment, trying to bribe someone else to do his job (17:25).

David, on an errand for his father, leaves his flocks and journeys to the battle lines. He hears the taunt of the Philistine and becomes enraged. David asks several fighters, "Who is this uncircumcised Philistine, that he should defy the armies of the living God?" (1 Sam. 17:26). His response is met with mockery and disdain. Undeterred, David comes before Saul and declares that he will go and fight Goliath. Saul cannot imagine such a thing, for Goliath has trained for war his whole life and is now a decorated veteran, while David is only an unskilled novice (v. 33). David's response is profound:

> Your servant used to keep sheep for his father. And when there came a lion, or a bear, and took a lamb from the flock, I went after him and struck him and delivered it out of his mouth. And if he arose against me, I caught him by his beard and struck him and killed him. Your servant has struck down both lions and bears, and this uncircumcised Philistine shall be like one of them, for he has defied the armies of the living God. (17:34–36)

David reasons in this way: if he, as a shepherd of the flocks, defended against the attacks of bear and lion—both champions in their own right—how much more should the king, the shepherd of Israel, defend God's people against the attacks of the champion who defies the living God?

David slays the Philistine champion with his shepherd's sling. The story shows that, while Saul fails to execute his kingly duties, David proves himself to be the shepherd-king that Israel needs (2 Sam. 5:2). Eventually, David assumes his office as king over Israel, at which point God covenants with him and all Israel to establish a King among them forever from David's own offspring. The King will be, like David, a Shepherd-King who will defend them from all attacks, bring rest from every enemy, and lead the people into peaceful dwelling places (7:14–16; Ps. 23:1–2).

From that point onward in Scripture, the promise of a King from David's lineage becomes interwoven with the promise of a Redeemer, the Messiah, the Anointed One, who would:

- Rule with a rod of iron (Ps. 2:9).
- Justly govern all the nations put under his feet by God (Pss. 2:8; 110:1; Isa. 11:1–5).

- Shepherd his people (Ezek. 34:11–31).
- Bring about peace and righteousness over all the earth (Ps. 110:1; Isa. 11:6–11).

When the story of Israel picks up in the New Testament, the Gospel writers identify Jesus Christ as this Messiah. Matthew opens his Gospel in this way: "The book of the genealogy of Jesus Christ, the son of David, the son of Abraham" (Matt. 1:1). From the outset, Matthew—as well as Mark, Luke, and John—portrays Jesus as the Promised One, the true offspring of Abraham and the heir to David's throne, who will restore the kingdom to God's people and secure it forever.

Battle Scene 4: Jesus the Messiah and His Definitive Victory

Jesus Is a Better Rescuer than Abraham. As mighty as Abraham was by God's blessing, Jesus, the Son of God, is far mightier. He declares that whoever keeps his word will never taste death (John 8:51). The religious leaders are incredulous: if Abraham, the greatest of all of God's people, died, they argue, how is it that keeping Jesus' word will prevent people from dying? "Are you greater than our father Abraham, who died?" they ask (v. 53). Their question betrays their belief that Abraham is in fact greater. Andreas Köstenberger aptly highlights the "thick . . . irony that laces [their] question"[8] and Jesus' response, which amounts to his saying: "As a matter of fact, I am" (John 8:58). By using *I am*, Jesus identifies himself with the Lord God—who is vastly more powerful than Abraham.

How does Jesus rescue his people? By dying and rising for them. In John's Gospel, he speaks of his saving death: "I am the good shepherd. The good shepherd lays down his life for the sheep" (John 10:11). He also speaks of his saving resurrection: "For this reason the Father loves me, because I lay down my life that I may take it up again" (v. 17). Jesus by his death and resurrection

8. Andreas J. Köstenberger, *John*, Baker Exegetical Commentary on the New Testament (Grand Rapids: Baker, 2004), 270.

overcomes the devil. With a view to those impending events, he asserts: "Now will the ruler of this world be cast out" (12:31) and "the ruler of this world is judged" (16:11).

The apostle Paul also has much to say about our mighty rescuer: "But thanks be to God, who in Christ always leads us in triumphal procession" (2 Cor. 2:14). Paul lifts up Christ's crucifixion: "He has delivered us from the domain of darkness and transferred us to the kingdom of his beloved Son, in whom we have redemption, the forgiveness of sins" (Col. 1:13–14). The apostle also extols Jesus' resurrection: "But thanks be to God, who gives us the victory through our Lord Jesus Christ" (1 Cor. 15:57).

Jesus Is a Better Deliverer than Moses. Isaiah spoke of a Deliverer who was to come, who would "bring good news to the poor; . . . bind up the brokenhearted, . . . proclaim liberty to the captives, and [open] the prison to those who are bound" (Isa. 61:1). Jesus claims to be this Deliverer (Luke 4:16–21). The author of Hebrews explains how Jesus accomplished this: "Since therefore the children share in flesh and blood, he himself likewise partook of the same things, that through death he might destroy the one who has the power of death, that is, the devil, and deliver all those who through fear of death were subject to lifelong slavery" (Heb. 2:14–15). The Son of God became a man to die to vanquish the evil one and provide the deliverance from the bondage of sin that God's people so desperately needed.

Paul teaches that Christ's death (and resurrection) accomplished the same two things that Hebrews 2:14–15 affirmed, only Paul reverses the order. Christ brought sinners forgiveness by paying the penalty for their sins, and God defeated our spiritual enemies through Christ and his cross:

> And you, who were dead in your trespasses and the uncircumcision of your flesh, God made alive together with him, having forgiven us all our trespasses, by canceling the record of debt that stood against us with its legal demands. This he set aside, nailing it to the cross. He disarmed the rulers and

authorities and put them to open shame, by triumphing over them in him. (Col. 2:13–15)

Through the exodus, Moses led the captives of Egypt to freedom at Sinai, but Moses could not set the people free from sin. What Moses' law was powerless to do, God did by sending his own Son (Rom. 8:1–3), and his death broke the bonds of slavery to sin once and for all for everyone who believes (Rom. 6:10, 18, 22; Gal. 4:4–7; 1 Peter 1:18–19).

Jesus Is a Better Shepherd-King than David. Ezekiel describes the future work of Christ, the Shepherd of God's people:

> And I will set up over them one shepherd, my servant David, and he shall feed them: he shall feed them and be their shepherd. And I, the LORD, will be their God, and my servant David shall be prince among them. . . . And they shall know that I am the LORD, when I break the bars of their yoke, and deliver them from the hand of those who enslaved them. They shall no more be a prey to the nations, nor shall the beasts of the land devour them. They shall dwell securely, and none shall make them afraid. (Ezek. 34:23–24, 27–28)

Jesus begins his public ministry in Mark's Gospel by declaring, "The time is fulfilled, and the kingdom of God is at hand" (Mark 1:15). The day of which Ezekiel spoke has arrived at last; the Son of David, the King, will conquer all the enemies of God's people. Day by day his ministry evidences his divine kingship in his authoritative teaching, supernatural healings, and authority over demons. People begin to suspect that he is the promised Davidic heir (Matt. 12:23). So the religious leaders attack him in desperation, accusing him of being possessed by a demon (v. 24; Luke 11:15). Jesus counters this charge by saying that the only way to enter a strong man's house and plunder it is to be stronger than the strong man (Matt. 12:29). Jesus, who is King over all, is stronger than the prince of this world. Jesus declares in Luke's Gospel that "if it is by the finger of God that I cast out demons, then the kingdom of God has come upon you" (Luke 11:20).

The Shepherd-King has come, died, and arisen, and he will protect and use his people, as Hebrews reminds us: "Now may the God of peace who brought again from the dead our Lord Jesus, the great shepherd of the sheep, by the blood of the eternal covenant, equip you with everything good that you may do his will" (Heb. 13:20–21; cf. 1 Peter 2:25). And when he comes again to gather his flock for eternity, then the promise to David will be fully realized: "The Lamb in the midst of the throne will be their shepherd, and he will guide them to springs of living water, and God will wipe away every tear from their eyes" (Rev. 7:17).

Already and Not Yet: The Warfare of a Defeated Foe

If Christ is already victorious through the cross and empty tomb, then as the New Testament asks, why do we not yet see everything made right (1 Cor. 15:23–28; Heb. 2:5–8)? Though the victory has been secured, and the defeat of sin, death, and the devil is certain, a battle still rages. Satan rages against his defeat, knowing that his time is short (Rev. 12:12). He and his forces prowl about, attempting to devour God's people (1 Peter 5:8).

We could also mistakenly think that the kingdom of darkness is advancing because of the way that the kingdom of God grows. The famous parables of the kingdom in Matthew 13 highlight reasons why it is hard to see kingdom growth at times:

- The gospel of the kingdom sometimes takes hold for only a little while (v. 21).
- The gospel of the kingdom is sometimes choked out by the cares of this world (v. 22).
- The kingdom of God and the kingdom of darkness grow up and flourish side by side (vv. 24–30, 47–50).
- The kingdom of God starts off small and reveals its fullness only in the end (vv. 31–32).
- The kingdom often multiplies invisibly (v. 33).

101

But Jesus teaches that this kingdom is indestructible: "And I tell you, you are Peter, and on this rock I will build my church, and the gates of hell shall not prevail against it" (Matt. 16:18). Christ's victory is assured. The kingdom has been given over to him, and he is now seated in power at the Father's right hand (Luke 22:69; Eph. 1:20; Heb. 12:2). Paul bases our confidence in Christ's victory in God himself:

> Who shall separate us from the love of Christ? Shall tribulation, or distress, or persecution, or famine, or nakedness, or danger, or sword? . . . No, in all these things we are more than conquerors through him who loved us. For I am sure that neither death nor life, nor angels nor rulers, nor things present nor things to come, nor powers, nor height nor depth, nor anything else in all creation, will be able to separate us from the love of God in Christ Jesus our Lord. (Rom. 8:35–39)

God's Word affirms that often things are not what they seem. The psalmist writes, "Fret not yourself because of evildoers; be not envious of wrongdoers," for "though the wicked sprout like grass and all evildoers flourish, they are doomed to destruction forever" (Pss. 37:1; 92:7). Likewise, "[Revelation] is meant to show us that things are not what they *seem*. The beast that comes up out of the abyss *seems* victorious. . . . Does it *seem* as if [the prayers of the saints] are not heard (Rev. 6:10)? . . . Do they *seem* to be defeated? In reality they reign!"[9] The saints reign because of the unparalleled victory of the Lamb. The enemies of the Lord "will make war on the Lamb, and the Lamb will conquer them, for he is Lord of lords and King of kings, and those with him are called and chosen and faithful" (Rev. 17:14).

We have viewed the kingdom of God as inaugurated (at creation), at war (after the fall), and as victorious (in redemption). In the next chapter, we will investigate the kingdom at peace (in the restoration).

---

9. William Hendriksen, *More than Conquerors* (Grand Rapids: Baker, 2000), 8–9 (italics in original).

6

The Kingdom at Peace

In sum, the kingdom of God cannot be understood apart from its eschatological element, because it is that which gives it its meaning and purpose. From our present point of view it will come in the future, but when it comes time will end and a new kind of life will be inaugurated. . . . In the new creation we shall dwell in a dimension of reality that is beyond change and decay, in which our identity and purpose will be defined by our union with Christ. He will be our king and our bridegroom, the one who reigns over us but who at the same time cherishes us as he cherishes his own body. What we see and know in this life is a foretaste of what is to come, but it cannot compare with the reality itself. For that we must await the coming of the kingdom and the revelation of the king who will come with judgment and with salvation to those who believe.[1]

Gerald Bray is correct; the final installment of God's kingdom is great beyond imagining. Previously, we explored the kingdom of God at creation (inaugurated), after the fall (at war), and in redemption (victorious). Now we explore it at peace at the restoration.

- Understanding Kingdom Battles in Revelation
- The Last Battle and the Victory of Christ

1. Gerald Bray, "The Kingdom of God and Eschatology," in *The Kingdom of God*, ed. Christopher W. Morgan and Robert A. Peterson, Theology in Community (Wheaton, IL: Crossway, 2012).

- Victory over the World: The Defeat of Seduction and Deception
- Victory over the Devil: The Defeat of the Accuser
- Victory over the Flesh: The Defeat of the Christian's Identity Crisis
- Victory over Death: The Defeat of the Last Enemy
- Transformation

It is no coincidence that the final battle in Revelation 16–20 acts as the prelude to the vision of renewed creation in chapters 21–22. How can the new kingdom, in which only righteousness and peace dwell (Isa. 65:24–25; 2 Peter 3:13), be established unless God first grants victory on every side? The construction of the first temple began only when Israel was at peace and rest (1 Kings 5:2–5). Similarly, the new creation, the whole of which is the temple of the Lord, will not be finally established until Christ's victory is consummated in fullness and every last enemy has been vanquished forever.

The climax of the book of Revelation is the final outcome of the war between good and evil.[2] The war is a struggle between two opposing powers, the Trinity and the counterfeit trinity of Revelation 12–13.[3] That is, it is a war between two thrones. Over three-quarters of the occurrences of the word *throne* in the New Testament are found in the book of Revelation.[4] The throne of the Father and the Lamb battles against the throne of Satan (Rev. 2:13; 13:2; 16:10), and the fate of the whole cosmos hangs in the balance. John uses throne language to direct readers' attention away from external components of a kingdom to the reigning

2. This is not to say that the two powers are equal in power—and this is important. The biblical story never depicts God and Satan as equal opposites of good and evil, fighting for an undecided outcome. Satan is a fallen angel, a creature (Gen. 3:1; Jude 5–7). Though Satan is stronger than we, he is subject to the will of the Lord just as everything else in all creation is (Job 1:6–12; Dan. 4:35). For more, see Sydney H. T. Page, *Powers of Evil: A Biblical Study of Satan and Demons* (Grand Rapids: Baker, 1995).

3. The counterfeit trinity includes the dragon (like the Father, Rev. 12:3), the beast of the sea with a "mortal wound [that] was healed" (like the Son, 13:1–3), and the false prophet (or beast of the earth, like the Spirit, 13:11–17).

4. Greek *thronos* occurs sixty-two times in the New Testament, forty-seven times (76 percent) in Revelation.

King instead. John's visions center on God the Father, who sits on the throne (Rev. 3:21; 4:2–5:1), and Jesus Christ his Son, the Lord and heir of David (22:16), who sits at the Father's right hand (3:21; 22:1, 3). John's visions also focus on the struggle between the Trinity and "the great dragon . . . , that ancient serpent, who is called the devil and Satan, the deceiver of the whole world" (12:9).

Understanding Kingdom Battles in Revelation

Revelation is replete with battles. But it is not clear how to synthesize the battles into a cohesive whole. There is much disagreement between scholars in various Christian traditions, especially in regard to the millennium of Revelation 20. Since this book is concerned with the eternal kingdom in the new creation, we will try to avoid debates and focus on the key points.[5]

The Battles Are Cosmic

Regardless of whether one associates the characters and prophecies in Revelation with actual political nations (e.g., Rome), one thing is clear: the acting power behind these agents is the devil. As the original readers understood in part that an evil force stood behind the serpent in Genesis 3, so the readers in Asia Minor would understand that the devil stands behind the conflicts in Revelation (12:9).[6] Plainly, the evil one will be defeated in the end. Revelation peels back the veil of earthly conflicts to reveal their supernatural foundations.

The Battles Are Escalating

We recommend reading the book of Revelation from start to finish in one sitting. This allows readers to see the big picture. So

5. For discussions of millennial perspectives, see Robert G. Clouse, ed., *The Meaning of the Millennium: Four Views* (Downers Grove, IL: InterVarsity Press, 1977); Darrell L. Bock et al., *Three Views on the Millennium and Beyond* (Grand Rapids: Zondervan, 1999).

6. Leon Morris, *Revelation: An Introduction and Commentary*, Tyndale New Testament Commentaries (Downers Grove, IL: InterVarsity Press, 2009), 156–57.

often we get caught up—especially in Revelation—in a verse-by-verse analysis and in so doing miss the author's main message. And when Revelation is read front to back, it is apparent that the conflict between good and evil intensifies as the book progresses. An easy way to recognize this is in the increasing scope of the plagues throughout. The visions escalate in scope of destruction, beginning with a quarter of the earth in chapter 6 (the seven seals), to a third in chapters 8–9 (the seven trumpets), and finally to everything in chapters 15–16 (the seven bowls).

The Battles Are Concluding

In the middle of Revelation, readers get the sense that things are coming to a conclusion: "And the angel . . . raised his right hand to heaven and swore by him who lives forever and ever . . . that there would be no more delay, but that in the days of the trumpet call to be sounded by the seventh angel, the mystery of God would be fulfilled" (Rev. 10:5–7). This is reaffirmed at the beginning of the last series of visions (15:1–22:5): "Then I saw another sign in heaven, great and amazing, seven angels with seven plagues, which are the last, for with them the wrath of God is finished" (15:1). John asserts that this last series of visions is the final outpouring of God's wrath and the consummation of Christ's victory, which then give way to the new heavens and the new earth.

The Last Battle and the Victory of Christ

Revelation 16–20 depicts, in varied ways, the great victory of the Lamb, Jesus Christ, the King from the line of David, who slays God's enemies and casts them into everlasting torment (19:20; 20:10). The kingdom of God will then exist as it was intended since creation. And over this the heavenly voices rejoice:

> "The kingdom of the world has become the kingdom of our Lord and of his Christ, and he shall reign forever and ever." And the

twenty-four elders who sit on their thrones before God fell on
their faces and worshiped God, saying,

> "We give thanks to you, Lord God Almighty,
>> who is and who was,
> for you have taken your great power
>> and begun to reign.
> The nations raged,
>> but your wrath came,
>> and the time for the dead to be judged,
> and for rewarding your servants, the prophets and saints,
>> and those who fear your name,
>> both small and great,
> and for destroying the destroyers of the earth." (11:15–18)

These foes, the "destroyers of the earth," are introduced at different
points throughout the book of Revelation:

- The dragon (12:1–17), Satan, who is also the scarlet beast
  (17:1–14).
- The beast of the sea together with the false prophet (13:1–10).
- Babylon (14:8).

Christ's victory over these enemies occurs in reverse order of that
in which they are introduced. This affirms what we stated above,
that Satan is ultimately the instigator behind the attacks on God's
people. This is further confirmed by the fact that Satan stands
behind the evil works of the other two enemies (13:4; 17:3). Of
course, death is an enemy as well—the last enemy, in fact (1 Cor.
15:26; Rev. 20:14; 21:4).

Victory over the World: The Defeat of Seduction and Deception

The two foes depicted as proceeding from Satan in Revelation remind Christians of the tactics of the evil one against the
kingdom of Christ. Remember that in the garden, Eve was deceived

107

by Satan and seduced by his false statements. Eve's temptation reveals the patterns that sin often follows: deceit seduces us with its lure (James 1:14). Christ breaks this pattern, first by defeating the seduction of the world, and then by doing away with deception altogether.

The Defeat of Seduction

The apostle John sees, in graphic detail, the fall of Babylon in Revelation 17–18. Babylon is portrayed as a woman sitting on a scarlet beast,

> arrayed in purple and scarlet, and adorned with gold and jewels and pearls, holding in her hand a golden cup full of abominations and the impurities of her sexual immorality. And on her forehead was written a name of mystery: "Babylon the great, mother of prostitutes and of earth's abominations." (Rev. 17:4–5)

The angel explains: "All nations have drunk the wine of the passion of her sexual immorality, and the kings of the earth have committed immorality with her, and the merchants of the earth have grown rich from the power of her luxurious living" (18:3). Even more, "in her was found the blood of prophets and of saints, and of all who have been slain on earth" (v. 24).

How can one "person" be guilty of the blood of all mankind throughout history? Robert Mounce explains: "Adorned in luxury and intoxicated with the blood of the saints, she stands for a dominant world system based on seduction for personal gain. . . . John's images are timeless in that they portray the essential conflicts of humanity from the beginning of time until the end."[7] In other words, Babylon represents the seduction of all manner of immorality—sex, power, wealth, pleasure, and so on—that opposes God's holy people from Genesis 3 until the last day. And on that day, she will be judged in answer to the prayers of the

---

7. Robert H. Mounce, *The Book of Revelation*, rev. ed., New International Commentary on the New Testament (Grand Rapids: Eerdmans, 1998), 308.

saints (Rev. 6:10), and her sentence will be carried out. She will be thrown down like a stone thrown into ocean depths (18:21–23), never to rise again to bewitch people with her seductions.

Seduction is a powerful weapon of Satan, as Christians know well. Our hearts are easily seduced. Why? Because seduction perverts the goodness of God's creation. This is why Paul fears for the Corinthians: "I am afraid that as the serpent deceived Eve by his cunning, your thoughts will be led astray from a sincere and pure devotion to Christ" (2 Cor. 11:3). Certainly each of us should have this same fear today.

C. S. Lewis helps us to understand the lure of seduction by explaining how all earthly pleasures are in reality shadows of the true pleasures that we will enjoy in the new heavenly creation:

> There have been times when I think we do not desire heaven, but more often I find myself wondering whether, in our heart of hearts, we have ever desired anything else. You may have noticed the books you really love are bound together by a secret thread . . . [or] you have stood before some landscape, which seems to embody what you have been looking for your whole life. . . . All the things that have ever deeply possessed your soul have been but hints of [your desire for heaven]—tantalizing glimpses, promises never quite fulfilled, echoes that died away just as they caught your ear.[8]

Lewis means that on their deathbeds, people never exclaim, "I wish I had made a little more money," or "I wish I had spent more Sundays at the office," though their lives might have been characterized by those very things. Why? Because people, when they do those things, are searching to satisfy the cravings of their souls and, in searching, are lured away by the seduction of this world's pleasures. But in the end, as the Preacher of Ecclesiastes discovers, all is vanity: the desires still remain because the world never really fulfilled them in the first place. God-given desires can be satisfied only by God himself.

8. C. S. Lewis, *The Problem of Pain* (San Francisco: HarperOne, 2001), 149–51.

This is why Babylon's future judgment and downfall should give our hearts great hope. Christ's victory over seduction means that there will no longer be things to draw our hearts away from the purity of devotion to Christ. The power of evil desire will be broken (1 John 2:15–17). The compulsion to acquire wealth will cease; the attraction of illicit sex will be no more; the draw of worldly praise will fade away; the lure of autonomous power will be shattered. Only the righteous desire to please the One for whom we were created will remain.

The Defeat of Deception

The second manifestation of Satan's attacks in Revelation is found in Revelation 13, where the beast of the sea and the beast of the earth—later identified as the "false prophet" (Rev. 16:13; 19:20)—create a system to lure people to worship Satan. The false prophet "exercises all the authority of the first beast in its presence, and makes the earth and its inhabitants worship the first beast, whose mortal wound was healed. It performs great signs, even making fire come down from heaven to earth in front of people, and by the signs that it is allowed to work in the presence of the beast it deceives those who dwell on earth" (13:12–14a). The two beasts cooperate in performing signs and miracles, even so far as imitating the resurrection of Christ, so as to deceive "those who dwell on earth," that is, unbelievers.[9]

The two beasts together, then, depict the worldly systems orchestrated by Satan to draw people away from true knowledge of the living God. Certainly the original readers recognized some of these patterns in their day, but John's vision transcends one particular culture or nation.[10] A number of systems around the world today oppose the worship of God, and there is no shortage

---

9. G. K. Beale, *The Book of Revelation: A Commentary on the Greek Text*, New International Greek Testament Commentary (Grand Rapids: Eerdmans, 1999), 290; Morris, *Revelation*, 166. The phrase "those who dwell on earth" is a technical term in Revelation for unbelievers (3:10; 6:10; 8:13; 11:10; 12:12; 13:8, 14; 14:6).

10. Beale, *The Book of Revelation*, 685–86; J. Ramsey Michaels, *Revelation*, IVP New Testament Commentary (Downers Grove, IL: InterVarsity Press, 1997), 158–60.

of this opposition in the United States, either. While Christians should always be cautious about definitively (and publicly) identifying specific individuals and entities with the work of Satan, we are called to be discerning (Rev. 13:9–10, 18). That is, we are called to exercise a proper Christian worldview. We are not to be naive and act as though the things we encounter in the world were morally or religiously neutral (Col. 2:8; James 4:4; 1 John 2:16). In Revelation 12–13, John reiterates what Jesus said in the Synoptic Gospels—that no system in the world can claim neutrality. We serve either God's system or Satan's (Matt. 6:24; Luke 16:13). For this reason, the Scriptures exhort believers to be of sober mind and judgment (Rom. 12:3; 1 Thess. 5:6, 8; 1 Peter 1:13), because the systems of the world in which we live actively oppose Christ and his kingdom.

During the course of a single day, Christian men and women face the foe of deception many times. Certainly we face the personal temptations to believe lies in the same way that Adam and Eve were tempted. In addition, there is also the multiplication of false teaching, both within and without the church, which already existed in the days of early Christianity (Mark 13:22; Acts 13:6; 2 Peter 2:1; 1 John 4:1). Aside from these obvious deceptions, Christians face the more subtle rationalization of their sins—which amounts to being deceived about their true identity (Gal. 6:3; 1 John 3:7).

Christ's victory over deception brings tremendous hope to the Christian life. It assures us that one day we will no longer wonder whether the voice we hear calling us is the voice of God or of the enemy. Scripture contains only one example to help us understand the true gravity of this victory. In chapter 1, we noted that Adam's work was perfect and free. Before the fall, neither Adam nor Eve hesitated to obey God in any endeavor because the deception of sin had not yet entered the world. Likewise, in the eternal kingdom, with deception destroyed forever, Christians will enjoy a similar freedom—the freedom to do as God asks without hesitation. We will finally let our guard down against sin because it will be gone forever.

Victory over the Devil: The Defeat of the Accuser

Not only is Satan disarmed and his servants defeated, but Satan himself is also defeated. John tells of heaven's celebration at his defeat: "Now the salvation and the power and the kingdom of our God and the authority of his Christ have come, for the accuser of our brothers has been thrown down, who accuses them day and night before our God. And they have conquered him by the blood of the Lamb and by the word of their testimony" (Rev. 12:10–11). The name *Satan* means "accuser." Satan is the one who began this whole war with his accusations in Genesis 3. And he is the one empowering and instructing his servants as the source of evil (Rev. 13:4). In fact, he is "the deceiver of the whole world" (12:9). After his minions are cast into the eternal lake of fire (19:20), he is likewise cast there to be tormented with them forever and ever (20:10). He who started the battle in the beginning will be once and for all expelled from the everlasting kingdom of God.

Victory over the Flesh: The Defeat of the Christian's Identity Crisis

What, then, remains to be disposed of? The enemies without have been conquered; the enemy within must be also. The conquering of sin within the hearts of God's people is also discussed in Revelation, though less obviously, since God's people themselves are already conquered by the love of Christ. What remains is to put away sin from within them entirely, to make them anew in true righteousness and holiness (Eph. 4:24). John's visions often depict this concept in God's people's donning white garments (Rev. 3:5; 6:11; 7:13–14; 19:6–8). The heavenly voices explain that the "bright and pure" (i.e., white) linens represent the righteous deeds of the people of God. The key to understanding Christ's victory here lies in the phrase "it was granted her" (19:8), as Leon Morris explains: "The [righteous deeds] were given to the saints, not provided by them. The white robes of the multitude in 7:9, 14 were not provided by a righteous act on the part of the wearers, but were the result of washing 'in the blood of the Lamb.' So it is here [in chapter 19]."[11] Christ conquered the enemy within us by his death and resurrection. The consummation of his victory will result in his presenting "the church to himself in splendor, without spot or wrinkle or any such thing, that she might be holy and without blemish" (Eph. 5:27).

The battle against the sin in our own lives sometimes manifests itself in doubt. "Is this what God wants me to do right now?" "Am I hearing God, myself, or the voice of the world?" Christ's victory over the sinful deeds of the flesh means that in that day internal warring will cease. The heart, mind, and body will all act in accord with our new identity in Christ (Rom. 8:14–17). Paul anticipates this new reality, when the "perishable puts on the imperishable" (1 Cor. 15:54). If Christians share in the victory of Christ's death, they will also share in the victory of his resurrection (v. 21). That victory means that our lives will be unified in all respects as they were in the garden of Eden. We will want to please God, and in all things we will. Not a hint of the old struggle will remain, for it will have passed away (1 Cor. 7:31; Rev. 21:1, 4).

Victory over Death: The Defeat of the Last Enemy

With all other enemies subdued by Christ, the last enemy remains: death (1 Cor. 15:26). Paul understands death well, explaining, "If, because of one man's trespass, death reigned through that one man, much more will those who receive the abundance of grace and the free gift of righteousness reign in life through the one man Jesus Christ" (Rom. 5:17). He knows that death was defeated by Christ (1 Cor. 15:54–57). Likewise, John sees death personified in Revelation 20:13–15 and destroyed; thus, "death shall be no more" (21:4). The poet John Donne expresses this truth exquisitely in his Divine Sonnet X:

Death be not proud, though some have called thee
Mighty and dreadful, for thou art not so;

11. Morris, *Revelation*, 216.

For those whom thou think'st thou dost overthrow
Die not poor Death nor yet canst thou kill me.
From rest and sleep, which but thy pictures be
Much pleasure, then from thee much more must flow;
And soonest our best men with thee do go,
Rest of their bones and soul's delivery.
Thou art slave to Fate, chance, kings, and desperate men,
And dost with poison, war, and sickness dwell,
And poppy or charms can make us sleep as well
And better than thy stroke; why swell'st thou then?
One short sleep past, we wake eternally
And Death shall be no more; Death, thou shalt die.[12]

Untimely or not, death is one of the deepest sorrows experienced on earth, and it leaves in its wake a pain that will be healed only in the resurrection to come. The destruction of death teaches Christians that death, while a large part of the experience of everyday life, is unnatural and contrary to God's design (Gen. 2:17). This is particularly important for us to remember. We should not become numb to death, should never allow ourselves to become accustomed to it. It is to be hated.

Christ's victory over death has further implications for believers when they experience the death of people they love. When a believer dies, it is correct to affirm that he or she is with the Lord (2 Cor. 5:6–9; Phil. 1:21–23). But the Christian hope for complete healing from the pain of death and for reunion with departed loved ones lies in the resurrection and the new creation (John 11:24–25; 1 Thess. 4:13–17). Only there will Christians find enduring victory over death, the last enemy.

Victory Everlasting

During discussions of heaven, the question arises, "What will keep the new heavens and the new earth from suffering the same curse as Eden?" While there are similarities between Eden and the

12. John Donne, *The Complete Poetry and Selected Prose of John Donne*, ed. Charles M. Coffin, Modern Library Classics (New York: Modern Library, 2001), 250.

114

new creation, it is crucial to remember that heaven is not a return to Eden's paradise but deliverance from Eden's curse. That is, redemptive history moves in one direction—toward restoration, not back to the beginning. Here are the two key differences between creation and the new creation that assure Christians of everlasting righteousness.

The Presence of Evil Is Removed. John closes his description of the New Jerusalem with these words: "nothing unclean will ever enter [the New Jerusalem], nor anyone who does what is detestable or false, but only those who are written in the Lamb's book of life" (Rev. 21:27). In the garden, evil was present in the form of a serpent. The possibility of sin was present in Eden because the presence of evil introduced an external factor. But without the presence of evil, the creation will for the first time exist without an influence pushing it away from God. The new creation is a place where only righteousness will flourish (2 Peter 3:13).

The Possibility of Rebellion Is Removed. The difference between Adam in the garden and believers in the new creation lies in the nature of their perfection. Was Adam perfect? Yes. But Adam was perfect with the possibility of losing his perfection. Based on Christ's saving work, God declares us righteous now (Rom. 4:5; 5:1; 2 Cor. 5:21) and will perfect us in righteousness in the life to come (Phil 3:21; 1 Thess. 5:23–24; 1 John 3:2–3). Resurrected and transformed believers are as incapable of sinning as they are of undoing Christ's death and resurrection.

Reigning in Victory with Christ in His Kingdom

Because believers are united to Christ in his death, they are also united to him in his resurrection life. The Scriptures attest to the coreign of all believers with Christ, from the moment of conversion by faith (Eph. 2:4–6; Rev. 5:9–10) into eternity future in the new creation (Dan. 7:26–27; 2 Tim. 2:12; Rev. 22:3–5). They will judge both fallen angels and rebellious humanity (Dan. 7:22; 1 Cor. 6:2; Rev. 20:4). That is, believers will sit enthroned with Christ as he carries out the judgment initiated by the Father, "probably by agreeing with and praising his judicial decisions. . . . Consequently, the saints are

115

pictured as beginning to reign and to execute the judicial function that they will carry out consummately at the end of the age."[13]

Transformation

How are we to live now in our fallen kingdom? Christ reigns, we are seated with him (Col. 3:1–3), and yet evil still abounds. The world still oppresses. Doubt still wars with faith. How can such things be if Jesus is seated as King? When will he make the kingdom perfect? The disciples wondered as much (Acts 1:6). Jesus' reply was to say that they were asking the wrong question. The question is not when he will come again, but how we are to live in the midst of this tension until he returns.

The short answer is for believers to put on the full armor of God (Eph. 6:10–18). That is, we must put on Christ himself and fight in his strength if we are to stand firm. It can hardly be said better than Puritan William Gurnall in his classic *The Christian in Complete Armour*:

> By armor is meant Christ. We read of putting on the Lord Jesus (Rom. 13:14), where Christ is set forth under the notion of armor. The apostle does not exhort them, for rioting and drunkenness, to put on sobriety and temperance . . . as the philosopher would have done, but bids them to put on the Lord Jesus Christ, implying this much, that until Christ is put on, the creature is unarmed. It is not a man's morality and philosophical virtues that will repel a temptation sent with a full charge from Satan's cannon. . . . The graces of Christ are the armor of Christ.[14]

Therefore, the means of victory—union with Christ—is also the means of battle, as Paul explains: "as you received Christ Jesus the Lord, so walk in him" (Col. 2:6).

13. Beale, *The Book of Revelation*, 997.
14. William Gurnall, *The Christian in Complete Armour: Or, a Treatise on the Saints' War with the Devil*, ed. John Campbell (London: William Tegg, 1862), 26 (adapted into modern English by the authors).

Battling Sin

We have already been freed from the power of sin (Rom. 6), but it still wages war against us (Rom. 7:15–20). So John hears the call of the angel, "Come out of her, my people, lest you take part in her sins, lest you share in her plagues; for her sins are heaped high as heaven, and God has remembered her iniquities" (Rev. 18:4–5). In their fight against evil, Christians sometimes spend their efforts battling the wrong enemy. Paul reminds us that in the kingdom of God, the true enemy is "the rulers, . . . the authorities, . . . the cosmic powers over this present darkness, . . . the spiritual forces of evil in the heavenly places" (Eph. 6:12). There are two key implications for the church.

Fight the Enemy, Not Your Brother. In a church riddled with disunity and internal conflict (1 Cor. 3:1–9), Paul urges the unity of believers by using the image of a physical body. He concludes the picture: "God has so composed the body . . . that there may be no division in the body, but that the members may have the same care for one another. If one member suffers, all suffer together; if one member is honored, all rejoice together" (1 Cor. 12:24–26). Does this typify your church, your small group, your family? To be united to Christ is to be united to each other—forever. As brothers and sisters, we all struggle to get along with fellow members of the body of Christ. Age, culture, socioeconomic status, even personal preferences all hinder the unity of the body. But Christ died that we might be reconciled not only to God, but also to each other: "For he himself is our peace, who has made us both one and has broken down in his flesh the dividing wall of hostility . . . , that he might create in himself one new man in place of the two, so making peace, and might reconcile us both to God in one body through the cross, thereby killing the hostility" (Eph. 2:14–16).

Fight the Enemy, Not Yourself. All believers struggle to see themselves as God sees them, and for good reason: we are keenly aware of our sin. But it is a tactic of the evil one to misdirect our efforts so that we fight against ourselves instead of him. That is, we make ourselves the enemy. We think, "I am such a failure. God cannot use me, and never will, especially after this. I might as well just give up now." The temptation is to define ourselves in terms of our weaknesses rather than in terms of our union with Christ. But because we are united to him, we share in his victory over the evil one (1 John 5:4–5). We have a new identity as children of the living God, and Satan can never destroy our heritage.

Overcoming Evil

How, then, do we overcome evil? Not by our strength. This, among other things, is how popular media has led the church astray. Fortunately, Jude provides a helpful corrective in this regard: "when the archangel Michael, contending with the devil, was disputing about the body of Moses, he did not presume to pronounce a blasphemous judgment, but said, 'The Lord rebuke you'" (Jude 9). Believers do not do battle with Satan directly; Jesus does. The mandate throughout the New Testament is not to conquer evil but to stand firm in the midst of it—Paul tells the Ephesians to stand firm three times in the context of putting on the armor of God (Eph. 6:11, 13, 14).

Rather, it is Christ who conquers on our behalf, and we share his victory. Countless Christians doubt that they are good or strong enough to conquer evil. But all are heirs of the kingdom (Matt. 25:34, 46). This is why Christians are not primarily described as "earners" of heavenly victory but as heirs of the kingdom with Christ (Rev. 21:7), as sons and daughters of the King (Rom. 8:16–17; Gal. 4:5–7). How do people become heirs? Again, not by their own doing, but by the work of the Father, who adopts them into his family by grace through faith. To be a Christian, then, is to have already conquered the enemy through the Lamb (Rom. 8:37). What remains is to appropriate that victory, leveraging it against the guerrilla warfare of the devil by the power of Christ in the Spirit. Sin has no authority over us except what we abdicate to it.

Enduring until the End

We all know brothers and sisters in the Lord who walked well with God, and then, because of some trauma or sin in their lives, experienced a great fall. Such things should not shock us. Do we really believe that Satan is always after us? Do we really understand that there is not a single redemptive thing about him? Even the most wicked persons are still made in the image of God and are decent at times to, say, their own families. But not Satan; his every thought and deed overflows with hatred for God. And he has had great success in terrorizing God's people.

But in the end, all of God's true children will conquer the devil, even those who outwardly do not seem to endure to the end. Can suicide (as tragic as it is) separate a Christian from the Lord? By no means! Can murder or hatred or adultery or addiction? No, even in the midst of these, those whom God has called will inherit the kingdom (Rom. 8:28–30). It is only those who never knew him—or rather, whom he never knew—who will be cast out of the eternal kingdom (Matt. 7:21–23). Certainly, the fight will be hard; it could cost a job, a loved one, even one's own life. Christians have been ridiculed, hated, beaten . . . and yet by God's grace they have endured.

How do we endure? Hebrews says that it is by imitating the lives of those who have gone before us. Consider first Jesus, "who endured from sinners such hostility against himself" (Heb. 12:3). What enabled him to do so? Yes, his divine power—but remember that he was also fully human. In his humanity, he had to endure the same trials as we do (2:10–18). But it was "for the joy that was set before him [that he] endured the cross" (12:2). That is, he looked beyond the cross to the inheritance in the kingdom beyond. By fixing our eyes on the coming kingdom, we imitate the godly men and women in Scripture who looked to God's future promises for strength to endure (6:10–12; 11:23–26). Because our inheritance is safe, we find strength to persevere, to press on toward the goal for which Christ Jesus first took hold of us (Phil. 3:14).

Having viewed three pictures of heaven (as creation, rest, and kingdom), we next turn our attention to a fourth picture: heaven as the presence of God.

Part 4

Presence

7

Banished from God's Presence

"IN YOUR PRESENCE there is fullness of joy; at your right hand are pleasures forevermore" (Ps. 16:11). Addressing these words to God, David knew that true life, joy, and satisfaction are found only in God's presence. Jonathan Edwards, in a sermon preached in 1733, explained:

> God is the highest good of the reasonable creature, and the enjoyment of him is the only happiness with which our souls can be satisfied. To go to heaven fully to enjoy God, is *infinitely* better than the most pleasant accommodations here. Fathers and mothers, husbands, wives, children, or the company of earthly friends, are but shadows. But the enjoyment of God is the substance. These are but scattered beams, but God is the sun. These are but streams, but God is the fountain. These are but drops, but God is the ocean.[1]

Our first parents enjoyed God's presence in the garden of Eden. God will supremely bless his people with his presence on the last day. In between Eden and the last day, human beings are driven out of God's presence, and many, believing in Christ, enjoy a renewal of that presence. But only in the resurrection will they

---

1. Jonathan Edwards, "The Christian Pilgrim," quoted in Alister E. McGrath, *A Brief History of Heaven* (Malden, MA: Blackwell Publishing, 2003), 115 (italics in original).

know the joys of being with God as never before. We will reflect on the first three categories here and on the restoration (being supremely blessed with the divine presence) in the next chapter.

- Creation: Serving in God's Presence
- Fall: Banished from His Presence
- Redemption: Renewed by His Presence
- Restoration: Blessed with His Presence

Creation: Serving in God's Presence

From the beginning, Scripture depicts God as a personal Creator with a vital interest in his creatures: "Then the LORD God formed the man of dust from the ground and breathed into his nostrils the breath of life, and the man became a living creature" (Gen. 2:7). Though man is not the only creature to possess the breath of life (see 1:30), he is the only one created in God's personal image, the only one endowed with such glory. And he is the only creature shaped directly by God's hand, emphasizing God's personal involvement with and care for his human creatures. But God does not create Adam and Eve and then forget them. The rest of Genesis 2–3 presents God as having an ongoing personal relationship with our first parents. This is characterized by his presence in the garden as they begin to fulfill their mutual calling to be fruitful and multiply and to cultivate the garden and keep it (2:15–24).

The Garden as God's First Temple Dwelling

For the ancient Israelite, reading Genesis 1–3 would have underscored the Lord's presence in the garden of Eden. While Christians today most commonly refer to the place in Genesis 1–3 as "the garden of Eden," the fact is that outside the creation narrative it is more commonly referred to in the way Lot refers to it, as "the garden of the LORD" (Gen. 13:10; Isa. 51:3), or as "the garden of God" (Ezek. 31:8, 9).[2] In fact, Gregory Beale successfully argues that the first audience in the wilderness would have understood the garden as the first dwelling place and temple of the Lord God, in which the first man both served and worshiped.[3]

The Garden as the Lord's Royal Palace. As God's creative act comes to a close in Genesis 2:3, the narrator shifts his focus to the garden, planted by God near Eden (v. 8). The language used by Moses suggests that the Israelites understood Eden and its garden as a sort of palatial domain, one that is fitting not only for God's perfect image-bearers, but also for the dwelling and enjoyment of the Creator-King and his interaction with his subjects.

Palace and temple complexes in Moses' day often had common features, in much the same way that capitol buildings today are similar, though each one is unique. One such feature was a royal garden. As the climax of a 180-day celebration of himself, King Ahasuerus of Persia "gave for all the people present in Susa . . . a feast lasting for seven days in the court of the garden of the king's palace" (Esth. 1:5). In an Old Testament context, only very powerful, important people would have had a garden; it was a luxury.[4] Thus, the simple fact that the Lord himself made a garden suggests that he is one such person. And like the royal and divine gardens of other ancient cultures, its beauty was magnificent: "And out of the ground the LORD God made to spring up every tree that is *pleasant to the sight* and good for food" (Gen. 2:9). Christians ought not to think of the garden as merely providing food for humankind. It is also the adornment of the first dwelling place of the Lord.

Additionally, the garden seems to have been an actual paradise. When Solomon recounts his kingly dwelling, he describes a paradise: "I built houses and planted vineyards for myself. I

2. The two occurrences of "the garden of Eden" outside the creation account are in Ezekiel 36:35 and Joel 2:3.

3. G. K. Beale, *The Temple and the Church's Mission: A Biblical Theology of the Dwelling Place of God* (Downers Grove, IL: InterVarsity Press, 2004), 66. Beale's treatment provides a framework for the rest of this subsection.

4. Similarly, Ahab, king of Samaria, sought to annex a vineyard from Naboth to have a garden near his house (1 Kings 21:2).

made myself gardens and parks, and planted in them all kinds of fruit trees. . . . I also gathered for myself silver and gold and the treasure of kings and provinces" (Eccl. 2:4–5, 8). Would not the dwelling place of the King of the universe be luxurious? Every tree, Moses writes, had both exquisite beauty and wonderful fruit (Gen. 2:9). The garden was surrounded by flowing water, which wandering Israel surely recognized as a luxury in the desert areas of the east. And it was located in an area abundant in gold and precious stones (2:11–12). Eden is truly a place of joy and gladness in the presence of the Lord (Ps. 16:11; Isa. 51:3).

One further indication that the garden of Eden was a royal palace of the Lord is the presence of his royal guard. Certainly any king or deity protected his dwelling from those who would defile it. So it is with Eden. As one would expect, the Lord stations his guardian cherubs at the edge of Eden to protect its sanctity against the return of a then impure Adam and Eve (Gen. 3:24).

The Garden as a Temple of Worship of the Lord. Not only was the garden of Eden the first royal dwelling place of the Lord God, but it was also the temple in which the first man and woman served and worshiped him. Geographically, the "entrance" to the garden was on the east (3:24), as was the entrance to the tabernacle courtyard (Ex. 27:13–16). This suggests that Moses was drawing a parallel between entering Eden and entering the tabernacle, a parallel that must have been striking for the original readers. Further, the language used by Moses in Genesis 2:15 to describe the work of Adam and Eve ("to cultivate," *abad*, and "keep/guard," *shamar*) is also found elsewhere in Scripture, the terms occurring together to refer to serving God and keeping his word (Deut. 11:16; Josh. 22:5) or to the task of the Levites' serving their brothers and guarding the tabernacle complex (Num. 3:7–8; 18:5–6; 1 Chron. 23:32). In effect, Moses "was portraying Adam against the later portrait of Israelite priests, and . . . he was the archetypal priest who served in and guarded (or 'took care of') God's first temple."[5] Thus, the work with which Adam

---

5. Beale, *The Temple and the Church's Mission,* 68.

was charged was not just manual labor. Rather, the charge given to Adam and Eve was nothing less than to serve God and worship him in his temple.

The Garden as the Place of the Lord's Presence. In ancient cultures, not unlike our own, prosperity—fertility, bountiful crops, many possessions, and great beauty—was commonly interpreted as a sign of the presence of a deity, and with his presence came his blessing. It is that way in Eden; the sheer opulence of the place "was a sign of God's presence in and blessing on Eden."[6]

More specifically, the narrative of Genesis 3 suggests that God himself regularly walked in the garden. Genesis 2:25 offers a concluding summary of the disposition of Adam and Eve after their coming together in the garden: "And the man and his wife were both naked and were not ashamed." Compare that with the way they are described after eating from the tree of the knowledge of good and evil: "and they knew that they were naked. And they sewed fig leaves together and made themselves loincloths" (3:7). In other words, it was not their physical nature that somehow changed—they were naked just as they were before eating. Rather, it was their moral character that was altered, damaged by their actions, as represented by their shame at their formerly unashamed nakedness.

This is significant, for it is *the reason* for their hiding from God's presence in the garden. Moses writes, "They heard the sound of the LORD God walking in the garden in the cool of the day" (Gen. 3:8). The picture is that of the Founder of the garden taking his usual evening stroll, enjoying the night air and the glory of his creation. Such a picture is right in line with the personal, loving Creator portrayed throughout the Genesis narrative. As the Lord is doing so, Adam and Eve hear a sound in the evening air, a sound that produces fear (v. 10). But what sound could possibly evoke such an emotion? Certainly not the sound of the beasts or the birds, since Adam has just named them (2:19–20). Such an act was a symbol of the authority of the name-giver over

6. Gordon J. Wenham, *Genesis 1–15*, Word Biblical Commentary (Waco, TX: Word, 1987), 61; cf. ibid., 76.

that which was named.[7] Who is afraid of something over which he has complete authority? The narrative points the reader to the one obvious fact: Adam and Eve are afraid of facing their Maker, the One who has authority over them. They hear the sound that he makes walking among the trees of the garden (3:8), and for the first time this sound puts fear in their hearts.

In sum, it is likely that Moses and the exodus community understood Eden as a temple-like place, a sanctuary and royal palace that the Lord built to dwell among his good creation. Paradise is secure. As long as Adam and Eve obey the command of the Lord, they will enjoy the prosperity of his presence. But the Lord's presence demands holiness, as is well pictured by the later ritual purification needed to worship him in the tabernacle and temple. Nothing impure can remain in Eden; it must be put out.

Fall: Banished from His Presence

When Eve took fruit from the tree of the knowledge of good and evil, she ate and gave some to her husband, who was with her (Gen. 3:6). This is in direct opposition to God's command (in 2:16–17). For many of us, the synopsis of the fall ends there. But if the garden of Eden was understood as God's first royal dwelling place, then the original audience would have been horrified—for in essence Adam and Eve would have robbed God's temple, God's palace. Like later thieves who would conquer Israel and carry away the vessels of gold used for the worship of God, in a single abominable act Adam and Eve defiled his sanctuary by stealing from it. Does this not further explain why they so quickly hid from the presence of the Lord walking in his garden?

Of course, it is impossible for Adam and Eve to hide from God's presence. The hiding serves as an opportunity for dialogue

7. Gerhard von Rad, *Genesis: A Commentary*, trans. John H. Marks, Old Testament Library (London: SCM Press, 1961), 83, quoted in George W. Ramsey, "Is Name-Giving an Act of Domination in Genesis 2:23 and Elsewhere?" *Catholic Biblical Quarterly* 50, 1 (1988): 24–35.

between Adam and God. That dialogue reveals that the holy presence of the Lord exposes disobedience to him, resulting in fear, shame, and guilt.[8] Now, it is not Adam and Eve's nakedness itself that is the problem. Rather, being naked before the Creator God is a picture of sin's exposure by the holiness of God.

After setting forth punishments for their disobedience, God then symbolizes the disconnect that sin has created by banishing Adam and Eve from the garden (Gen. 3:24), and thus by implication from his presence and blessing there. The severity of the sentence is evident: the Lord God "drove out the man, and at the east of the garden of Eden he placed the cherubim and a flaming sword that turned every way to guard the way to the tree of life" (v. 24). Such supernatural guards highlight the priority of keeping God's dwelling place free from the defiling presence of our first parents. The fellowship of God and man dwelling together in perfect harmony in paradise has been irreparably broken.

Redemption: Renewed by His Presence

Genesis 1–3 sets forth a picture of life and communion with God: when humanity is living according to his will, his presence brings protection, favor, and joy. When men and women rebel against the Lord, however, his presence becomes a source of fear, guilt, and shame. God has put humankind away from his presence because his holiness cannot tolerate their sin. But in addition, the banishment of Adam and Eve from the garden was an act of his grace, so that they would not be destroyed by their own folly. The first humans and their progeny are banished from the garden so that they may not "take also of the tree of life and eat, and live forever" (3:22). Sin has introduced death (2:17). To allow Adam and Eve to live forever in their condemnation would be cruel, for it would imprison them in a life of misery. The damage caused by their sin must be remedied. To remedy the problem that sin

8. C. John Collins, *Genesis 1–4: A Linguistic, Literary, and Theological Commentary* (Phillipsburg, NJ: P&R Publishing, 2005), 174.

has created, God must now provide a way to once again dwell among his people without contaminating his own holy presence.

The Presence of God in the Tabernacle and Temple

The first form of God's provision for his presence comes directly after he rescues his people from slavery in Egypt. Now that God has redeemed them, he reaffirms his covenant with them, and they with him (Ex. 19–24). God meets with them on Mount Sinai, and his holy presence descends in fire, smoke, and lightning. But some problems linger.

Israel Is Still a Sinful People. Before God descends to Mount Sinai, he tells Moses to warn the people, "Take care not to go up into the mountain or touch the edge of it. Whoever touches the mountain shall be put to death. No hand shall touch him, but he shall be stoned or shot; whether beast or man, he shall not live" (Ex. 19:12–13). Their consciousness of their own sin is evident by their collective response: "The people were afraid and trembled, and they stood far off and said to Moses, 'You speak to us, and we will listen; but do not let God speak to us, lest we die'" (20:18–19). Like Adam and Eve, their sin makes them tremble before the Lord's holy presence and retreat in fear and guilt. Yet God's coming is not a coming in judgment but a coming in redemption, for now that the Israelites have been delivered from Egypt, they can worship God at his holy mountain (3:12; 19:4).

Israel Is Still Far from the Promised Land. Further complicating the situation is that Mount Sinai is not Israel's final destination. The Israelites have been promised the land of Canaan that the Lord showed Abraham (Gen. 12:1–9), the land that he promised would be theirs after four hundred years of captivity (15:13–14). God's presence is on the mountain, but that is not the place where they are to remain. They are to journey onward, cross the Jordan River, and take possession of the land promised to Abraham, Isaac, and Jacob.

God's Solution Is the Tabernacle. God commands Moses to take up a contribution from the people, that they may "make me a sanctuary, that I may dwell in their midst" (Ex. 25:8). This is to be a dwelling place designed by the Lord himself (25:40; 27:8). God's presence at Sinai needs to be made portable if God is to go with Israel as the people journey to the Promised Land. For this is the purpose of their redemption by God: "I will dwell among the people of Israel and will be their God. And they shall know that I am the LORD their God, who brought them out of the land of Egypt that I might dwell among them. I am the LORD their God" (29:45–46). The tabernacle contains echoes of Eden, where the Lord God walked freely among his people.

But in order for the Most Holy God to dwell with his sinful people, God had to make provision for them to be present with him without defiling his holiness. And the book of Leviticus sets forth his solution. When all is said and done, God sets forth the blessings of obedience (Lev. 26:3–13) and the curses for disobedience (26:14–45), following a similar covenant formula as with Adam (Gen. 2:15–17; Hos. 6:7),[9] Noah (Gen. 9:8–17), and Abraham (12:1–3; 15:7–21; 17:1–21). God promises Israel a kind of renewal of Eden by the restoration of his presence among them, conditioned on covenantal faithfulness: "I will make my dwelling among you, and my soul shall not abhor you. And I will walk among you and will be your God, and you shall be my people. I am the LORD your God, who brought you out of the land of Egypt" (Lev. 26:11–13).

The Israelites thus understood from Leviticus 26 that faithful living from the heart would result in the continued presence of the Lord among them, ongoing protection from their enemies, conquest and possession of the Promised Land, and rest from oppression. But disobedience would result in military defeat, plagues and famines, untold hardships, and ultimately banishment into the hands of their enemies, with the Israelites' once more being cast out from the Lord's presence.

After many years, Israel obtains possession of the Promised Land, and God eventually establishes a permanent dwelling place

---

9. Though the term *covenant* is not found in the account of Adam and Eve, later biblical authors in both Testaments nonetheless recognize our first parents as being under a covenant (Hos. 6:7; Rom. 5:12–21; 1 Cor. 15:22, 45).

in Jerusalem through King Solomon (1 Kings 5–8). Solomon places the ark of the covenant within the temple, and the glory cloud of the Lord's presence fills the temple (1 Kings 8:10–11), just as his presence filled the tabernacle (Ex. 40:34–38). When Solomon sees this, he dedicates the temple in the sight of all Israel and prays for his people, that they may always be faithful to the covenant (1 Kings 8:22–61). He prays that when the people sin and the curses of Leviticus 26 are levied against them, God will forgive the people when they repent and restore his favorable presence among them. He prays this way so that the Israelites might experience the full measure of the Lord's promise to dwell among them forever as their God (Lev. 26:11–13).

Israel, however, wavers and goes after other gods. The people do not walk in the Lord's way, nor do they keep his statutes, commands, and ordinances (1 Kings 8:58). And the Lord, faithful to his covenant, gives Israel into the hands of its enemy—Nebuchadnezzar, king of Babylon—who burns down the temple (2 Kings 25:9), symbolizing the departure of the Lord's presence from among his rebellious people (Ezek. 10:1–22).

The Presence of God in the Son of God

With the temple destroyed and the people of God enslaved by other nations, what hope is there for Israel? The hope is that though we are faithless, God remains faithful to his covenant throughout all generations, even as Solomon prayed in his benediction to God's people at the dedication of the temple: "The LORD our God be with us, as he was with our fathers" (1 Kings 8:57). The apostle John records the answer to Solomon's prayer and hope: the return of the presence of God among his people in the person of Jesus Christ: "In the beginning was the Word, and the Word was with God, and the Word was God. . . . And the Word became flesh and *dwelt* among us, and we have seen his glory, glory as of the only Son from the Father, full of grace and truth" (John 1:1, 14). John describes Jesus as "tabernacling" ("dwelling") among us, a reference that first-century Christians would understand as alluding to the Old Testament tabernacle and temple. God's people were unfaithful to the covenant, and his presence departed from among them. What our hearts were powerless to perform God did himself through his own Son, Jesus Christ, who humbled himself to be made like us so that he might once and for all renew the presence of God among his people (Rom. 8:3; Heb. 9:23–27).

The Presence of God in the Lives of His People

After declaring that he is about to depart from them, Jesus explains to his disciples how he will establish his presence among them forever: "And I will ask the Father, and he will give you another Helper, to be with you forever, even the Spirit of truth, whom the world cannot receive, because it neither sees him nor knows him. You know him, for he *dwells with you and will be in you*. . . . If anyone loves me, he will keep my word, and my Father will love him, and we will come to him and make our *home* with him" (John 14:16–17, 23). By the indwelling of the Holy Spirit, poured out at Pentecost (Acts 2), is how Jesus erects the true temple—a temple not made with human hands—in which Father, Son, and Holy Spirit will dwell with their people forever (Eph. 2:18–22; Heb. 9:11–24).

The Church as the True Temple Dwelling of God. All those indwelt by the Holy Spirit are the true temple, the true house of the living God: "you yourselves like living stones are being built up as a spiritual house, to be a holy priesthood, to offer spiritual sacrifices acceptable to God through Jesus Christ" (1 Peter 2:5). Despite divisions that Christians make among themselves, there is but one church and one true temple of the living God (1 Cor. 3:16). There is no room for divisions because of the Holy Spirit's presence (Eph. 4:1–6). There is no other place, and there is no other people of God. Transferring membership from one church to another or changing denominations does not dissolve the bond of the Holy Spirit any more than turning eighteen changes one's biological relationship to his or her parents. God has chosen people to believe in Jesus Christ and likewise gifted them each to play a role in the grand story of redemption (Acts 13:48)—whether we like them, agree with them, or see them. All are one, united by the indwelling presence of God's Spirit.

The Renewing Power of the Presence of God. The building of this New Testament temple of God is not an end unto itself, but like the Old Testament tabernacle and temple, the indwelling presence of God has a redemptive purpose. Solomon declared it, as we have seen above, and Peter affirms it also: "you yourselves like living stones are being built up as a spiritual house, to be a holy priesthood, to offer spiritual sacrifices acceptable to God through Jesus Christ" (1 Peter 2:5). God has renewed his presence among his people so that they might experience his holiness. Paul says it this way: "What agreement has the temple of God with idols? For we are the temple of the living God; as God said, 'I will make my dwelling among them and walk among them, and I will be their God, and they shall be my people'" (2 Cor. 6:16, quoting Lev. 26:11–12). The charge to faithfulness and holiness in Leviticus 26 is now applied to the church in the new covenant. Because God has chosen people to believe in him and made them to be his people, building them into an everlasting temple, they should be holy in all they do.

And just as in the Old Testament, obedience is not an end in itself. But progressive sanctification—the transformation brought about by the renewal of God's presence in the lives of his people—serves to identify Christians as God's people to the watching world. Obedience is intended to differentiate the people of God from those who do not know him. And although it looks different in different contexts, obedience ultimately serves the purpose of bringing people into relationship with Jesus Christ.

Jesus himself hints at this purpose in the Great Commission (Matt. 28:18–20):

> All authority in heaven and on earth has been given to me. Go
> therefore and make disciples of all nations, baptizing them in
> the name of the Father and of the Son and of the Holy Spirit,

134

teaching them to observe all that I have commanded you. And behold, I am with you always, to the end of the age.

Compare this to the words of Solomon to Israel at the conclusion of his prayer of dedication of the temple in 1 Kings 8:57–58, and 60:

> The LORD our God be with us, as he was with our fathers. May he not leave us or forsake us, that he may incline our hearts to him, to walk in all his ways and to keep his commandments, his statutes, and his rules, which he commanded our fathers . . . , that all the peoples of the earth may know that the LORD is God; there is no other.

By declaring, "I am with you always," Jesus puts himself in the place of God as the answer to Solomon's prayer, proclaiming his own divine character and power. But more than that, Jesus assures the disciples that they themselves are recipients of the presence of God promised in the Old Testament. Jesus builds on the theological foundation of the presence of God with his people from the garden of Eden until that very day:[10]

> "God is with you," says Abimelech to Abraham (Gen. 21:22).

> "I am with you and will bless you," says the Lord to Isaac (26:24).

> "I am with you . . . wherever you go," says God to Jacob (28:15).

> "God will be with you," says Jacob, blessing Joseph (48:21).

> "I will be with you," says the Lord to Moses at the burning bush (Ex. 3:12).

> "I will make my dwelling among you," the Lord promises Israel (Lev. 26:11).

10. This formula is later echoed in Acts 18:10 when the Lord declares to Paul, "I am with you, and no one will attack you to harm you, for I have many in this city who are my people."

"And I . . . will be your God," he declares to his people Israel (26:12).

"As I was with Moses, so I will be with you," says the Lord to Joshua (Josh. 1:5).

"I will be with you," the Lord promises Solomon (1 Kings 11:38).

"I am with you to deliver you," the Lord promises Jeremiah (Jer. 1:8).

"Be strong, . . . for I am with you," the Lord assures all his people (Hag. 2:4).

"The Lord is with you!" Gabriel declares to Mary, the mother of Jesus (Luke 1:28).

When Jesus concludes his earthly ministry with the apostles, therefore, he is not merely reassuring them of his help. Rather, he is weaving the disciples—and all other New Testament believers—into the ongoing story of the redemption of God's people from the disharmony created by the fall and banishment from the presence of the Lord.

The story of redemption is completed only at the restoration, when believers will enjoy the fullness of God's presence forever. And that is the subject of our next chapter.

Blessed with God's Presence

IN THE PRECEDING CHAPTER, we traced the biblical story of God's presence from creation (Adam and Eve served in his presence) to the fall (they were banished from his presence) to redemption (believers are renewed by that presence). Now we follow the story to its end and view Christians as joyous in God's presence forever.

- Interpreting Visions of God's Presence in Revelation
- Revelation 21: A Picture of the Bride of Christ
- The New Jerusalem as the Bride: A Picture of God's Presence with His People
- Transformation

What did Jesus go to do when he left his disciples and ascended into heaven? To prepare a place for them in the Father's coming kingdom (John 14:1–3). This is where he desires for us to be—with him (17:21)—for now he has been glorified with his rightful splendor. His worthiness is rightly proclaimed: "Worthy are you . . . , for you were slain, and by your blood you ransomed people for God from every tribe and language and people and nation, and you have made them a kingdom and priests to our God, and they shall reign on the earth" (Rev. 5:9–10).

From Genesis into the New Testament, God has *stated* that he is with his people; but in Revelation, which is a series of visions that God gave to the apostle John on Patmos, God *pictures* his presence with his people. For example, it is one thing for John to hear Jesus state matter-of-factly, "All authority in heaven and on earth has been given to me" (Matt. 28:18), but it is quite another for him to see his authority in action as in Revelation 5 above, a picture so moving that it causes John to weep (Rev. 5:4)! There is something very powerful and compelling about the pictures in Revelation. One of the primary blessings of the book is that it paints pictures of many of the things that have been told throughout the biblical story. So it is with the presence of God. The Bible is full of statements about God's presence. But Revelation 21 in particular shows God's people how he will fulfill his promise to dwell among them forever—in a fullness never experienced before—in a way that statements alone cannot describe.

Interpreting Visions of God's Presence in Revelation

The question arises, "What is Revelation 21 picturing?" Is it a real, physical city, to be centered in modern-day Jerusalem, or a mere symbol with no real, tangible sense? At least, this is how the question is sometimes posed! Let us consider the following as we attempt to answer this important question.

John Intended His Message to Be a Blessing

The term *apocalypse*, from which the title *Revelation* comes, means "uncovering" or "revealing."[1] This is why John writes, "Blessed is the one who reads aloud the words of this prophecy, and blessed are those who hear, and who keep what is written in it, for the time is near" (Rev. 1:3). God blessed John by giving him revelation in visions while he was in exile on Patmos. But God did not intend these visions to be for him alone. John was commanded to write down what he saw and pass it

---

1. Gerhard Kittel and Gerhard Friedrich, eds., *Theological Dictionary of the New Testament*, trans. Geoffrey Bromiley (Grand Rapids: Eerdmans, 1985), 405–13.

along so that other believers might be blessed as well (1:11, 19; 14:13; 21:5). Jesus has a message for his church, and John was to communicate that message to the churches in first-century Asia Minor. John, then, wrote down what he saw in the form of a letter that could be easily distributed along a well-traveled Roman postal route.[2]

The Original Readers Understood What John Wrote

This is not the first time that John has written a letter. He knows how to communicate his message in a way that will be readily received by his readers. In order for the visions to have their intended effect on believers through the Holy Spirit, readers must first understand them. When Christians today read the book of Revelation, it is often like reading Homer's *Iliad* or Shakespeare's *Much Ado about Nothing*; they have a difficult time of it. Perhaps this is because two of every three verses refer to the Old Testament—and many of us are deficient in our knowledge of the Old Testament, especially books that John uses heavily, including Exodus, Isaiah, Ezekiel, Daniel, Joel, and Zechariah.

So in order for John's message to have meaning for the original audiences in Asia Minor, the imagery must make sense to them based on their knowledge at the time.[3] This is not to say that they understood everything—we certainly do not! But it does mean that we, who have the same Holy Spirit as they, must read the text of Revelation as if we were in the first century, receiving it from John himself. Only by doing so will we understand the meaning and receive the intended encouragement.

2. William Mitchell Ramsay, *The Letters to the Seven Churches of Asia, and Their Place in the Plan of the Apocalypse* (Grand Rapids: Baker, 1963), 15–34. Though some details are speculative, Ramsay offers a compelling argument that, in principle, the order of the letters recorded in Revelation conformed to John's intended order of circulation using well-known Roman trade routes.

3. When John wrote, written publications were few compared to the modern digital age. Though writing technology had certainly come a long way since the days of Abraham, Greco-Roman and Jewish cultures alike were still primarily oral-learning cultures: if you heard something that you valued, you had to remember it.

Prophetic Visions Use the Understandable to Explain the Heavenly

If someone told you that he caught a "big fish" and that it was thirty inches long, you would need more information to understand how big that fish really was. In order to understand the concept of "big," the hearer needs a point of reference. If the fish were a rainbow trout, thirty inches would be fairly large for such a fish.

Visions in the book of Revelation also provide a point of reference with which the original readers would be familiar, and then against that reference point explain the idea that each vision intends to communicate. G. K. Beale explains: "On one level the seer sees visions composed of earthly pictures that he can understand, whether lions, human figures, books, or someone measuring a wall in an ordinary manner. But the purpose of the visionary images is to reveal to John the deeper meaning of heavenly or spiritual truths that the earthly images symbolize."[4] In other words, God accommodates himself to his people. He speaks in language and imagery that they comprehend—otherwise, the visions in the book of Revelation would be incomprehensible.

Consider an example from the opening chapter of Revelation. John sees the risen Christ standing in the midst of seven lampstands with seven stars in his hands (Rev. 1:12–16). Falling at his feet, John is comforted by Jesus, who commands him to write what he sees (vv. 17–20). Then Jesus explains what John just saw: "the seven stars are the angels of the seven churches, and the seven lampstands are the seven churches" (v. 20).[5] Jesus wants to communicate that he is among his people. But how could he draw a picture of the invisible church? John sees the lampstands, and Jesus says that these are the seven churches. John understands the notion of lampstands—objects from the tabernacle and temple that symbolized the presence of God among his people—and Jesus

---

4. G. K. Beale, *The Book of Revelation: A Commentary on the Greek Text*, New International Greek Testament Commentary (Grand Rapids: Eerdmans, 1999), 1077.

5. The "this is that" prophetic pattern is present elsewhere in Revelation: 4:5; 5:6, 8; 7:13–14; 11:4, 8; 16:13–14; 17:9, 12, 15, 18; 19:8; 20:2; 21:8.

explains that they represent the seven churches, among which Jesus is pictured as standing (v. 13).

Sometimes someone in the vision gives the interpretation; sometimes not. But either way, the pattern remains the same. This is why it is crucial that John writes "Then I saw" or "And I saw," because these words indicate that John is not interpreting the visions himself. John does not present the visions in the form of propositions because they are not propositional; they are metaphorical. So the very nature of the text, received in the form of visions to John, points the reader toward a symbolic interpretation.

Revelation 21: A Picture of the Bride of Christ

John's Readers Would Assume That Bride Refers to a People, Not a Place

Both the Old and New Testaments contain implicit references to God's people as his bride (Isa. 61:10; Jer. 2:2; John 3:29). Outside these contexts, all other uses of *bride* refer to a woman who is (or is to be) married. For those familiar with the Old Testament, this predisposes the reader to understand the bride as the collective worshipers of God. Furthermore, John has already prepared his readers to understand "the Bride" by writing about her in chapter 19, where God's people are pictured as purified, enjoying the consummation of their union with Christ (vv. 7–8).

But the text says that John "saw the holy city, new Jerusalem, coming down out of heaven from God, prepared as a bride adorned for her husband" (Rev. 21:2). How can the city of Jerusalem refer to a people? In the Old Testament, *Jerusalem* was often used as a name for the people of God (e.g., Isa. 40:9; 52:1; 62:6).[6] For those familiar with the Old Testament, then, this would not have posed an obstacle to understanding but would harmonize well with John's description of his vision of "a bride adorned for her husband."

6. This figure of speech is called *metonymy*.

141

John Links Revelation 21:2 with 21:9-10

In terms of structure, Revelation 21:1–27 forms a cohesive narrative unit; John is not describing two different visions. Consider the following verses in Revelation 21:

> And I saw the holy city, new Jerusalem, coming down out of heaven from God, prepared as a bride adorned for her husband. (21:2)

> Then came one of the seven angels . . . , saying, "Come, I will show you the Bride, the wife of the Lamb." And he . . . showed me the holy city Jerusalem coming down out of heaven from God, having the glory of God. (21:9–11)

The striking parallels between the two passages alert readers. And this is intentional. John uses repetition to indicate that the scene in Revelation 21:9–27 is related to the text of 21:1–2. Why, then, do verses 3–8 "interrupt" John's recounting of the vision? Because there he records what he *heard*. He writes, "And I heard a loud voice from the throne saying . . . And he who was seated on the throne said . . ." (vv. 3, 5). For John, all of this happens very quickly. When he retells the vision, however, he writes it in an orderly fashion. In this case, John signals in verse 1 that he sees the New Jerusalem in the new heavens and new earth. As he sees this part of the vision, he twice hears a voice from the throne. John tells us about the voice before he returns to the vision of the New Jerusalem and provides specific details.

The New Jerusalem as the Bride: A Picture of God's Presence with His People

The imagery of the bride communicates that God is united to his people and dwells among them, a conclusion supported by John's quoting Leviticus 26:11–12 in Revelation 21:3. But God is not pictured here as dwelling in a separate tent, approachable only after sacrificial purification, but as living among his people as a husband lives with his wife. This is astounding! The Lord of the universe, the everlasting God, has sovereignly worked throughout world history to bring about an intimate union with his people. Our God is both the transcendent Creator and a loving husband.

Revelation 21: A Picture of the Temple of God

In addition to functioning as narrative links, Revelation 21:1–2 and 21:9–10 function as headings for the verses that follow. Revelation 21:3–8 is the part of the chapter that seems easiest to most Christians. This is because it is written in a style common in the New Testament—in propositional statements. There is no confusing imagery, just references to the Old Testament pointing readers to the conclusion that God is fulfilling his ancient promises. He is remedying the problem of sin that began in Eden. He is redeeming all things in perfect righteousness.

Revelation 21:11–27 is different. The text shifts from propositional statements to the description of a vision that John saw, and we are left to pick up clues along the way. Helpfully, John links the two sections. What John heard from the voice on the throne in 21:3–8 he sees pictured in verses 11–27. Thus, the whole of Revelation 21 is describing the same heavenly reality, "the dwelling place of God . . . with man" (v. 3).

If the focus of Revelation 21 is on God's dwelling with his people, does this not point readers to understand the New Jerusalem as a future, physical city? This is a great question, one often advanced in defense of such an interpretation. And this underscores the importance of keeping the genre of the passage in mind. John recounts the vision that he saw. Remember how visions function in Scripture: the familiar symbolizes the spiritual point behind it. John does not intend to suggest that a nearly 1,380-mile[7] cube will descend one day and land on modern Jerusalem. The question is not "Isn't Jerusalem a real

---

7. This conclusion assumes that a *stadion* measures about 607 feet, or 185 meters.

place?" but "How does this description of the New Jerusalem differ from the Jerusalem familiar to the original readers?" And additionally, "What would those differences signify to those readers?"

The New Jerusalem: A Place of Perfect Holiness. The description of the city throughout chapter 21 is derived in part from Isaiah 52:1, "Awake, awake, put on your strength, O Zion; put on your beautiful garments, O Jerusalem, the holy city; for there shall no more come into you the uncircumcised and the unclean." The imagery of the bride, together with the description of the holiness of this new place—a place where "nothing unclean will ever enter it, nor anyone who does what is detestable or false" (Rev. 21:27; see also 22:3)—portrays this new, sin-free state. All those who are meek, who are found in the Lamb's Book of Life, will inherit the New Jerusalem (Matt. 5:5; 25:34; Rev. 21:7) and will dwell together with the Lord and each other in perfect righteousness (2 Peter 3:13).

This is further emphasized by the fact that the city's "gates will never be shut by day—and there will be no night there" (Rev. 21:25). The gates of an ancient city were shut at the first hint of danger. Because of increased dangers at night, cities normally closed their gates at sundown. But there is no such need in the new city that John sees. The total righteousness of this renewed creation means that there is no more opportunity for evil to arise— there is no more danger. Consequently, there is no need to close the gates for fear of impending harm. Because sin and death have passed away, defeated forever by Christ (19:11–21; 21:1, 4–5), the people of God in the new heavens and the new earth will be free to move about without any of the fears we face today because of the lingering presence of evil.

The New Jerusalem: A Thorough Transformation. The description of the city is that of a lavish paradise, unequaled in magnitude by anything in history. John's vision is vibrant. The appearance of the New Jerusalem boggles the imagination to grasp the glory, wonder, and perfection of believers' eternal dwelling with God. John adds descriptions of precious materials:

144

And he . . . showed me . . . Jerusalem . . . , having the glory of God, its radiance like a most rare jewel, like a jasper, clear as crystal. (21:10–11)

The wall was built of jasper, while the city was pure gold, clear as glass. (21:18)

And . . . the street of the city was pure gold, transparent as glass. (21:21)

Why? If we think about how this differs from the temple structures that the original readers knew—both Herod's temple in the first century and Solomon's temple in the Old Testament—then the answer becomes clear. While the vessels and smaller objects within the tabernacle and temple were made of pure gold, the larger elements such as the walls, pillars, and altar were overlaid with gold, which signified their consecration for God's holy purposes (Ex. 25:11–13, 24–28; 26:29, 37). But in Revelation 21, the city, its streets, its gates, and its wall are not merely overlaid with precious materials—they are gold or jasper or another precious jewel through and through. The scale of the New Jerusalem is beyond imagining, especially to first-century readers. Consider: "And the twelve gates were twelve pearls, each of the gates made of a single pearl" (v. 21)!

The point, then, is this: John describes the city as precious, clear, and transparent to further symbolize the absolute purity and beauty of the New Jerusalem and its inhabitants. The city in which God dwells is itself the picture of perfection. Consequently, in the New Jerusalem, not a single element needs a covering of gold. Everything is set apart to the Lord as purified and glorious.

The New Jerusalem: The True Holy of Holies. When reading Revelation 21:9–27, we cannot help but wonder about the measuring of the New Jerusalem. What does the scene depict? The framework above continues to provide answers to our questions. What would have been familiar and understandable to the original audience? Five points are offered in response.

First, John intentionally focuses the reader's attention on the *shape* of the city more than its measurement: "The city lies four-square, its length the same as its width. And he measured the city with his rod, 12,000 stadia. Its length and width and height are equal" (v. 16). John knows that the measurement of 12,000 stadia is an attention-getter; anyone reading that in the first century would have been astonished at the enormousness of the New Jerusalem. So John refocuses readers' attention by repeating his first description of the city and adding that not only are its length and width equal, but also its height. Only one cubical structure is recorded in the Old Testament—the Holy of Holies. First Kings 6:20 records that the Holy of Holies built by Solomon was a perfect cube, twenty cubits long, wide, and high, and overlaid with pure gold. The singular shape of the New Jerusalem leads readers to connect that city with the Old Testament dwellings of the Lord. This means that the New Jerusalem itself functions as a Holy of Holies where the presence of God dwells, but on a vastly grander scale.

Second, further supporting the notion that the New Jerusalem functions in this way is the fact that it was common for objects assigned to holy service in the tabernacle and temple to be foursquare, reflecting the square dimensions of the Holy of Holies on two sides. In fact, the word *foursquare* in the Greek Old Testament is used exclusively with respect to the dimensions of the sacred objects in the tabernacle and temple with one exception.[8]

Third, the adornments of the city wall described in Revelation 21:14, 19–20 approximate the precious stones that adorned the breastplate of the high priests who served in the tabernacle and temple (Ex. 28:15–30). The exact colors of the stones in Revelation are difficult to determine precisely, and they are in a different order from those in Exodus. Additionally, the precious stones are associated with the names of the twelve apostles and not the twelve tribes (Rev. 21:14), as one might expect. Yet the point here

8. The word is *tetragōnos*. In the Greek Old Testament, it describes sacred objects in Exodus 27:1; 28:16; 30:1–2; 36:15–16; 1 Kings 7:40–42; Ezekiel 41:21; 43:16–17; 45:2; 48:20. The lone exception is in Genesis 6:14.

146

is not a detail-for-detail identification but the overall picture. Compare the two descriptions:

Description of the Breastplate	*Description of the Foundation Stones*
Twelve Precious Stones	Twelve Precious Stones
Four Rows with Three Stones Each	Four Walls with Three Stones Each
Set in Gold Filigree	Set in Gold Stone
Inscribed with a Tribe's Name	Inscribed with an Apostle's Name

The purpose of the "breastpiece of judgment" in the Levitical system was "to bring [Israel] to regular remembrance before the LORD" (Ex. 28:29). That is, when the high priest entered the Holy of Holies once a year on the Day of Atonement to make atonement for the sins of the people of Israel, he wore the breastplate. His doing so symbolized the fact that the sins of the people were before the Lord, and the high priest was to atone for them. This action also symbolized how precious the Lord's people were in his sight—the breastplate gives a pictorial representation that they were his "treasured possession among all peoples" (19:5). This description further links the New Jerusalem with the Holy of Holies.

Fourth, the setting of the vision itself also suggests a link to the temple dwelling of the Lord. John's description of his vision aligns very closely with Ezekiel's vision of the temple in chapters 40–48 and is probably partially drawn from it:

> The hand of the LORD was upon me, and he brought me to the city. In visions of God he brought me . . . and set me down on a very high mountain, on which was a structure like a city. . . . (Ezek. 40:1–2)

> And he carried me away in the Spirit to a great, high mountain, and showed me the holy city Jerusalem coming down out of heaven from God. (Rev. 21:10)

147

Ezekiel then encounters someone with a measuring reed (sound familiar?) and proceeds to measure the structure. Though the structure looks like a city, it is in fact a temple, as the rest of Ezekiel 40–48 describes in detail. Even more, in both cases the seer is shown the vision of a great mountain. Throughout Scripture, mountains frequently are places where people encounter God's presence.

- The prophet Ezekiel describes Eden, where the Lord God walked with Adam and Eve, as "the garden of God" and "the holy mountain of God" (Ezek. 28:13–14).
- Noah's ark comes to rest on the mountains of Ararat, where God makes a covenant with him, and Noah there builds an altar and worships him (Gen. 8–9).
- Abraham, about to sacrifice his only son on a mountain in the land of Moriah, is dramatically stopped by the angel of the Lord, and Abraham and Isaac build an altar there and worship the Lord (Gen. 22:1–19).
- Moses encounters the Lord at the burning bush on Horeb, "the mountain of God" (Ex. 3:1–2).
- Israel is brought out of captivity to worship at "your own mountain, the place, O LORD, which you have made for your [dwelling], the sanctuary, O Lord, which your hands have established" (Ex. 15:17). This is Mount Sinai, where the glory cloud of the Lord descends for seven days, after which Moses enters it for forty more days (24:16–18). Before this, the Lord God celebrates a meal with the elders of Israel (vv. 9–11), a precursor to the marriage supper of the Lamb (Rev. 19:6–10).
- Elijah meets with the Lord on Horeb, where he does not find the Lord in the mighty wind, the earthquake, or the fire, but in the soft whisper (1 Kings 19:8–18). Shortly before, Elijah had defeated the 450 prophets of Baal on Mount Carmel (18:20–40).
- Solomon built "the house of the LORD in Jerusalem on Mount Moriah, where the LORD had appeared to David his father" (2 Chron. 3:1).

- The psalmist prays that he might be brought "to your holy hill and to your dwelling" (Ps. 43:3), that he might worship the Lord there.
- Isaiah, foreseeing the wedding supper of the Lamb, prophesies, "On this mountain the LORD of hosts will make for all peoples a feast of rich food, a feast of well-aged wine, of rich food full of marrow, of aged wine well refined. . . . He will swallow up death forever; and the Lord GOD will wipe away tears from all faces, and the reproach of his people he will take away from all the earth, for the LORD has spoken" (Isa. 25:6, 8).
- The prophet Daniel sees a vision of a statue, which is obliterated by "a stone . . . cut from a mountain by no human hand" (Dan. 2:45), which then becomes "a great mountain and fill[s] the whole earth" (v. 35). What he sees depicts the eternal, heavenly kingdom, handed over to the Son of Man, described in a corresponding vision in Daniel 7.
- While they were "on the holy mountain," the disciples heard the voice of the Lord from heaven saying, "This is my beloved Son . . ." (2 Peter 1:17–18).
- Jesus himself was transfigured on this "high mountain" (Matt. 17:1–8), and later ascended into heaven from the Mount of Olives (Acts 1:9–12).
- In the vision of the great multitude, John ultimately sees the Lamb standing with his people on Mount Zion (Rev. 14:1, built upon 7:1–17).

Mountains are places where throughout history God's people meet with and worship him. "As symbols," mountains "declare the nature of God. As the place where humans encounter the divine, they epitomize how God and people relate to each other, both in history and in the [life to come]."[9]

Fifth, like most narrative scenes—and visions are usually told in narrative form, as here—the climax of the story comes near the end: "And I saw no temple in the city, for its temple

9. Leland Ryken et al., eds., *Dictionary of Biblical Imagery* (Downers Grove, IL: InterVarsity Press, 1998), 574.

is the Lord God the Almighty and the Lamb" (Rev. 21:22). The Old Testament temple was modeled in large part on the tabernacle. The tabernacle itself was built according to "the pattern" shown to Moses while he met with the Lord on Mount Sinai (Ex. 25:9, 40; Acts 7:44). The author of Hebrews explains: "Now the point . . . is this: we have such a high priest, one who is seated at the right hand of the throne of the Majesty in heaven, a minister in the holy places, in the true [tabernacle] that the Lord set up, not man" (Heb. 8:1–2). The earthly tabernacle and temple were shadows, representations of the true tabernacle, the true Holy of Holies, the true dwelling place of the Lord God. It is the true dwelling place of God that is portrayed in Revelation 21: "For Christ has entered, not into holy places made with hands, which are copies of the true things, but into heaven itself, now to appear in the presence of God on our behalf" (Heb. 9:24).

This is precisely why there is no temple in John's vision: the temple was a representation of the true reality that John is now privileged to see. There is no more structure to separate the holy presence of God from the sinfulness of his people because there is no sin in the holy city. The fullness of the presence of the Most Holy God extends unabated throughout the new creation so that God dwells with his people in a way not experienced since before the fall in Eden.

Revelation 21: A Picture of the Presence of God Dwelling with His People

The image of the church as the bride of the Lamb pictures the intimate union between God and his people. The picture of the city-temple of God, the New Jerusalem, portrays the people of God as experiencing the fullness of the Lord's presence in a way once possible only in the Holy of Holies. Each of the images communicates the intimate, personal presence of God with his people. Taken together, they portray a scene that astonished believers' minds in the first century—and our minds today.

Transformation

Sometimes we wish that we could see Jesus. We fool our-selves into thinking, "If I could just see him, I would be more diligent in living as he wants me to." But Christ *is* really with us, always, and we just do not comprehend the reality of that truth on a daily basis.

God's Presence Is Our Strength

Brother Lawrence was a humble man who became a Carmel-ite monk in the seventeenth century. Monastic life was tedious for him. But he found that while he went about his daily chores, especially in the kitchen, he could meditate on God's presence in ways that fueled his walk with God. He explains:

> When we are faithful to keep ourselves in His holy Presence, and set Him always before us, this not only hinders our offend-ing Him, and doing anything that may displease Him, at least willfully, but it also begets in us a holy freedom, and if I may so speak, a familiarity with GOD, wherewith we ask . . . [for] the graces we stand in need of . . . by often repeating these acts, they become habitual, and the presence of GOD is rendered as it were natural to us.[10]

Brother Lawrence is applying the idea of the psalmist: "in your presence there is fullness of joy; at your right hand are pleasures forevermore" (Ps. 16:11). The problem is not that God is absent from our lives—how could he be? The problem is that we do not appropriate by faith the reality of his presence. If we really believed that God is with us now, that nothing can dam-age our salvation, that there is nothing to fear from life around us (Rom. 8:33–39), how would that change the way we act at home . . . at school . . . at work . . . at the gym . . . or at church? Understanding that God is with us always—even as we anticipate

10. Brother Lawrence, *The Practice of the Presence of God: Being Conversations and Letters of Nicholas Herman of Lorraine* (New York: Revell, 1895), 29.

his eternal presence—strengthens us when we are weak and assures us that we can stand firm.

God's Presence and Our Sin

In addition, how does the Lord's presence through his Spirit within us affect how we view our sin? Daniel foretells "the abomination that makes desolate" (Dan. 11:31), an act that mortified God's people for centuries to come. His prophecy was fulfilled when a wicked Syrian ruler named Antiochus Epiphanes entered the Holy of Holies in 167 B.C. along with some of his troops and sacrificed unclean animals to their gods. Paul writes of something just as ugly: "What agreement has the temple of God with idols? For we are the temple of the living God" (2 Cor. 6:16). Our lives are as sacred as the Holy of Holies once was. Our lives are to be as holy as the Most Holy Place was, since the presence of God dwells in each of us. How abominable does that make our sin! We lust in our minds, envy in our hearts, and feed our idols of comfort, greed, power, and fame—all in the very presence of the Lord God. And while such thoughts sadden our hearts, they also exalt our praise for the glorious sacrifice of the Lamb, who paid the penalty for our abominations and united us forever with himself and the Lord. "Thanks be to God for his inexpressible gift!" (2 Cor. 9:15).

God's Presence and Community

Life in the community of Christ is often very difficult because we are sinful people. We defraud each other emotionally, financially, and sexually. We speak ill of one another in ways that we never would if we were face-to-face. We compete with one another for recognition and praise. We secretly, and at times openly, covet what others have instead of rejoicing with them at the Lord's goodness in their lives.

But the presence of God within us unites us not only to himself, but also to each other. As brothers and sisters in the Lord, we are irrevocably united in Christ, and with all of God's people

152

in all places and at all times. There is no other people of God to which we can change our membership. Switching Sunday school classes or community groups, changing churches, or even moving to another denomination does not dissolve the eternal bond of Christ between us and those whom we leave. Our disagreements, conflicts, and feuds cannot dissolve our union with one another. How, then, should we relate to one another? Do we really understand that this person who just took advantage of us or stabbed us in the back will be our friend on the new earth for all eternity?

We understand that there are appropriate times to separate for protection and healing in various circumstances among the body of Christ. But we are just that—one body. There is one faith and one Lord, and "God has so composed the body . . . that there may be no division in the body, but that the members may have the same care for one another. If one member suffers, all suffer together; if one member is honored, all rejoice together" (1 Cor. 12:24–26). Although we await the time when that unity will be perfected on the new earth, in the meantime our hearts cry: Oh, that the watching world would see such love and commitment within the body of Christ and thereby see the love of God made manifest in us![11]

We have now treated four of our five themes of heaven (creation, rest, kingdom, and God's presence). We turn to our last theme in the next section: glory.

11. For more on God's presence, see Lanier Burns, *The Nearness of God: His Presence with His People*, Explorations in Biblical Theology (Phillipsburg, NJ: P&R Publishing, 2009).

Part 5

Glory

9

Exchange of Glory

PERHAPS THE MOST FAMOUS—and justly so—twentieth-century meditation on ultimate salvation is C. S. Lewis's *The Weight of Glory*, which summarizes the Bible's promises for believers. One of these is the promise of glory, which Lewis correctly asserts is prominent in Scripture. Glory in turn has two aspects: glory as fame and glory as luminosity. He admits frankly that initially he found the first idea wicked and the second ridiculous.[1]

But as he further reflected on these ideas, Lewis changed his mind and came to agree with Christians through the ages who found great comfort in heaven as their glory:

> When I began to look into this matter I was shocked to find such different Christians as Milton, Johnson, and Thomas Aquinas taking heavenly glory quite frankly in the sense of fame or good report. . . . I saw that this view was scriptural; nothing can eliminate from the parable the divine *accolade*, "Well done, thou good and faithful servant." . . . And that is enough to raise our thoughts to what may happen when the redeemed soul, beyond all hope and nearly beyond belief, learns at last that she has pleased Him whom she was created to please. . . . The promise of glory is the promise, almost incredible and only possible by the work of Christ, that some of us . . . shall actually survive that examination, shall find approval, shall please God. To please

1. C. S. Lewis, *The Weight of Glory and Other Addresses* (San Francisco: Harper San Francisco, 1980), 35–36.

God . . . to be a real ingredient in the divine happiness . . . to be loved by God, not merely pitied, but delighted in as an artist delights in his work or a father in a son—it seems impossible, a weight or burden of glory which our thoughts can hardly sustain. But so it is.

And this brings me to the other sense of glory—glory as brightness, splendour, luminosity. We are to shine as the sun, we are to be given the Morning Star. . . . We want something else which can hardly be put into words—to be united with the beauty we see, to pass into it, to receive it into ourselves, to bathe in it, to become part of it. . . . For if we take the imagery of Scripture seriously, if we believe that God will one day *give* us the Morning Star and cause us to *put on* the splendour of the sun, then we may surmise that both the ancient myths and the modern poetry, so false as history, may be very near the truth as prophecy. . . . The load, or weight, or burden of my neighbor's glory should be laid on my back, a load so heavy that only humility can carry it, and the backs of the proud will be broken. It is a serious thing to live in a society of possible gods and goddesses, to remember that the dullest and most uninteresting person you can talk to may one day be a creature which, if you saw it now, you would be strongly tempted to worship, or else a horror and a corruption such as you now meet, if at all, only in a nightmare.[2]

As we follow the theme of glory through the Bible's story, we will see that it contains Lewis's ideas of fame and luminosity and even more. In this chapter, we concentrate on the first three stages of glory: at creation, at the fall, and in redemption. In the next chapter, we will concentrate on the final stage of glory—at the restoration.

- Creation: Coronation in Glory
- Fall: Exchange of Glory
- Redemption: Transformation in Glory
- Restoration: Brilliance in Glory

2. Ibid., 36–45 (italics in original).

Creation: Coronation in Glory

When God created men and women, he gave them his own glory. "Then God said, 'Let us make man in our image, after our likeness'" (Gen. 1:26). The historic writings of the church are filled with debate concerning the precise nature of this image. Is it primarily something we *are* as human beings, given from God when he created us, or is it primarily something we *do*, reflecting God's nature as we live out his mandate to be fruitful and rule over the world (1:28)?[3] We will not enter the debate here, but will focus on two truths: it is the whole human being, not only a part, who bears God's image, and human glory is inseparably tied to humankind's role as stewards over the earth.

First, we need to understand that the image of God in the Old Testament—apart from two figurative uses—always has physical form in view.[4] David Clines summarizes: "The body cannot be left out of the meaning of the image; man is a totality, and his 'solid flesh' is as much the image of God as his spiritual capacity, creativeness, or personality."[5] The body—skin, bones, and muscles—bears the marks of its Creator. This is the foundation for the doctrine of resurrection and its centrality to life in the new heavens and new earth. The value of the human body to God is greater than we often realize; it is neither something to be escaped from nor something to be casually exploited. The image of God is nothing less than God's likeness imprinted into flesh, mind, heart, spirit, and all things human: a divine cast of the invisible into the visible, like sculpting the music of Beethoven's Ninth Symphony into a beautiful statue.[6]

In addition, humankind's dominion is tied to this image. "When the author of Genesis 1 claimed that man was made as

---

3. For a good synopsis of debate concerning the image of God, see David J. A. Clines, "The Image of God in Man," *Tyndale Bulletin* 19 (1968): 54–61. See also Anthony A. Hoekema, *Created in God's Image* (Grand Rapids: Eerdmans, 1986), 33–65; R. Larry Overstreet, "Man in the Image of God: A Reappraisal," *Criswell Theological Review* 3, 1 (Fall 2005): 43–70.

4. Bruce K. Waltke, *An Old Testament Theology: An Exegetical, Canonical, and Thematic Approach* (Grand Rapids: Zondervan, 2007), 215.

5. Clines, "The Image of God in Man," 86.

6. Derek Kidner, *Genesis: An Introduction and Commentary*, Tyndale Old Testament Commentaries (Downers Grove, IL: Inter-Varsity Press, 1967), 51.

the image of God, he meant that man was to be God's representative on earth, ruling, or having dominion, on God's behalf, like a king."[7] Both the background of ancient Near Eastern culture and the grammar of Genesis support this conclusion.[8] But in contrast to the dominant mind-set of the time, it is not only the king who bears God's image, but all. Male and female alike share this kingly privilege and responsibility to rule. The dominion we have is alien to every other creature; it is something that only humanity possesses. Our royal stewardship over creation is derived from the sovereign dominion that God exercises over all things as he "does according to his will among the host of heaven and among the inhabitants of the earth" (Dan. 4:35). God has, as David says, "put all things under [our] feet," that we might exercise "dominion over the works of [God's] hands" (Ps. 8:6–7). David celebrates the creation of men and women in the image of God with royal language, saying that God has crowned all humankind "with glory and honor" (v. 5). Bearing God's image is man and woman's coronation in glory, their ruling as stewards of all creation. This is manifested in two spheres: in the unique, personal glory we have as individuals and in the communal glory of the one people of God.

Personal Glory

The most basic of all human glories is the glory of being created: "So God created man in his own image, in the image of God he created him" (Gen. 1:27). Many young children have unknowingly asked a very profound question, "Why did God make us?" After all, Scripture tells us that God is not "served by human hands, as though he needed anything, since he himself gives to all mankind life and breath and everything" (Acts 17:25). Scripture leaves us with one conclusion: God created because he desired to create; it was his good pleasure. And if

<hr />

7. Ian Hart, "Genesis 1:1–2:3 as a Prologue to the Book of Genesis," *Tyndale Bulletin* 46, 2 (1995): 319–20.

8. Hoekema, *Created in God's Image*, 19.

he desired us so much as to create us, then we must be valuable to him—not because of what we do, for we did nothing to be created. Every person is valuable to God—and thus should be valuable to us as Christians, too—simply because he or she exists.

Genesis 1:27 does not end there but states that "male and female he created them." Many read Genesis 1:27 and gloss over a question corresponding to the one above: Why did God create men *and* women instead of just men or just women? If the mere fact of creation bestows humanity with glory, how much glory is conferred on us individually as unique men and women? One prominent truth in the story of Adam and Eve is that Eve was not made for all men; she was made for Adam (2:18–25). "This [one] . . . is bone of my bones" (v. 23), declares Adam, and the Hebrew conveys the idea of "this time,"[9] referring to the prior attempts by Adam at God's behest to find a suitable helper among the (other) animals of creation (vv. 18–20). It is apparent from the text that Eve is not only different from the rest of creation, but also different from Adam.[10]

This, then, is the question: why did God create so many individual differences between people, even between Adam and Eve? Why have we received from our Creator differing temperaments, talents, and tolerances? Furthermore, why endow men and women with the ability—even the responsibility (1:28)—to reproduce *another* unique man or woman? The story of creation impresses on us a glorious thought: since I am a unique human among all humans, I must be personally, individually special in the eyes of the Creator, in the same way that each painting holds special meaning to its artist. You yourself matter to God because he personally created you and loves you, and because in all of human history there is no one else exactly like you. You are a unique manifestation of the glory of God.

9. C. John Collins, *Genesis 1–4: A Linguistic, Literary, and Theological Commentary* (Phillipsburg, NJ: P&R Publishing, 2005), 108.
10. One should not take "different" as implying better or worse, but simply as meaning "not the same." On the equality of men and women as bearers of God's image from creation, see Waltke, *An Old Testament Theology*, 239–41; Collins, *Genesis 1–4*, 107n26.

Communal Glory

Just as Genesis 1:27 has many glorious implications for individuals, it also has implications for the whole people of God. For the responsibility of dominion does not fall simply on the shoulders of men but on women also as fellow image-bearers. The author of Genesis gives the clear meaning of the plural *them*—in the expression "and let them have dominion"—in the context and structure of Genesis 1:26–28:

> Then God said, "Let us make man in our image. . . . And let them have dominion over the fish . . . and over every creeping thing that creeps on the earth." (1:26)

> So God created man in his own image,
>   in the image of God he created him;
>   male and female he created them. (1:27)

> And God blessed them. And God said to them, "Be fruitful and multiply . . . and have dominion over the fish . . . and over every living thing that moves on the earth." (1:28)

Verses 26 and 28 bracket verse 27. "Man" is thus clarified by verse 27, the focal point of the three verses, where Moses says, "God created man in his own image . . . ; male and female he created them." The "man" (*adam*) made in the image of God is thus a generic term for male and female human beings, i.e., humankind. The necessary implication of this is that men and women collectively glorify God in a way otherwise impossible if only one or the other existed.

Consider the end of Genesis 2, for example. Adam has exhaustively searched creation for a helper suitable for him in humankind's global task, and sadly has found none. But God intervenes and creates a woman, a helper suited specifically to him. Upon seeing her, Adam marvels at this wonderful helper made especially for him. United they enjoy each other and so gloriously image the triune God in whose image they were made (v. 24).

We do not mean that people must be married to reflect God's glory. Was not Jesus, *the* image of God himself, unmarried (John 1:14; Col. 1:15; Heb. 1:3)? Rather, this is to say that humankind was created in and for community, even as God himself exists in community: Father, Son, and Holy Spirit. And when the people of God come together, they reflect his glory in a way that none of them individually can. A world-class violinist may render amazing melodies on her instrument, but when she joins a whole symphony of gifted musicians, the sound produced exceeds the sum of their individual abilities.

Fall: Exchange of Glory

Honey is one of the sweetest and tastiest natural substances on earth. But eat too much of it and it will make you sick (Prov. 25:16). A good thing, used improperly, leads to ruin (v. 27). For that reason, Francis Schaeffer accurately characterizes the fallen human condition as "glorious ruins." Glory is a good thing—a great thing, in fact. But instead of seeking glory according to God's purposes, we exchange it for that which is not really glory at all. Just as Esau traded away his birthright for a single meal (Gen. 25:29–34), we pawn God's precious gift so that we might indulge our desires in enjoyment as feeble as it is fleeting.

Jeremiah describes the double-edged folly of self-glorification:

> Has a nation changed its gods,
>   even though they are no gods?
> But my people have changed their glory
>   for that which does not profit.
> Be appalled, O heavens, at this;
>   be shocked, be utterly desolate,
>   declares the LORD,
> for my people have committed two evils:
> they have forsaken me,
>   the fountain of living waters,
> and hewed out cisterns for themselves,
>   broken cisterns that can hold no water. (Jer. 2:11–13)

We forsake the Creator and run to the creation, which by its very nature is no god at all (Hab. 2:16–20). We trade our true glory for a pseudo-glory that has no hope of ever really glorifying us. As Paul says, each of us has "exchanged the truth about God for a lie" (Rom. 1:25). We think we will find glory in places other than God—that's why we go to them. And no sooner have we drunk this counterfeit glory than it dissolves, leaving us as empty as before, just like the empty jar in Jeremiah's indictment. Because of the fall, every man, woman, and child is left with a glory-vacuum in the core of his or her being; we all have traded away our glory—our beauty, our honor—*for nothing.*

Not only do all individuals fall short of God's glory (Rom. 3:23), but so do the people of God as a whole. The first commandment, "You shall have no other gods before me" (Ex. 20:3), is not only an injunction for each of us personally, but God's demand for his people communally. The first commandment warns the covenant community not to put any part of creation in place of the Creator (Col. 1:16; Heb. 11:3), whether it be natural elements such as wind and fire, supernatural beings such as angels, or even animals, fellow creatures of the sixth day. And yet those who know the story of Sinai know that in just a few days the entire camp of Israel abandoned that commandment and exchanged the glory of God for a golden image in the shape of a calf (Ex. 32:1–6). Psalm 106 walks through Israel's adulterous history, and one can almost hear the sadness in the author's voice: "They made a calf in Horeb and worshiped a metal image. They exchanged the glory of God for the image of an ox that eats grass" (vv. 19–20). And ultimately God would judge this fall from glory by removing his glorious presence from the temple and sending the people into exile because of their sins.

In sum, we both individually and communally have received the just consequence for our sin: our glory has been turned into shame (Hos. 4:7), and we all share this shame together. But Psalm 106 does not end with an endless indictment against Israel, for God is merciful. Instead, despite humanity's unfaithfulness, God remembers his covenant and brings glory from dust, beauty from ashes.

Redemption: Transformation in Glory

Since God's glory is embedded in our very creation as men and women, in the image of God that we bear, there is still hope for human glory (Col. 1:27). Though thoroughly corrupted, the image of God was not annihilated by Adam's sin (Gen. 9:6; James 3:9). All human beings in some way still reflect the glory of God in which they were created. For "both the human race and individual men [and women] . . . do not cease to be the image of God so long as they remain [human]; to be human and to be the image of God are not separable."[11] The problem of the fall is not a problem with God's glory; it is with our inability to live according to our created purpose. We need to "put on the new self" and to be "renewed in knowledge after the image of [our] creator" (Col. 3:10). As Christians, we know that as we draw nearer to God, we more clearly reflect (image) his glory. That is, the more we progress in holiness and are conformed to the image of Christ, the more the creational glory—damaged though it was by the fall—shines forth in our lives, visible to those around us (2 Cor. 3:18; 4:6). We need someone to cleanse the pollution of our hearts and restore the shine to our tarnished lives. We need a Redeemer—a Glory-Redeemer.

The Glory-Redeemer

Who alone can restore our lost glory? Scripture answers loudly and clearly:

> In their case the god of this world has blinded the minds of the unbelievers, to keep them from seeing the light of the gospel of the glory of Christ, who is the image of God. (2 Cor. 4:4)

> He is the image of the invisible God, the firstborn of all creation . . . , that in everything he might be preeminent. (Col. 1:15, 18)

11. Clines, "The Image of God in Man," 101. Scripture teaches that all human beings are created in God's image and are thus worthy of dignity, even unbelievers (James 3:9). God himself exemplifies this fact through his common grace, whereby he "makes his sun rise on the evil and on the good" alike (Matt. 5:45).

> . . . his Son, whom he appointed the heir of all things, through
> whom also he created the world. He is the radiance of the glory
> of God and the exact imprint of his nature. (Heb. 1:2–3)

Our Restorer of glory must be both God and man. Only One meets those qualifications. The eternal Son of God is both Creator and heir of all things. And he became incarnate as the true image of God and the radiance of his glory to rescue us.

The author of Hebrews draws the portrait of this Glory-Redeemer, Jesus Christ, the Son of God (Heb. 2:5–10). It was humans—not the angels (v. 5)—who were given original glory and dominion on earth (vv. 6–8). So why is the earth not yet in subjection to humans (v. 8b)? The reason: because of our sin. In order to restore our glory—the glory that we exchanged for nothing—Jesus had to become human so that he might defeat the power of sin (v. 9). At his ascension, he was crowned with everlasting glory and honor, and Jesus' "coronation and investiture with priestly glory and splendor provide assurance that the power of sin and death has been nullified and that humanity will yet be led to the full realization of their intended glory."[12] Christ's coronation as King at God's right hand secured for his people a glory that can never be diminished or lost (1 Peter 1:3–5). Christ's death and resurrection have irreversibly set in motion the final events of this age, which will bring every child of God into the redemptive fullness of his or her glory (Heb. 2:10).

The Goal of Glory

This personal restoration of glory has a common purpose for all believers: to unite us under one Father in one Spirit by one Lord and Savior, Jesus Christ (Eph. 4:4–5). Jesus prays to the Father for all believers:

> The glory that you have given me I have given to them, that
> they may be one even as we are one, I in them and you in me,

12. William L. Lane, *Hebrews 1–8*, Word Biblical Commentary (Dallas: Word, 1991), 50.

that they may become perfectly one, so that the world may know that you sent me and loved them even as you loved me. (John 17:22–23)

One purpose of Christ's redemption of our creational glory is for unity, not as an end in itself but for the sake of God's glory in the world. All of God's people are recipients of his special grace, not that we may spend it on ourselves (James 4:3) but that we might be a blessing to others (Gen. 12:2–3; Matt. 5:13–16). God intends for his work in his people to have evangelistic import. God manifests his glory in them so that the world might look upon them and praise him.

Our redemption in glory is applied to us through the Holy Spirit, who enables us to commune with the Father through the Son. As we gaze upon Christ, we gaze upon the image of God the Father himself (John 14:9; Col. 1:15), and as we do, we are transformed into his image with ever-increasing glory (2 Cor. 3:18). The glory given to our first parents at creation is being increased in us as we become more like Christ. Our guarantee of the completion of this work of glory is the completed glorification of Christ as the first instance of redemption (1 Cor. 15:23). Because he has been glorified, we also will be! And the Bible paints a clear picture of this process: now, we are being formed in part, but at the moment of Christ's royal coming, we will be changed and will be like him (1 Cor. 15:51–53; 1 John 3:2).[13] We will not be seen in our full glory until all the consequences of sin have been made right. And when all evil is abolished, perfection will ensue.

Those things will occur only at the restoration, when all believers will be brilliant in glory. And that is the exalted theme of our next chapter.

13. See also 1 Cor. 13:9–13; Phil. 3:21; Col. 3:3; 1 John 3:2–3.

Brilliance in Glory

IN THE PREVIOUS CHAPTER, we considered the first three stages of glory: coronation in glory (at creation), exchange of glory (at the fall), and transformation in glory (in Christ). Here we finish the story of glory by focusing on our brilliance in glory at the restoration.

- The Glory of Bodily Resurrection
- The Glory of Perfect Righteousness
- The Glory of Divine Love
- The Glory That Does Not Fade
- Transformation: God's Enabling Glory

Now we are walking toward our glorious eternity with Jesus on the new earth. Where will that path end? Back in Eden? A common misunderstanding among believers is that heaven in eternity future is merely a return to Eden. But remember the way the Bible works: Eden is the beginning of the story, not the end. Our future is not a simple restoration of creational glory. Rather, an even greater glory awaits (Hag. 2:9). Although we were made "a little lower than the angels" in terms of glory (Ps. 8:5 NKJV), our eternal heavenly glory will exceed theirs. As the author of Hebrews asks concerning Christ, "And to which of the angels has [God] ever said, 'Sit at my right hand until I make your enemies a footstool for your feet'?" (Heb. 1:13). Amazingly, to each believer,

Jesus declares, "I will grant him to sit with me on my throne, as I also conquered and sat down with my Father on his throne" (Rev. 3:21), from where we will then, along with Christ, judge the angels (1 Cor. 6:3). This is certainly a greater glory than in Eden. Throughout Scripture God permits us glimpses into our future glory. Only in that day will we be "a crown of beauty in the hand of the LORD, and a royal diadem in the hand of [our] God" (Isa. 62:3).

The Glory of Bodily Resurrection

During a fellowship time at our church recently, I (Dan) spoke with a sweet older woman sitting behind me. I grasped her hand and asked her how she was doing. She replied, "I am doing so well. I just lost the sight in my left eye, but I am doing so well." While I rejoiced in her sweet spirit, my heart grew heavy. The destruction of our bodies is all around us: frailty, genetic defects, cancer, and so on. Yet in my sadness at that moment, the Word of God sprang to mind:

> So we do not lose heart. Though our outer self is wasting away, our inner self is being renewed day by day. For this light momentary affliction is preparing for us an eternal weight of glory beyond all comparison, as we look not to the things that are seen but to the things that are unseen. For the things that are seen are transient, but the things that are unseen are eternal. (2 Cor. 4:16–18)

> If then you have been raised with Christ, seek the things that are above, where Christ is, seated at the right hand of God. . . . For you have died, and your life is hidden with Christ in God. When Christ who is your life appears, then you also will appear with him in glory. (Col. 3:1, 3–4)

We believers are *already* seated with Christ in the heavenly places. A glorious life and a glorious inheritance are ours now, guaranteed by the Spirit who indwells us (Eph. 1:13–14). And one day, when Christ comes to abolish sin and death forever, then every eye will be healed, every disease destroyed, and every evil abated forever (Rev. 21:4).

The resurrection of Jesus Christ is the chief source of hope for Christians (1 Cor. 15:3–8, 12–22). Christ's atoning death, life-giving resurrection, and ascension (Rom. 5:10) announce him as both King and Savior of all humankind (Acts 2:36). Perhaps this is why every evangelistic speech in the book of Acts prominently features the resurrection of Christ.[1] In fact, the author of Hebrews considers the doctrine of our resurrection an "elementary teaching" (Heb. 6:1–2 NASB). And the members of the early church believed that bodily resurrection is so basic to Christianity that they included it in the Apostles' Creed.[2] Christ is the firstfruits; everything has its order. He first died for us, and now we participate in his death. When he returns, we will participate in his resurrection (Rom. 6:4–5; 1 Cor. 15:20–23; Phil. 3:21). But not only is Christ the *means* by which we are resurrected, he is also the *model* for our future resurrected bodies (Rom. 6:5; Phil. 3:21; Col. 3:4) because the same Spirit who raised Jesus from the dead also dwells in us (Rom. 8:9–11).[3]

So this is our hope, the redemption of our mortal bodies (Rom. 8:9–11, 23). But what does it mean that we will "be like him" in the resurrection? Does the Bible provide any clues about what physical resurrection entails?

Bodies Characterized by Brightness

The first thought that probably comes to mind is that of brightness. Jesus in Matthew 13:43 quotes Daniel 12:3, "the righteous will shine like the sun." Most popular scenes of heaven

1. See Acts 2:32; 3:26; 4:10; 5:30–31; 10:40; 13:30; 17:31.
2. Timothy George, "Heavenly Bodies: If After Death We Are Already in the Joy of God's Presence, What Exactly Do We Gain from a Bodily Resurrection?" *Christianity Today* 47, 2 (2003): 84.
3. N. T. Wright, *Surprised by Hope: Rethinking Heaven, the Resurrection, and the Mission of the Church* (New York: HarperOne, 2008), 149.

involve bright white lighting. Is this just Hollywood theatrics? Actually, the basis for this portrayal is Scripture itself: "And the city [the New Jerusalem] has no need of sun or moon to shine on it, for the glory of God gives it light, and its lamp is the Lamb" (Rev. 21:23, echoing Isa. 60:19). The apostle John metaphorically describes how the righteous will "shine." He does not say that light will "beam out" from a single source as artistry depicts, but rather that the glory of God, primarily manifested in Christ, is reflected in us (Rev. 21:11). It is true that the heavenly city will be illumined by God's glory, but not only by the glory of his presence but also by the image of Christ gloriously perfected in his people.

For saints with failing bodies, however, maybe their first thought regarding resurrection is: "What will my new body be like?" Apparently the Corinthians wanted to know the answer to that question, too: "But someone will ask, 'How are the dead raised? With what kind of body do they come?'" (1 Cor. 15:35). Jerry Seinfeld once characterized Hollywood's visions of the future as portraying people who wear exactly the same things and style their hair in the same way: "The individuality thing is over. It's just the one-piece . . . with the boots."[4] But Paul's response in the subsequent verses is that we will indeed be unique. In fact, we will be more ourselves than ever. Whereas the body now is characterized by this sin-cursed world, the resurrection body will be characterized by the glorious world to come (1 Cor. 15:36–39). Paul tells his readers that our bodies now are the seed that in the resurrection will grow into a flourishing plant.

Bodies Characterized by Power

Perhaps you, like us, resonate with the words of Paul, "For I have the desire to do what is right, but not the ability to carry it out" (Rom. 7:18). And with the apostle we each cry out, "Who will deliver me?" Though our bodies now are characterized by weakness because of sin (Matt. 26:41), in the resurrection they will be characterized by power (1 Cor. 15:43). Some suggest that this

---

4. Jerry Seinfeld, *I'm Telling You for the Last Time*, audio CD (Umvd Labels, 1998).

power means we will be able to imitate Christ's ability to appear and disappear at will, as he does in the upper room (John 20:19) and on the road to Emmaus (Luke 24:31). Now, this suggestion may or may not be true. What is certain is that our bodies will be empowered for perfect service to Christ. No more struggling to focus on the task at hand, no more weariness at the end of a day. As the inner man will be perfected for righteous thinking (Heb. 12:23), the body will be likewise perfected for righteous living. Our bodies and our desires will finally harmonize, displaying the glory of our Creator and Lord.

Bodies Characterized by Beauty

No matter what emotions you feel now at the sight of your body in the mirror, your resurrection body will be beautiful. What does that mean, specifically? Some, such as Augustine and Jonathan Edwards, believed that no matter when we actually die, each of us will be raised to look as though we were in our prime.[5] But as the saying goes, "beauty is in the eye of the beholder"— or, in this case, "beauty is in the eye of the Creator." Each of us has different ideas of beauty, but ultimately God himself defines beauty. Here is what we know for sure: "You shall be a crown of beauty in the hand of the LORD, and a royal diadem in the hand of your God. . . . For as a young man marries a young woman, so shall your sons marry you, and as the bridegroom rejoices over the bride, so shall your God rejoice over you" (Isa. 62:3, 5). Because our hearts and minds will be perfected, we will—some of us for the first time—truly see ourselves as God sees us through Christ (1 Cor. 13:12). Each of us personally will be reunited with our own bodies, bodies that will be more powerful and more beautiful than ever.

Note that we will be resurrected in *our own bodies*. We will not have someone else's body, as if that were possible, or a body

5. Augustine, *The City of God*, trans. Thomas Merton (New York: Modern Library, 1994), 22:16, 839; John H. Gerstner, *Jonathan Edwards on Heaven and Hell* (Grand Rapids: Baker, 1980), 39.

that is completely foreign to us. Scripture teaches that our individuality continues in the resurrection. We see this when Paul promises that the Father who raised Jesus will do the same for our mortal bodies: "If the Spirit of him who raised Jesus from the dead dwells in you, he who raised Christ Jesus from the dead will also give life to your mortal bodies through his Spirit who dwells in you" (Rom. 8:11). Paul also uses the analogy of celestial bodies to teach that as "star differs from star in glory," so each of us will shine a little differently—not better or worse, but uniquely, personally (1 Cor. 15:41–44).

It is an error to conclude that in the resurrection humans will be neither male nor female but asexual, based on Jesus' words: "For in the resurrection they neither marry nor are given in marriage, but are like angels in heaven" (Matt. 22:30).[6] Jesus himself, the first human being to be resurrected, is still male. And when Scripture says that we will be resurrected "like him" (1 John 3:2), it does not mean that we will all be males, but that we will be made perfect and incorruptible like him. We will retain our gender in the resurrection.

The Glory of Perfect Righteousness

There are not many days, to be honest, when we wake up and think, "Wow! I am so excited to be about the Lord's work, I just can't wait to get started!" Don't misunderstand; we love serving the Lord, but living in a fallen world is fraught with difficulty and discouragements. Now consider what life on the new earth will be like. Listen as Paul prays and promises: "Now may the God of peace himself sanctify you completely, and may your whole spirit and soul and body be kept blameless at the coming of our Lord Jesus Christ. He who calls you is faithful; he will surely do it" (1 Thess. 5:23–24).

6. See also the corresponding passages in Mark 12:18–27 and Luke 20:27–38. One might also point to Paul's statement in Galatians 3:28 that "there is neither Jew nor Greek, there is neither slave nor free, there is no male and female, for you are all one in Christ Jesus." Paul's point, however, is the unity of all believers in the church, regardless of gender, race, or social status; he is not teaching about gender in the resurrection.

God is faithful, and he will sanctify us completely when Jesus returns, equipping us for life on "a new earth in which righteousness dwells" (2 Peter 3:13). The apostle John uses a different idiom, but his teaching agrees with Paul's:

> Beloved, we are God's children now, and what we will be has not yet appeared; but we know that when he appears we shall be like him, because we shall see him as he is. And everyone who thus hopes in him purifies himself as he is pure.
>
> Everyone who makes a practice of sinning also practices lawlessness; sin is lawlessness. You know that he appeared to take away sins, and in him there is no sin. (1 John 3:2–5)

When Jesus comes again, God will enable us to see the glorified Christ, and we will be changed by that seeing. We will be transformed, and as a result, we will share his moral likeness. Such a hope purifies us now. But on that day, the full harvest of righteousness will be reaped for all those who know him who "appeared to take away sins" (1 John 3:5).

Our hearts, minds, and bodies will be made perfect. Whatever we attend to, it will be done right; whatever we think, it will be glorifying to God; whatever we undertake, it will be accomplished in perfect joy, and our Creator will fully approve. There will be no more indecision, doubt, or regret. It will be impossible to do anything wrong for the rest of eternity. It is difficult for our frail minds now to grasp such glorious thoughts!

The Glory of Divine Love

Jesus says, "He who loves me will be loved by my Father, and I will love him and manifest myself to him" (John 14:21). Paul likewise declares, "Whoever believes in him will not be put to shame" (Rom. 9:33). Despite these reassuring words of Scripture, many Christians today have mixed emotions at the thought of standing before God. Why? Because they have been taught that unless they attain a certain level of faithfulness on earth, they will experience regret and loss at the coming of Christ.[7] It is true that we all will stand before Christ, whose eyes are like a penetrating fire, and be examined (Rev. 1:14). But when Christ our Advocate confesses us before his Father, we will come away not just unscathed, but approved, overflowing with divine love and joy (Matt. 10:32; Jude 24).

Approval and Reward

One reason Christians today are uneasy about God's judgment is that they fail to distinguish divine love and approval from heavenly reward, as Scripture does. Certainly these topics overlap, but God's love is much more than what we simply receive—either now or in heaven. Here is what just a few passages say about the scope of divine love:

- God's love draws us near to him (John 6:44; 14:21, 23).
- God's love gives us his Holy Spirit (Rom. 5:5).
- God's love unites us to Christ's life, death, resurrection, and ascension (Eph. 2:4–7).
- God's love adopts us into his family (1 John 3:1).
- God's love enables us to follow his commands (1 John 4:9–12).

This discussion, however, is sometimes clouded when passages about God's love and approval are misunderstood as teaching about heavenly rewards. The quintessential example of this is Matthew 25:14–30, the parable of the talents. Some conclude on the basis of this parable that only some Christians—the completely faithful—will hear, "Well done, good and faithful servant. . . . Enter into the joy of your master" (v. 21). But we should not exaggerate the faithfulness of the first two servants, for the passage

7. For example, Tim Stevenson, *The Bema: A Story about the Judgment Seat of Christ* (Gainesville, TX: Fair Havens Publications, 2001); Erwin W. Lutzer, *Your Eternal Reward: Triumph and Tears at the Judgment Seat of Christ* (Chicago: Moody, 1998).

does not indicate that there is a proportional heavenly equivalent to the 100 percent returns on investment.[8]

The primary point of the parable is not Christians' degrees of faithfulness, but that every true Christian will bear the fruit of faithfulness. By contrast, every unbeliever will be seen as squandering God's gifts. In fact, this parable should be of great comfort to God's people! Notice that it is the master (God himself) who causes the increase in talents (Matt. 25:26–27). Ultimately the faithfulness of Christians is not dependent on our own works, but on the power of God, who works mightily within us (Col. 1:29).

Because of God's Love, We Are Approved by Faith

"There is therefore now no condemnation for those who are in Christ Jesus" (Rom. 8:1). Christ's propitiation on the cross has made us acceptable to God; he has brought us near to God by his own blood (3:25). And we will never be disappointed, because "hope does not put us to shame, because God's love has been poured into our hearts through the Holy Spirit who has been given to us" (5:5). Repeatedly the New Testament authors affirm that through Christ, we not only are forgiven but also are accepted by God.[9]

Because of God's Love, We Cannot Lose His Approval

Our acceptance before God is based on God's freely given salvation, and therefore it can never be lost. This is Paul's argument in Romans 8:

> Who shall bring any charge against God's elect? It is God who justifies. Who is to condemn? Christ Jesus is the one who died—more than that, who was raised—who is at the right hand of God, who indeed is interceding for us. Who shall separate us

8. Craig Blomberg, *Interpreting the Parables* (Downers Grove, IL: InterVarsity Press, 1990), 216.
9. For example: Rom. 5:8–11; Gal. 3:13–14; Eph. 1:3–8; Col. 2:8–15; 3:2–4; Titus 2:11–14; 3:5–7; Heb. 2:9–11; 1 Peter 1:3–9.

177

from the love of Christ? Shall tribulation, or distress, or persecution, or famine, or nakedness, or danger, or sword? As it is
written, "For your sake we are being killed all the day long; we
are regarded as sheep to be slaughtered." No, in all these things
we are more than conquerors through him who loved us. For I
am sure that neither death nor life, nor angels nor rulers, nor
things present nor things to come, nor powers, nor height nor
depth, nor anything else in all creation, will be able to separate
us from the love of God in Christ Jesus our Lord. (Rom. 8:33–39)

Because of God's eternal election, we have been united to Christ
through faith, and nothing can ever separate us from the love
of Christ. Nothing, therefore, can hinder God's gaze of approval
upon us in the final examination. This is not to say that our sins
please God—far from it. But our life is hidden with Christ in
God (Col. 3:3), who bore all our sins in his own body on the cross
(1 Peter 2:24). And when we stand before God, Christ will confess
our name before the Father (Rev. 1:6), and our approval will be
found in Christ.

But what about the promises in Revelation 2–3 to "the one
who conquers"?[10] The answer is twofold. First, the image of "one
who conquers" is just another way of describing a true Christian.
John defines the one who conquers for us: "For everyone who has
been born of God overcomes the world. And this is the victory that
has overcome the world—our faith" (1 John 5:4). Likewise Paul, in
the passage above, describes all believers as "more than conquerors" (Rom. 8:37). Most importantly, Revelation itself clarifies the
meaning of "the one who conquers." Each of the seven promises
in Revelation 2–3 pertains to all true believers. For example: "To
the one who conquers I will grant to eat of the tree of life, which
is in the paradise of God" (2:7); and again, "The one who conquers
will not be hurt by the second death" (v. 11). All Christians will eat
of the tree of life, and all will escape the second death (20:14–15).

Thus, Scripture assures all believers that they will one day
enter eternally into the Father's joy and love. But God's love in

10. The NIV translates as "him who overcomes."

heaven is more than the mere absence of shame or loss; it produces overflowing joy because of the glory that divine love has conferred on us. To be publicly honored by the mayor of your city for doing something worthwhile is desirable. To be recognized by the governor of your state would be unusual and memorable. To be praised by the president of the United States would be amazing. By contrast, how will it feel to be commended by almighty God on the last day?

Jesus gives us a feel for such an honor in the parable of the talents. The master in the parable is God himself. To both good servants his words overflow with praise: "Well done, good and faithful servant. You have been faithful over a little; I will set you over much. Enter into the joy of your master" (Matt. 25:21, 23). This is living by faith in Jesus Christ, "for whoever would draw near to God must believe that he exists and that he rewards those who seek him" (Heb. 11:6). The Lord of the universe cares much about what his faithful servants have done. He praises them, rewards them, and promises them great joy. His words will mean more than his servants will be able to express. Here is complete fulfillment—to be praised by God at the end of the age. And every child of God will receive the Father's praise on that day. Surely this is something to look forward to!

When Paul describes our glory in heaven, it is likely that the glory of divine love and approval is the weightiest of them all (2 Cor. 4:17). It is a glory that every person who stands before God will receive. We repeat: the hope of hearing "well done, good and faithful servant; enter into the joy of your master" (Matt. 25:14–30) is not only for "super-Christians." Let no one take the hope of the gospel and the joy of Christ from you, for these things have been written to us in order that "through the encouragement of the Scriptures we might have hope" (Rom. 15:4).

The Glory That Does Not Fade

Peter exhorts the elders, "Shepherd the flock of God that is among you, exercising oversight, not under compulsion, but willingly, as God would have you; not for shameful gain, but eagerly; not domineering over those in your charge, but being examples to the flock. And when the chief Shepherd appears, you will receive the unfading crown of glory" (1 Peter 5:2–4). Though some think that this is one of the "five crowns" of heaven, which only some believers will receive, this is an error.[11]

Throughout the letter Peter has contrasted this world's decaying nature with all believers' imperishable, unfading inheritance (1 Peter 1:3–7, 18–25). He continues this theme in 5:1–5, exhorting elders to clothe themselves with humility and not to use their office for personal gain or to exalt themselves. Why? Because their true glory lies in Jesus' appearing, when all believers will share in his glory forever. J. Ramsey Michaels explains:

> The [emphasis in 5:1–5] is not on the elders as individuals, as if each will have his or her own "crown," but rather on the common glory in which all are "sharers" (cf. . . . "sharer," in v. 1). This would be true even if Peter had spoken of "crowns" in the plural, but the fact that "crown" as well as "glory" is singular puts it beyond question. The other uses of "glory" in 1 Peter make it clear, in fact, that the "crown of glory" promised here is not for elders alone, but for all who share in the Christian hope. The elders will receive their "crown" like everyone else in the congregation, for doing what they are called to do (cf. 3:9).[12]

Many people in this world appear glorious, but their glory is temporary and has already begun to fade (James 1:11) because this world is passing away (1 Cor. 7:31; 1 John 2:17). But the glory of the redeemed image of God is only beginning to manifest itself in us (2 Cor. 3:18; Col. 1:27) as we continue to gaze intently upon Jesus and seek glory only in him (John 5:39–44; Rom. 2:7). When Jesus returns to make all things right, he will share his glorious inheritance—imperishable, undefiled, and unfading—with us (1 Peter 1:3–4).

11. For a fuller discussion, see Frequently Asked Questions, pp. 203–5.
12. J. Ramsey Michaels, *1 Peter*, Word Biblical Commentary (Waco, TX: Word, 1988), 287.

Transformation: God's Enabling Glory

Thoughts of our future perfection are nearly impossible to believe because they are so wonderful. Nonetheless, this is the sure end of all believers. We lack space to explore the vast implications of our future glory. And while no area of life is left untouched by the promise of glory, we will mention four key areas.

God's Gift of Glory Enables Us to Truly Love Him

The call on humankind as God's image-bearers to live holy lives is impossible to carry out because of sin, for "whoever keeps the whole law but fails in one point has become accountable for all of it" (James 2:10). Such a weight crushes each of us, and indeed, that is good if it leads us to Christ. But it is not healthy to remain crushed. Scripture's assurance that God loves us, accepts us, and freely gives us his glory through Christ enables us to relate to God not out of the fear of punishment, but in love. And "by this is love perfected with us, so that we may have confidence for the day of judgment. . . . There is no fear in love, but perfect love casts out fear. For fear has to do with punishment, and whoever fears has not been perfected in love" (1 John 4:17–18). So what is our response to such amazing love? "We love because he first loved us" (v. 19). Our hope of future glory frees us to love God in worship, work, and play.

God's Gift of Glory Enables Us to Truly Love One Another

One of the most distressing aspects of the reality shows on television today is the hateful attitudes of contestants toward one another. One of the reasons for such attitudes is that the contestants have nothing to lose and everything to gain.

Imagine for a moment that you are a contestant. Before the first show, the producers tell you that no matter what happens—as long as you participate—they will give you the grand prize in the end. How would that affect your attitude throughout each challenge? How would your relationships with the other

181

contestants change? How would you handle the pressures of the game differently?

God's gift of unfading glory should have a similar effect on our lives. Instead of clamoring for glory among ourselves (John 5:44; Gal. 5:26), we are freed to serve one another in Christlike love. Instead of competing with one another for spiritual or material glory, we can share with fellow believers, for we know that our true inheritance is reserved in heaven (1 Peter 1:4). And instead of judging and condemning one another, we can see others as coheirs of the glorious inheritance of Christ Jesus our Lord.

God's Gift of Glory Enables Us to Truly Love Ourselves

Many Christians think that humility consists primarily in acknowledging to God how wretched we are and thereby magnifying how great he is. But when we put on the lenses of Scripture and see ourselves as those who have received Jesus' glory—in part now, in fullness at the resurrection—then we no longer have to debase ourselves and dishonor the image of God in us. Instead, we can rightly confess our sins and magnify him for his gifts to us.

One particular problem area is physical self-image. We have both heard men and women confess disgust at their bodies! But the promise of glory is that though our bodies may not be as we want now, through Christ's work we—including our bodies—are accepted by God. We do not mean that we can just let ourselves go and sinfully indulge every physical appetite; that is not how grace works. Rather, grace frees us from the bondage of yielding to every urge. It also frees us from worshiping a perfect appearance. Moreover, the promise of bodily resurrection assures us that one day we will have bodies that the Lord himself has perfected, and because our minds and hearts will be perfected as well, we will finally see our physicality as God does—through Christ (1 Cor. 13:12).

God's Gift of Glory Enables Us to Invite Others to Love Him

A difficult evangelistic question to answer is "Why do non-Christians sometimes act better than Christians?" The answer is not difficult because it is mysterious; it is difficult because Christians say one thing and do another—something that we all are guilty of at times. And one reason for this is that we do not appropriate the promise of heavenly glory. That promise promotes Christlike living. When we live trusting in the guarantee of our future glory in Christ, we present a contrast to the pattern of the world, which says, "Get all you can now, because you can't take it with you." This contrast is one of the main purposes of God's glorious image in us, as Jesus said: "so that the world may know that you sent me and loved them even as you loved me" (John 17:23). This is one way that we function as priests of God in the world (Ex. 19:5–6; 1 Peter 2:9; Rev. 1:6). By transformed lives we make Christ known to those who do not know him. God's blessing of glory through Christ is ours so that through us all the nations of the earth will also be blessed and brought into the family of God.

We have now looked at five biblical pictures of final salvation or heaven. Heaven is resurrection and righteousness in the new heavens and new earth, enjoying perfect rest, being a citizen at peace in the kingdom of God, fullness of joy in God's presence, and brilliance in glory. Heaven is a wonderful prospect indeed!

Conclusion

SCOTT OLIPHINT AND SINCLAIR FERGUSON share the following story and their insightful comments on it:

> Some time ago we heard a fascinating radio program in which a number of famous people were asked what they thought heaven would be like. A consistent three-point pattern began to emerge in their answers, although its most significant element seemed to pass unnoticed by the program makers:
>
> 1. All those interviewed believed in heaven.
> 2. All those interviewed assumed they would be there.
> 3. When asked to describe heaven, not one of those interviewed mentioned that God was there.
>
> But it is the presence of God in holy, loving majesty that makes heaven what it is. It can even be said that heaven *is* the presence of God—being in heaven means living with him forever.[1]

Oliphint and Ferguson are right on both counts: people too easily forget about God—even when thinking about heaven—and heaven is all about God. As we draw matters to a close, then, we want to fulfill two desires: to underline that it is the God of glory and grace who makes heaven to be heaven, and to apply the five pictures of heaven to real life. We attempt the first because to write about heaven and not focus on God is to distort the Bible. God is far and away the most important person in the biblical

---

1. K. Scott Oliphint and Sinclair B. Ferguson, *If I Should Die before I Wake* (Grand Rapids: Baker, 1995), 44 (italics in original).

story, and it is our role as creatures to exalt him. We attempt the second because it is our prayer that our writing about heaven will strengthen us and readers.

- We Will Know Our Covenant Lord as Resurrected Persons on the New Earth
- We Will Enjoy the Eternal Sabbath Rest with our Divine Lover
- We Will Serve Our Great King as Subjects in His Eternal Kingdom
- We Will Delight in the Presence of the Holy One
- We Will Be Transformed in Glory to Glorify Our Glorious Triune God

We Will Know Our Covenant Lord as Resurrected Persons on the New Earth

We began this book with two chapters dealing with creation for good reasons. First, they lay a foundation on which the other chapters build. And second, many believers have the mistaken idea that we will live eternally as disembodied souls in a spiritual heaven. We affirm the intermediate state—that at death believers are "away from the body and at home with the Lord" (2 Cor. 5:8). But we do not extend that intermediate situation into the eternal state. Rather, we affirm with Scripture that in the final state we will be resurrected whole persons who know and serve the Trinity on the new earth.

The biblical theme of the new heavens and the new earth has deep Old Testament roots. Near the beginning of the biblical story, God swore by himself to bless and multiply Abraham, "since he had no one greater by whom to swear," and promised Abraham "all the land of Canaan, for an everlasting possession" (Heb. 6:13–14; Gen. 17:8). The patriarch believed God's promises and looked "forward to the city that has foundations, whose designer and builder is God" (Heb. 11:10). By faith father Abraham, "having seen them [the things promised] and greeted them from afar" (11:13), saw dimly the fulfillment of the Promised Land of Canaan in the new earth. At the other end of the biblical story, the image of "the holy city Jerusalem coming down out of heaven from God" (Rev. 21:10) speaks of heaven coming down to earth, and heaven and earth becoming one. The most basic way to view heaven, then, is as our being raised from the dead, transformed, and equipped to live forever, knowing and loving our great covenant Lord in the new heavens and earth.

So What?

The single most important thing that we want readers to take away from this book is that "the central message of Scripture about the future of man is that of the resurrection of the body."[2] This is the Christian hope: eternal life with God and all the saints on the new earth. We can learn from John Calvin, who devoted a chapter in his famous *Institutes of the Christian Religion* to "Meditation on the Future Life." Calvin believed that "no one has made progress in the school of Christ who does not joyfully await the day of death and final resurrection."[3]

This truth transforms the way we view our lives and work. It is no wonder that Paul puts these words at the end of "the resurrection chapter": "Therefore, my beloved brothers, be steadfast, immovable, always abounding in the work of the Lord, knowing that in the Lord your labor is not in vain" (1 Cor. 15:58). Our work for God now is not in vain because he will transform this present world into the new heavens and earth. And what we do now for God counts for eternity because he will transform us and his creation so that both will last forever.

We Will Enjoy the Eternal Sabbath Rest with Our Divine Lover

One beautiful facet of the precious stone of final salvation is the Sabbath rest for God's people. In contrast to the temptations,

2. Anthony A. Hoekema, *The Bible and the Future* (Grand Rapids: Eerdmans, 1979), 91.
3. John Calvin, *Institutes of the Christian Religion*, ed. John T. McNeill, trans. Ford Lewis Battles (Philadelphia: Westminster, 1960), 3.9.5.

struggles, and failures that God's people have endured over the ages, God our Father has promised us rest, everlasting hospitality in his house. Heaven means knowing and enjoying the company of him who said, "I have loved you with an everlasting love" (Jer. 31:3). Heaven is loving him "because he first loved us" and "sent his Son to be the propitiation for our sins" (1 John 4:19, 10). Heaven is enjoying the fellowship of the One who "in love . . . predestined us for adoption as sons through Jesus Christ . . . , to the praise of his glorious grace" (Eph. 1:4–6).

We have brothers and sisters in Christ in China, North Korea, Indonesia, and South Sudan, to name four hot spots, who have suffered in ways that we will never know—including persecution, displacement, and even death. We should pray for them more often than we do. And we should rejoice that they and we one day will enjoy—with our divine Lover—the everlasting Sabbath rest of all of God's people. That is a glorious prospect!

So What?

At the checkout counter of the grocery store, I (Robert) was recently reminded of the need for a biblically based book on heaven. The checker, a sweet Christian woman, when hearing that I was writing a book on heaven, asked: "What was your experience?" She wanted to know about my firsthand trip to glory from which I would share sure knowledge of the afterlife. To her disappointment, I told her that my coauthor Dan and I had not taken a trip to heaven, but instead had spent years studying the Bible.

This prompts a key question: Where do we learn of the delicious promise of future rest? And of other pictures of heaven? The only reliable source for such things is the written Word of God. It alone can be trusted to teach truth about final salvation, including our eternal Sabbath rest. Only in the Bible do we find the promise of eternal peace that means that Christians will never be disturbed or displaced again.

Therefore, we will not seek to learn of future things through dreams, visions, near-death experiences, or the like. Instead, we will study and believe the Word of God. In it our dear Father declares that he has loved us, that by grace he made us to be his sons and daughters, and that greater manifestation of our sonship awaits (Rom. 8:23; 1 John 1:1–2). It is critical for readers to know where we go to learn about heaven—the Holy Scriptures.

We Will Serve Our Great King as Subjects in His Eternal Kingdom

God's people have fierce and powerful enemies who are bent on destroying them. The "dragon, that ancient serpent, who is the devil and Satan" (Rev. 20:2), hates God and his saints. Though many Christians seem unaware of it, "we do not wrestle against flesh and blood, but . . . against the spiritual forces of evil in the heavenly places" (Eph. 6:12). Other foes include the world as a system set against God with its weapons of deception and seduction, our own sinful tendencies ("the flesh"), and "the last enemy . . . death" (1 Cor. 15:26).

These foes are much too strong for us to overcome. From Genesis to Revelation, the kingdom of Satan rages against the kingdom of God. But the true and living God is the everlasting King over all the earth (Pss. 10:16; 47:7; Jer. 10:10), and his Son is "King of kings and Lord of lords" (Rev. 19:16). God's people conquer through Christ, who loved them and gave himself for them (Gal. 2:20). "The Lion of the tribe of Judah" who "has conquered" is the Lamb (Rev. 5:5–6)!

So What?

The triumph of the kingdom of God in Christ's death and resurrection guarantees a great victory to Christians. This victory involves serving our great King as subjects of his kingdom now and forever. Christ speaks of this when he says: "The one who conquers, I will grant him to sit with me on my throne, as I also conquered and sat down with my Father on his throne" (Rev. 3:21). Indeed, the One "who loves us and has freed us from our sins by his blood" has also "made us a kingdom, priests to his God and Father, to [whom] be glory and dominion forever and ever" (Rev. 1:5–6).

Christ has defeated our powerful enemies without and within. The evil one is a defeated foe who will one day be thrown into the lake of fire (John 12:31; Rev. 20:10). Christ's death and resurrection vanquished seduction and deception so that our sinful drives need no longer dominate us. We are not at the mercy of thoughts and doubts that draw our hearts away from purity of devotion to Christ (2 Cor. 11:3). But we must do battle against them and overcome evil. Internal warring continues, but by God's grace we are able to live soberly and to persevere to the end (1 Peter 1:13; Heb. 6:9–12). In Christ there is victory over false teaching and rationalization of our sins. We have overcome death, so that at death we go to be with Christ (Phil. 1:23), and in the resurrection death will be no more (1 Cor. 15:26; Rev. 21:4). There will be complete healing *only* in the new creation, but the good news is that there will indeed be complete healing in the new creation!

The present real and ultimate comprehensive victory of the kingdom of God tremendously impacts our values in this life. In this way, heaven teaches us what things to hold on to and what things to let go. This is a critical message for a Western audience in the twenty-first century. Jesus, contrasting earthly and heavenly treasures, warned: "Where your treasure is, there your heart will be also" (Matt. 6:21). We ask ourselves and readers alike: Where is our treasure?

We Will Delight in the Presence of the Holy One

Both Old and New Testaments resound with affirmations of the holiness of the true and living God:

Who is like you, majestic in holiness,
awesome in glorious deeds, doing wonders? (Ex. 15:11)

Holy, holy, holy is the LORD of hosts;
the whole earth is full of his glory! (Isa. 6:3)

You shall be holy, for I am holy. (1 Peter 1:16, quoting Lev. 11:44)

For you alone are holy.
   All nations will come
   and worship you. (Rev. 15:4)

Such perfect divine holiness strikes fear into the heart of any sensible creature. That is why the Israelites trembled at the foot of Mount Sinai and begged Moses, "You speak to us and we will listen; but do not let God speak to us, lest we die" (Ex. 20:19). That is why Isaiah cried, "Woe is me! For I am lost; for I am a man of unclean lips . . . ; for my eyes have seen the King, the LORD of hosts!" (Isa. 6:5). That is why Peter fell down before Jesus, exclaiming: "Depart from me, for I am a sinful man, O Lord" (Luke 5:8). And that is why John, upon seeing the exalted Lord Jesus, "fell at his feet as though dead" (Rev. 1:17).

How, then, can sinful human beings ever come into the presence of this awesome and holy Being? How can Scripture exhort believers: "Let us then with confidence draw near to the throne of grace, that we may receive mercy and find grace to help in time of need" (Heb. 4:16)? The answer lies in the person and work of Christ. He is our Great High Priest who made "purification for sins," rose from the dead so that he "continues forever," "passed through the heavens," and saves "to the uttermost those who draw near to God through him" (Heb. 1:3; 7:24; 4:14; 7:25).

As a result of Christ's saving accomplishment, believing sinners "have redemption through his blood, the forgiveness of" their "trespasses" (Eph. 1:7). And because of that same saving accomplishment, we will delight in the presence of the Holy One forever. God was present in the garden of Eden before the fall and afterward lived in the midst of his people in the tabernacle and the temple. In the incarnation, the Son of God "became flesh and dwelt among us" (John 1:14). The Holy Spirit indwells believers individually and the church corporately (1 Cor. 3:16; 6:19).

Moreover, the Bible's story ends on this astounding note: "Behold, the dwelling place of God is with man. He will dwell with them, and they will be his people, and God himself will be with them as their God" (Rev. 21:3).

It is no wonder that Scripture ascribes great joy to the people of God privileged to be in his holy presence forever:

> You make known to me the path of life;
>   in your presence there is fullness of joy;
>   at your right hand are pleasures forevermore. (Ps. 16:11)

> Then the King will say to those on his right, "Come, you who are blessed by my Father, inherit the kingdom prepared for you from the foundation of the world." (Matt. 25:34)

> He will wipe away every tear from their eyes, and death shall be no more, neither shall there be mourning, nor crying, nor pain anymore, for the former things have passed away. (Rev. 21:4)

> Blessed are those who wash their robes, so that they may have the right to the tree of life and that they may enter the city by the gates. (Rev. 22:14)

So What?

What should our lives look like in the light of such a prospect? Surely it should promote joy and holiness in us now!

Joy. Even with all our issues, struggles, and sins, it is possible for us to rejoice now in the presence of the living God through his Son Jesus. This happens in a special way when the church gathers on Sunday. But God's grace and Spirit empower us to walk with God and enjoy his fellowship every day as we look for the great day of "our blessed hope" (1 John 1:3; Titus 2:13).

Holiness. The fact that heaven will mean enjoying a holy God's presence forever should cause us to walk away from sin and toward glory today. Scripture is plain: "Beloved, we are God's children now, and what we will be has not yet appeared; but we know that when he appears we shall be like him, because we shall see him as he is. And everyone who thus hopes in him purifies himself as he is pure" (1 John 3:2–3).

Here is the true story of a vulnerable Christian friend, whom we will call Roy, who asked us to share it to help other men and women struggling with the sin of pornography.

Roy had been sexually active before his conversion, without shame. After becoming a Christian and knowing that this behavior was unacceptable to God, he stopped having physically inappropriate relationships with women. But the seduction of sexual pleasure was a very strong force in his life, and so his public sins now became his private addiction. Roy's life was the embodiment of Jesus' words: "Everyone who commits sin is a slave to sin" (John 8:34).

He became desperate and asked friends for books to help him. He considered throwing out his computer, but knew that if he did, he would still find other outlets for his sin. Instead of trying to fix his computer or his behavior, Roy came to realize that he needed to fix his heart, and that his behavior would change as a result.

We encouraged Roy to study heaven in his devotions, to meditate on what personal holiness looked like in heaven *and why*. He found in the biblical picture of heaven a redeemed humanity free from the bondage of all that enslaves. And to his surprise, Roy learned that this picture of heaven in the future showed him the pathway to true joy through holiness in the present. Roy began to see that God had created him for righteousness, and so to live in righteousness—not in sin—was to live better and more fully. Roy realized that his sexual sin, ironically, was not leading him to a fulfilled life; rather, it was destroying it! Ultimately, Roy's study of heaven was the means that God used to recapture his heart and his love for God in a way that drove out sexual sin and others. Do you know a friend who needs to hear Roy's story?

We Will Be Transformed in Glory to Glorify our Glorious Triune God

The glory of God in Scripture is so overwhelming that we can understand it only in part.[4] The Bible describes God's glory in exalted language. When "the glory of the LORD filled the tabernacle . . . Moses was not able to enter" (Ex. 40:34–35). Isaiah exclaimed: "The whole earth is full of his glory!" (Isa. 6:3). At his transfiguration, when Jesus' divine glory was revealed, his "face shone like the sun" and his "clothing became dazzling white" (Matt. 17:2; Luke 9:29). Furthermore, the new heavens and earth do not need the light of sun or moon, "for the glory of God gives it light, and its lamp is the Lamb" (Rev. 21:23).

Amazingly, this glorious God chose to share his glory with human beings! As Adam and Eve came from the hand of their Maker, they were "crowned . . . with glory and honor" (Ps. 8:5). Of course, this creational glory was marred in our first parents' fall. But Christ, our Glory-Redeemer, reversed the effects of the fall by dying on the cross and being coronated at God's right hand (Heb. 2:9). As a result, he prayed to the Father this way concerning his disciples: "the glory that you have given me I have given to them" (John 17:22). Although it is difficult for us to imagine, Paul describes the Christian life in these terms: "And we all, with unveiled face, beholding the glory of the Lord, are being transformed into the same image from one degree of glory to another" (2 Cor. 3:18).

Scripture speaks frequently of final salvation in terms of glory:

> For I consider that the sufferings of this present time are not worth comparing with the glory that is to be revealed to us. (Rom. 8:18)

> For this light momentary affliction is preparing for us an eternal weight of glory beyond all comparison. (2 Cor. 4:17)

4. See an attempt: Christopher W. Morgan and Robert A. Peterson, eds., *The Glory of God*, Theology in Community (Wheaton, IL: Crossway, 2010).

When Christ who is your life appears, then you also will appear with him in glory. (Col. 3:4)

To this he called you through our gospel, so that you may obtain the glory of our Lord Jesus Christ. (2 Thess. 2:14)

So I exhort the elders among you, as a fellow elder and a witness of the sufferings of Christ, as well as a partaker in the glory that is going to be revealed. (1 Peter 5:1)

And after you have suffered a little while, the God of all grace, who has called you to his eternal glory in Christ, will himself restore, confirm, strengthen, and establish you. (1 Peter 5:10)

If this is the glorious future that all believers anticipate, how should that impact our lives now?

So What?

We can think of at least five ways. First, identity. Many Christians find their identity in the wrong places—in their jobs, bank accounts, friends, or pursuit of pleasure, to name common examples. Consequently, some think too much of themselves and others too little. Both too high a view and too low a view of self-esteem are misguided. Believers are to find their identity in Christ, our Glory-Redeemer who loved us unto death and rose again, promising us glory on the new earth. This is the identity of every Christian: we are winners—every single one is heading for eternal glory.

Second, unity. Because all believers will one day be transformed in glory so as to enjoy their glorious Lord forever, they ought to seek greater unity with one another now. Our goal is the same, and because of God's grace and power, we will not fail to reach that goal. Our hearts should overflow with joy at this bright prospect and with love for fellow believers with whom we will share the Glorious One forever.

Third, bodies. All those who love Christ will be raised with bodies that are incorruptible, powerful, beautiful, and perfect in righteousness. This should motivate us to care for our bodies now but not to be overly concerned with body-image issues.

Fourth, love. Because God loved us with an everlasting love and destined us for glory, we are assured of his love. Consequently, we are freed to love him, one another, and ourselves, and to invite others to love him, too.

Fifth, *sola Scriptura*. Our deepest prayer as we finish this book is that readers will be motivated to seek God where he is to be found—in his holy Word. We are not to be distracted with stories of near-death experiences and the like. Rather, we are to be devoted to God and his Word, where alone we are taught correctly about heaven and much else.

Frequently Asked Questions about Heaven

We will address these questions:

- What Common Questions about Heaven Does Scripture Not Answer?
- What Happens When Believers Die?
- What about Purgatory?
- Should People Talk to the Dead?
- What about Near-Death Experiences?
- What Are the Crowns That Believers Receive in Heaven?
- Are There Levels in Heaven according to Rewards?
- Will We Be All-Knowing in Heaven?
- Will the Current Earth Be Completely Destroyed and a Brand-New Earth Created?
- Will We Recognize Others in Heaven?
- Will We Be Married and Enjoy Sex in Heaven?
- What Kind of Bodies Will We Have in Heaven?
- What Happens to Babies Who Die?
- Will There Be Sorrow in Heaven over Those in Hell?
- Will Everyone Go to Heaven?

What Common Questions about Heaven Does Scripture Not Answer?

We sometimes ask questions of Scripture that it does not answer. Peter tells us that God "has granted to us all things that pertain to life and godliness" (2 Peter 1:3). God spoke forth his holy Word to give us all we need for eternal life and to live godly lives. The Bible is not a reference work that answers every conceivable question but is the book that tells God's story and our place in it. As such, it answers questions that pertain to our knowing God and living for him.

Concerning the life to come, God does not answer every question. What age will we be? We simply do not know. When God's Word speaks about the future, it tells mostly about the resurrection and life thereafter; it does not say as much about what happens when we die.

So for some questions we simply have little or no information. We could generate answers by extrapolating from broad biblical principles, but that would produce only educated guesses. Some questions that the Bible does not answer are these:

- What age will we be?
- Will we live as families or as one family of God?
- What will we be doing day in and day out?
- How will we interact with other Christians?

We respond to questions that we have been asked frequently and that Scripture answers. We simply do not have answers to every question.[1]

What Happens When Believers Die?

While this book focuses on believers' eternal state, we will briefly respond to a common question: What happens when we die? The Scriptures affirm that after death believers' spirits immediately go to be with the exalted Christ (Luke 23:43; Phil. 1:23). This is a great comfort, for we know that while death is often painful, Jesus never leaves us or forsakes us (Matt. 28:20). When believers die, they immediately enter into the joyous presence of

1. Dan invites readers to e-mail him questions that he will try to answer at questions@thestoryofheaven.com.

God. There is no period of unconsciousness,[2] but Christians enjoy the peace of heaven with the risen Savior. Our souls are made perfect in holiness (Heb. 12:23), and we enjoy all the benefits of being with Christ in perfect joy.

What about Purgatory?

The Roman Catholic doctrine of purgatory does not offer a chance for salvation after death. Instead, it enables Catholics to purge sins not atoned for in this life.[3] Purgatory is not a final destination, but all who go to purgatory eventually reach heaven. This consoles many who hope after death to go to purgatory and eventually reach heaven. But today many Catholics have abandoned belief in it. Nevertheless, their church still holds to this doctrine, as the documents of Vatican II show.[4]

Catholic theologian Zachary Hayes admits: "Roman Catholic exegetes and theologians at the present time would be inclined to say that although there is no clear textual basis in Scripture for the later doctrine of purgatory, neither is there anything that is clearly contrary to that doctrine."[5] But this is an inadequate basis for believing in purgatory, and Scripture does in fact contradict it.

Catholics have appealed to three texts in support of purgatory—Matthew 12:32; 1 Corinthians 3:15; and 2 Maccabees 12:42–45 from the Apocrypha—but these are not a sound basis for it. In Matthew

2. The Bible uses the language of "sleep" to describe the death of believers (1 Thess. 4:14). This does not imply that our souls are not awake, but highlights that bodily decay is but a temporary condition from which we will awaken in the resurrection.

3. Ludwig Ott, *Fundamentals of Catholic Dogma*, 4th ed. (Rockford, IL: Tan Books, 1960), 482.

4. "The doctrine of purgatory clearly demonstrates that even when the guilt of sin has been taken away, punishment for it or the consequences of it may remain to be expiated or cleansed. They often are. In fact, in purgatory the souls of those who died in the charity of God and truly repentant, but who had not made satisfaction with adequate penance for their sins and omissions[,] are cleansed after death with punishments designed to purge away their debt." Austin P. Flannery, ed., *Vatican Council II: The Conciliar and Post Conciliar Documents*, new rev. ed., Vatican Collection, vol. 1 (Northport, NY: Costello Publishing; Dublin: Dominican Publications, 1996), 64.

5. Zachary Hayes, "The Purgatorial View," in *Four Views on Hell*, ed. William Crockett (Grand Rapids: Zondervan, 1992), 107.

12:32, Jesus does not say that some sins will be forgiven after death, but declares that he who commits the unpardonable sin will never be forgiven. Concerning 1 Corinthians 3:15, "the Day" mentioned in verse 13 refers not to the time of death but to Christ's return and the last judgment. Also, there is nothing here about sins being purged after death or of people moving from purgatory to heaven.

We reject the appeal to 2 Maccabees 12:42–45 from the Apocrypha as evidence for purgatory because the Jews, the custodians of the Old Testament, never accepted the Apocrypha as a part of Scripture, and neither do we. In fact, Roman Catholic scholars base their belief in purgatory on church tradition, but we do not put tradition on the same plane as the Bible. Instead, we evaluate all human teachings on the basis of God's Word and find the doctrine of purgatory wanting.

Furthermore, purgatory insults Christ's saving work. All believers "have been sanctified through the offering of the body of Jesus Christ once for all" (Heb. 10:10; cf. 13:12). It is by his suffering on the cross, not our suffering after death, that sins are purged. There is no purgatory, but when we enter Christ's presence, he will immediately and entirely purify us: "May God himself, the God of peace, sanctify you through and through. May your whole spirit, soul and body be kept blameless at the coming of our Lord Jesus Christ" (1 Thess. 5:23 NIV). Purgatory offers a false hope, for Scripture speaks of only *two* destinies for human beings: heaven and hell (Matt. 25:46; John 5:28–29; Rev. 21:7–8).

Should People Talk to the Dead?

This one is easy to answer: the Bible repeatedly condemns attempts of the living to contact the dead. The Lord's message is unmistakable (*mediums* and *necromancers* often appear together in the Old Testament to indicate those who inquire of the dead):

> Do not turn to mediums or necromancers; do not seek them out, and so make yourselves unclean by them: I am the LORD your God. (Lev. 19:31)

200

> If a person turns to mediums and necromancers, whoring after them, I will set my face against that person and will cut him off from among his people. (20:6)

The Lord commands his people, before occupying the Promised Land, to destroy the Canaanites and to shun their sinful spiritual practices that he detests, including inquiring of the dead:

> There shall not be found among you anyone who burns his son or his daughter as an offering, anyone who practices divination or tells fortunes or interprets omens, or a sorcerer or a charmer or a medium or a necromancer or one who inquires of the dead, for whoever does these things is an abomination to the LORD. And because of these abominations the LORD your God is driving them out before you. (Deut. 18:10–12)

Second Kings contrasts the many evil kings who reigned in Jerusalem with the few good kings. Manasseh, an evil king, "dealt with mediums and with necromancers. He did much evil in the sight of the LORD, provoking him to anger" (2 Kings 21:6). Josiah, a good king, "put away the mediums and the necromancers . . . and all the abominations that were seen in the land of Judah and in Jerusalem, that he might establish the words of the law" (23:24).

God's denunciations of those who talk to the dead are also in the Prophets, where Isaiah contrasts those who "inquire of the dead on behalf of the living" with those who give heed to "the teaching and . . . the testimony," that is, the Word of God (Isa. 8:19–20).

The New Testament does not explicitly mention these practices, but they are included in its condemnations of sorcery (see Gal. 5:19–21; Rev. 21:8). Jesus' parable of the rich man and Lazarus is also important. Some claim appearances of their departed loved ones or seek them in dreams, but Jesus teaches us in Luke 16 to turn our attention to a much more reliable source of comfort—the promises of God's Word.[6]

6. See our treatment of it in the introduction on p. 5.

What about Near-Death Experiences?

The reported incidence of near-death experiences (NDEs) has skyrocketed since the 1970s along with the advancement of resuscitation techniques.[7] The list of people having NDEs in the last forty years is large and growing. Our ability to prolong life and accurately determine death is improving. J. I. Packer says that he used to speak of "heart-stop day," but now he thinks in terms of "brain-stop day," since on average the brain remains alive thirty minutes after the body ceases to function.[8] We should not assume that we can definitively estimate the time of death.

Scripture says, "It is appointed for man to die once, and after that comes judgment" (Heb. 9:27). There is not a single account in the Bible of a person who died, came back, and provided knowledge of heaven. This should make us cautious concerning NDE claims.

Deceased believers at the moment of death are ushered into God's presence (Luke 16:22). To remain in his holy presence requires perfect purity, which the Bible affirms our disembodied souls obtain at death (Heb. 12:23). Once made perfect, we do not come back to an imperfect (sinful) state.[9]

Second Corinthians 12:1–5 recounts Paul's experience when he was "caught up" to heaven. This is not a good example of an NDE, as some claim. Why? Because NDEs by definition are out of the body, and Paul twice writes this of his experience: "whether in the body or out of the body I do not know" (vv. 2, 3).

People told Jesus, "We wish to see a sign from you" (Matt. 12:38). But he rebuked them: "An evil and adulterous generation seeks for a sign" (v. 39). And Jesus is emphatic in Luke 16:29–31 that Scripture is sufficient. The Savior wants us to place our faith

7. Mario Beauregard and Denyse O'Leary, *The Spiritual Brain: A Neuroscientist's Case for the Existence of the Soul* (New York: HarperOne, 2007), 153.

8. J. I. Packer, "A Guided Tour of Heaven and Hell," discussion panel, Christian Book Expo, Dallas, 2009, video available at http://www.epm.org/resources/2010/Mar/24/guided-tour-heaven-and-hell/.

9. Some people object and cite the raising of Lazarus. But this should not be taken as setting a precedent, for Jesus treats the raising of Lazarus as a singular event, given as a witness for himself as "the resurrection and the life" (John 11:4, 15, 25).

not in signs but in the Word of God, and this means that NDEs have no further value to strengthen faith beyond the Bible.

Christians are told to examine all claims about God (Deut. 18:15–22; 1 John 4:1–3) because there are many false claims (1 Tim. 4:1–3; 1 John 4:3–6). Many accounts of NDEs not only contradict one another but also contradict God's Word.

It seems that NDEs are significant experiences in persons' lives and as such are under the same biblical authority as any other events. Most importantly, NDEs do not reveal any new information about heaven or its inhabitants that we do not already possess in God's Word.

What Are the Crowns That Believers Receive in Heaven?

Many have been taught that there are "five crowns" of heaven that only some believers will receive for accomplishing certain tasks during their lives:

- *The Incorruptible Crown* (1 Cor. 9:25) for those who die strong in the faith.
- *The Crown of Rejoicing* (1 Thess. 2:19) for those who evangelize well.
- *The Crown of Righteousness* (2 Tim. 4:8) for those who long for Christ's return.
- *The Crown of Life* (James 1:12) for those who are steadfast under persecution.
- *The Crown of Glory* (1 Peter 5:4) for those who govern God's people faithfully.

Some hold that the twenty-four elders cast these crowns before Jesus (Rev. 4:10–11).

This approach is not based on careful Bible study and has sometimes fostered spiritual competition and elitism. These crowns are not tangible, physical objects that a special few will receive but are symbols that describe the inheritance of all believers.

This is true for five reasons. First, in three passages the words following "crown" in English define it:

- The crown of righteousness (2 Tim. 4:8).
- The crown of life (James 1:12).
- The crown of glory (1 Peter 5:4).

That is, the crown that is righteousness, the crown that is life, and the crown that is glory. Thus, in these three instances the crowns are not literal but figurative of final salvation.

Second, in 1 Corinthians 9:25 Paul alludes to the Isthmian games that were held in Corinth in A.D. 49 and 51. He contrasts the winning runner's "perishable wreath" with an "imperishable" one. A literal "imperishable wreath" is an impossibility; they were made of plastered pine or celery leaves that suffered decay and destruction. By "imperishable wreath" Paul means the never-ending eternal life and blessing that all believers will enjoy.

Third, three of the occurrences speak of blessings that all true believers, not only the elite, will receive. All will be given righteousness (Rom. 5:19; Gal. 5:5), life (John 3:16; Rom. 6:23), and glory (Rom. 8:18; 2 Thess. 2:14).

Fourth, it is a mistake to include the "crown of boasting" (1 Thess. 2:19) in a list of crowns that we are to seek. Paul says that the Thessalonian believers are his, Silvanus's, and Timothy's hope, joy, or crown (vv. 19–20; cf. 1:1). This does not refer to a literal crown; Paul simply expresses affection and praise for the Thessalonian Christians.

Fifth, we could argue that, technically, the "crowns" in 1 Corinthians 9:25 and 1 Peter 5:4 are promised to apostles and elders, respectively. But when viewed in light of the Bible's teaching concerning salvation and "crowns," these church leaders are representative of God's people.

We conclude that the teaching concerning the "five crowns" of heaven should be abandoned. In the four passages that speak of something to be won (1 Cor. 9:25; 2 Tim. 4:8; James 1:12;

1 Peter 5:4), the prize is not only for super-saints, but for garden-variety believers in the Christ.

Are There Levels in Heaven according to Rewards?

The concept of levels in heaven gained popularity in the fourteenth century as a result of Dante's epic poem *Divine Comedy* and is still with us today, in Mormon teaching, for example. The poem includes hell, purgatory, and paradise, all of which Dante visits through guided tours. He experiences seven levels of hell, seven levels of suffering and spiritual growth in purgatory, and nine spheres of heaven. The levels of hell and spheres of heaven correspond to persons' wickedness or righteousness on earth.

When Jesus' disciples argue about who will be the greatest in the kingdom of heaven (Matt. 18:1), Jesus rebukes their one-upmanship. Such clamoring for the best places in the kingdom will be absent in heaven, for we will be completely sanctified and completely satisfied with our great God and his great salvation.

The idea of levels of heaven is misleading. First, Dante envisions believers as living on various planets, and some Christians have similar nonearthly conceptions of heaven. But this is wrong because, as we saw in chapter 2, the final destination of all of God's people is the new *earth*.

Second, rather than speaking of levels of heaven, we should think like this: all believers will be equal in *possession*, but there will be variety in *position*. We tend to think in individualistic terms (my car, my house, and the like), and some extend this way of thinking to heaven. But Paul teaches that each member of Christ's body already belongs to every other member (1 Cor. 12:12–26). And in glory, the unity of God's people will be complete.

Every Christian will be equal in possession of final salvation. Each of us will enjoy the Trinity, the new heavens and earth, and eternal life (Matt. 20:1–16; Luke 18:30; Rom. 8:17, 32)! Paul summarizes: "For all things are yours, whether . . . the world or life or death or the present or the future—all are yours, and you are Christ's, and Christ is God's" (1 Cor. 3:21–23).

This essential point is often overlooked in discussions of believers' rewards. And that is a big mistake, for this one point changes everything. If we are assured that everything will belong to us because we belong to Jesus, then compared to that, variations in position are unimportant.

Scripture also teaches that there will be differences in our positions on the new earth. Jesus' parables indicate that there will be greater and lesser positions of service (Matt. 25:14–30; Luke 19:12–27). But they will be just that—positions of *service*. Because heaven is perfect in righteousness, differences in positions of service will not cause pride or envy.

In sum: heaven's grand reward is the privilege of knowing, loving, serving, and enjoying God and one another for all eternity. And in this great reward all believers will share. Under that stupendous blessing, we will gladly embrace the positions of service to which we are assigned, to the glory of him who saved us freely by his grace.

Will We Be All-Knowing in Heaven?

This one is easy. First, God alone is the infinite Creator; we are his finite creatures. Even when we are glorified, we will remain finite creatures. We will never know all things as God does, for he alone is omniscient (Ps. 147:5; Heb. 4:13). This makes the prospect of everlasting life on the new earth so exciting: we will never exhaust the knowledge of the Holy One. We will never be bored in the presence of him who is infinitely interesting.

Yet Paul says, "Now I know in part; then I shall know fully, even as I have been fully known" (1 Cor. 13:12). He does not say that we will become omniscient like God. Rather, he means that we will see God directly and have a mature understanding of him compared to our current immature understanding:

> For we know in part and we prophesy in part, but when the perfect comes, the partial will pass away. When I was a child, I

spoke like a child, I thought like a child, I reasoned like a child. When I became a man, I gave up childish ways. For now we see in a mirror dimly, but then face to face. Now I know in part; then I shall know fully, even as I have been fully known. (13:9–12)

What does Paul mean by "the perfect," by seeing "face to face," by knowing "fully" (1 Cor. 13:10–12)? The key to answering correctly lies in noting his big contrast. He likens these three descriptions to adults' knowing over against children's knowing. That is, Paul does not contrast infinite knowledge with finite knowledge. Instead, he contrasts the immature knowledge of childhood with the mature knowledge of adulthood. So when he writes, "Then I shall know fully, even as I have been fully known" (v. 12), he does not anticipate one day being divine, but one day being mature. And that maturity is compatible with our creaturely finiteness.

At present, our minds are dimmed by sin. But when perfection comes, our minds will apprehend God, ourselves, and our friends with righteous clarity. Only then will we fulfill the great commandment in the Law: "You shall love the Lord your God with all your heart and with all your soul and with all your *mind*" (Matt. 22:37; cf. Deut. 6:5)!

Will the Current Earth Be Completely Destroyed and a Brand-New Earth Created?

This question is so important that we include it here and point readers to pages 36–40 of chapter 2, "Creation Renewed," where it receives extensive treatment.

Will We Recognize Others in Heaven?

While all believers will make many new friends over the course of eternity on the new earth, Scripture provides good reason to believe that we will recognize those we have known. People who ask this question often confuse what happens to believers at death with their eternal destiny. At death our bodies rest in the grave while our souls go immediately to be with Jesus. But this spiritual or nonphysical heaven is temporary. At the end we will be raised from the dead, God will unite our resurrected bodies and our souls, and we will enjoy him and one another forever. Resurrection means physicality, which means recognizability.

The risen Christ was recognizable, as Scripture attests (Matt. 28:9–10, 16–17; Luke 24:31–43; John 20:28). Some will object that at times his followers did not recognize him. But these are exceptions, not the rule. The disciples on the road to Emmaus did not recognize him because God prevented their doing so (Luke 24:16). Mary mistook Jesus for the gardener because she was not expecting him to rise. When he spoke her name, she immediately knew him (John 20:16). Oliphint and Ferguson are right: "Like Christ, we too will be recognizable after the resurrection. Indeed, who and what we really are will be clearer than ever."[10]

Will We Be Married and Enjoy Sex in Heaven?

We have addressed this question, which is on many minds, in chapter 2, "Creation Renewed," on pages 43–46.

What Kind of Bodies Will We Have in Heaven?

We direct readers to pages 41–43 of chapter 2, "Creation Renewed," where this important question is answered in some detail.

What Happens to Babies Who Die?

Infants and the mentally handicapped are unable to comprehend the knowledge of God. What is their fate? First, we affirm

10. K. Scott Oliphint and Sinclair B. Ferguson, *If I Should Die before I Wake* (Grand Rapids: Baker, 1995), 84.

that they are indeed persons. There are many today who deny that they are real persons, citing the ability to reason as being what truly makes us human. We disagree and affirm that human beings produce other human beings, and that a person is a person from conception.

Second, we affirm that all who are saved are chosen by the Father, are redeemed by the Son, and have their hearts opened by the Holy Spirit (Eph. 1:4–5, 7, 13–14).

Third, Scripture gives us a hint when it shows Jesus' attitude toward babies. Especially poignant is Luke 18:15: "Now they [the people] were bringing even infants to him that he might touch them." In Greek there are several words denoting children, but the word that Luke uses means "baby, infant," a word indicating babes at the breast (1 Peter 2:2).[11] Luke says that Jesus blessed infants, those who could not survive on their own (Acts 7:19).

Finally, we have every reason to believe that God cares for our infants and disabled persons more than we do: "Evangelicals generally agree that such persons will be in heaven."[12]

Will There Be Sorrow in Heaven over Those in Hell?

A hard question is whether believers will miss their loved one and friends who did not trust Christ as Savior. Scripture presents us as finally being on the new earth and so in love with God that all other loves pale by comparison. Still, the question nags at us.

First, we know that God and his judgments are just, as the Scripture affirms (Deut. 32:4; Rom. 2:2–5). But God is also a reluctant Judge: he "is patient toward you, not wishing that any should perish, but that all should reach repentance" (2 Peter 3:9). And so Christians pray, asking God to save those whom they love most.

11. William F. Arndt and F. Wilbur Gingrich, *A Greek-English Lexicon of the New Testament and Other Early Christian Literature*, 2nd ed. (Chicago: University of Chicago Press, 1979), 147.

12. Christopher W. Morgan and Robert A. Peterson, *Faith Comes by Hearing: A Response to Inclusivism* (Downers Grove, IL: InterVarsity Press, 2008), 243–44. One example is Ronald H. Nash, *When a Baby Dies: Answers to Comfort Grieving Parents* (Grand Rapids: Zondervan, 1999).

Second, it is on the basis of this righteous judgment that God sends people to hell. The blood of the righteous, slain by those opposed to God, calls out to him for justice (Rev. 6:9–11). And justice is what God finally gives to all those who refuse his offer of salvation, consigning them to eternal punishment.

Third, the Scriptures affirm something that is inconceivable at present: we will praise God for showing his justice. We all want justice, especially when we are victims. And justice is what John sees in his vision of the future. The angel calls the saints to praise God for the fall of Babylon: "Rejoice over her, O heaven, and you saints and apostles and prophets, for God has given judgment for you against her!" (Rev. 18:20). God is both just and loving, and we will praise him for both attributes on that day—for his justice toward the wicked and his grace toward the righteous.

Moreover, the great multitude in heaven will praise God: "Hallelujah! Salvation and glory and power belong to our God, for his judgments are true and just; for he has judged the great prostitute . . . and has avenged on her the blood of his servants" (Rev. 19:1–2). Oliphint and Ferguson help us: "so clear will be our vision of the holiness of God and the sinfulness of man, and so full our deliverance from the presence of sin in our own hearts, that we will be able unhesitatingly to recognize God's absolute righteousness in his acts of judgment."[13]

So, then: Will there be sorrow in heaven over those who are in hell? No, since in the new creation God "will wipe away every tear from their eyes, and death shall be no more, neither shall there be mourning, nor crying, nor pain anymore, for the former things have passed away" (Rev. 21:4).

Will Everyone Go to Heaven?

Universalism holds that all humanity will be saved. Its history and details are beyond our present scope.[14] We will focus on the

13. Oliphint and Ferguson, *If I Should Die before I Wake*, 93.
14. See J. I. Packer, "Universalism: Will Everyone Ultimately Be Saved?" in *Hell under Fire*, ed. Christopher W. Morgan and Robert A. Peterson (Grand Rapids: Zondervan, 2004), 169-94..

three biblical arguments that universalists use to support their position. First, universalists use texts expressing God's desire to save all. Their favorite is: "This is good, and it is pleasing in the sight of God our Savior, who desires all people to be saved and to come to the knowledge of the truth" (1 Tim. 2:3–4; see also 1 Tim. 4:10; 2 Peter 3:9).

Paul urges that prayers be made "for all people, for kings and all who are in high positions," that Christians might enjoy "a peaceful and quiet life" (1 Tim. 2:1–2). Roman officials opposed the churches; the infamous Nero was emperor when Paul wrote 1 Timothy. In verse 4, Paul motivates readers to pray even for ungodly rulers. He does not teach that all will eventually be saved but that God wants the gospel to reach all.

Second, universalists also argue from passages that allegedly speak of the unlimited outcome of Christ's crucifixion. They most frequently cite: "Therefore, as one trespass led to condemnation for all men, so one act of righteousness leads to justification and life for all men" (Rom. 5:18; see also John 12:32; Col. 1:20).

The "one act of righteousness" in Romans 5:18 refers to Jesus' death. But this verse does not support universalism, as the next verse reveals: "For as by the one man's disobedience the *many* were made sinners, so by the one man's obedience the *many* will be made righteous" (Rom. 5:19). We cannot press the two occurrences of "all" in verse 18 ("condemnation for all . . . justification and life for all") any more than we can press the two occurrences of "many" in verse 19. Rather, "many" and "all" here are relative terms that are contrasted with the "one" trespass of Adam and with the "one" act of righteousness of Jesus Christ. These contrasts emphasize the great effects of Adam and Christ on the human race. In fact, Paul restricts salvation to "those who receive the abundance of grace and the free gift of righteousness" (v. 17).

Third, the most popular argument for universalism is that Paul teaches the final restoration of all people. The favorite text is: "For as in Adam all die, so also in Christ shall all be made alive. . . . Then the Son himself will also be subjected to him who put all things in subjection under him, that God may be all in all" (1 Cor. 15:22, 28).

These verses do not teach universalism. First Corinthians 15:22 should be understood in light of the following verse, which qualifies "so also in Christ shall all be made alive" when it says, "But each in his own order: Christ the firstfruits, then at his coming those who belong to Christ" (v. 23). "All" of verse 22, then, is equivalent to "those who belong to Christ" (v. 23).

Last, we turn to 1 Corinthians 15:28, which speaks of God's being "all in all." This and similar passages (Eph. 1:10; Phil. 2:9–11), if taken alone, are compatible with universalism. But it is plain from other verses in the books where these verses appear that they do not teach that all will be saved. Universalists argue their case from only a portion of the biblical data and fail to take the whole Bible into account. As a result, universalism offers a false hope that inhibits Christian missions.

Questions for Study and Reflection

Introduction

1. Why do people seek information about heaven in the wrong places (pp. 2–3)?

2. What does *sola Scriptura* mean (pp. 4–5)? Why is it important when discussing heaven?

3. Do you ever resemble the person with his eyes "in the gutter" (p. 9)?

4. In what three ways does the Bible speak of *heaven* (pp. 10–12)?

5. Why is the intermediate state not our final home (p. 12)?

6. With which of the five pictures of heaven are you most familiar? Least familiar?

Chapter 1—Creation Marred

1. In what ways does his creation reflect the Creator (pp. 20–21)?

2. Why is it essential to include our bodies when we think of the image of God (pp. 22–23)?

3. Describe the effects of the curse on the world, human beings, and their work (pp. 24–26).

4. How do Jesus' miracles in the Gospels anticipate the new heavens and earth (pp. 30–31)?

5. Why are our lives in this fallen world such a struggle (pp. 28–29)? What is our source of hope amid the struggle?

6. Why is it important to understand common grace (p. 29)?

Chapter 2—Creation Renewed

1. Explain how Paul regards the redemption of believers as a microcosm of the redemption of creation (pp. 35–36).

2. If 2 Peter 3 does not speak of the annihilation of our present world, what does it speak of (pp. 36–38)?

3. Describe our resurrection bodies (4pp. 1–42).

4. How will our relationships be enhanced on the new earth (pp. 43–45)?

5. Revelation 21:24 says that "the kings of the earth will bring their glory into" the city (p. 48). What cultural artifacts will you be eager to see on the new earth?

6. How should our hope for the new heavens and earth affect our view of ecology (pp. 48–49)?

Chapter 3—Disturbed Rest

1. What does it mean for God to rest (Gen. 2:2–3; pp. 55–57)?

2. Does *rest* mean "inactivity" (p. 57)? Explain.

3. Explain the connection between God's presence and rest (pp. 58–59).

4. Tell how the fall disrupted harmony, work, and having a home (pp. 59–61).

5. How was the Promised Land both rest and the promise of greater rest (pp. 62–63)?

6. In what ways does King Jesus bring rest that King David could not bring (pp. 65–66)?

Chapter 4—Perfect Rest

1. In what sense will our works done now endure in heaven (pp. 71–72)?

2. Are inheritance and rewards the same (pp. 73–74)? Explain.

3. What did God do to remove the curse from us (pp. 74–75)?

4. How will the last judgment bring rest from wars (p. 76)?

5. What is God's final solution to the problem of homelessness (pp. 77–80)?

6. What aspect of rest are you most looking forward to (pp. 70–80)?

Chapter 5—The Kingdom at War

1. How does the creation account show that God is King over his people (pp. 86–88)?

2. In what sense are human beings servant-kings (pp. 88–90)?

3. How did the tempter employ his two favorite weapons— deception and seduction—in the garden of Eden (pp. 90–91)? How does he still employ them today?

4. Tell how the story of the exodus is a story of warfare (pp. 94–96).

5. How was Jesus' death a mighty victory over Satan and the deliverance of God's people (pp. 98–99; pp. 101–2)?

6. Explain how the parables of the kingdom help us to make sense of God's work in our world (p. 101).

Chapter 6—The Kingdom at Peace

1. Do some Christians focus on Satan too much? Do some of us do so too little? Explain.

2. How should it affect our present attitudes that God's enemies and ours will meet certain defeat in the end (pp. 116–19)?

3. How do you encounter seduction and/or deception? What does Christ's victory mean for these two foes in the future? Now?

4. Tell why death is so hurtful now. How will it be overcome in the future (pp. 113–14)?

5. Why do Christians fight one another? How can this be corrected (p. 117)?

6. Why do some endure and others do not? What is the antidote to the poison of apostasy (pp. 118–19)?

Chapter 7—Banished from God's Presence

1. What difference does it make to understand Eden as God's first temple and royal palace (pp. 124–27)?
2. Why do Adam and Eve try to hide from God (pp. 127–28)?
3. Why is God's banishment of our first parents from Eden an act of grace (p. 129)?
4. Tell how the tabernacle enables God to dwell among his people without defiling his holiness (pp. 130–32).
5. Explain how Jesus is the true tabernacle and temple (pp. 134–36).
6. What are God's goals for dwelling in his temple, the church (pp. 129–36)?

Chapter 8—Blessed with God's Presence

1. It is reasonable to assume that the first readers of Revelation could understand the book. How does this fact help us (p. 139)?

2. Show how the New Jerusalem pictures the people of God (Rev. 21:2, 9–10; pp. 141–42).

3. What does John's description of the city teach us about the final salvation of God's people (pp. 144–46)?

4. What is John's point when he describes the New Jerusalem in terms of gold and precious jewels (p. 145)?

5. What does the fact that the city is modeled after the temple and the Holy of Holies say about the city (pp. 143–50)?

6. Why is there no tabernacle or temple in the New Jerusalem (p. 150)?

Chapter 9—Exchange of Glory

1. Explain how being created in God's image involves human beings' ruling as stewards of all creation (p. 150).

2. How does humankind collectively reflect God's glory in a greater way than individuals do (pp. 162–63)?

3. Tell how individually and collectively we have exchanged God's glory for pseudo-glory (pp. 163–64).

4. What is the significance of the fact that fallen men and women still reflect God's glory in part (p. 165)?

5. Tell how Christ restores our glory (pp. 165–67).

6. Explain how one of God's grand purposes in restoring our glory is to perfect the church in unity (p. 167).

Chapter 10—Brilliance in Glory

1. How can our anticipation of bodily resurrection help us to deal with weakness, illness, and disability now (pp. 170–71)?

2. Tell how Christ's death *and* resurrection guarantee our glory (p. 171).

3. What does it mean that "the righteous will shine like the sun" (Matt. 13:43) (pp. 171–72)?

4. Imagine what it will be like to be confirmed in perfect righteousness (pp. 174–75).

5. Why is it imperative to distinguish God's acceptance from heavenly reward (pp. 175–77)?

6. What does it mean to you that because of God's glory we will be able to love God, one another, and ourselves truly (pp. 181–83)?

Conclusion

1. How can our hope of future bodily resurrection transform our lives now (pp. 186–88)?

2. Why is it so vital to underline the necessity of learning about heaven from Scripture (pp. 188–89)?

3. What impact should Christ's triumph in his death and resurrection have on our struggles (pp. 189–90)?

4. Explain how God's presence will produce perfect joy in the end and how it can increase our joy now (pp. 190–92).

5. Do we see the connection between heaven and holiness? How can Roy's story help us all? How can it especially help males (pp. 190–92)?

6. In what sense will we share God's glory at the end? How can this knowledge help us now (pp. 194–96)?

Select Resources on Heaven

Alcorn, Randy. *Heaven*. Wheaton, IL: Tyndale, 2004.

Augustine. *The City of God*, translated by Thomas Merton. New York: Modern Library, 1994.

Bavinck, Herman. *The Last Things: Hope for This World and the Next*. Grand Rapids: Baker Academic, 1996.

————. *Reformed Dogmatics*, edited by John Bolt, translated by John Vriend. 4 vols. Grand Rapids: Baker, 2004.

Beale, G. K. *The Book of Revelation: A Commentary on the Greek Text*. New International Greek Testament Commentary. Grand Rapids: Eerdmans, 1999.

Boa, Kenneth, and Robert M. Bowman Jr. *Sense and Nonsense about Heaven and Hell*. Grand Rapids: Zondervan, 2007.

Conyers, A. J. *The Eclipse of Heaven*. Downers Grove, IL: InterVarsity Press, 1992.

Davies, Eryl. *Heaven Is a Better Place*. Darlington, UK: Evangelical Press, 1999.

Dixon, Larry. *Heaven: Thinking Now about Forever*. Camp Hill, PA: Christian Publications, 2002.

Hoekema, Anthony A. *The Bible and the Future*. Grand Rapids: Eerdmans, 1979.

Lewis, C. S. *Made for Heaven: And Why on Earth It Matters*. San Francisco: Harper, 2005.

————. *The Weight of Glory and Other Addresses*. San Francisco: Harper San Francisco, 1980.

McDannell, Colleen, and Bernhard Lang. *Heaven: A History*. 2nd ed. New Haven, CT: Yale University Press, 2001.

McGrath, Alister E. *A Brief History of Heaven*. Malden, MA: Blackwell Publishing, 2003.

Metzger, Bruce M. *Breaking the Code: Understanding the Book of Revelation*. Nashville: Abingdon Press, 1999.

Oliphint, K. Scott, and Sinclair B. Ferguson. *If I Should Die before I Wake*. Grand Rapids: Baker, 1995.

Poythress, Vern Sheridan. *The Returning King: A Guide to the Book of Revelation*. Phillipsburg, NJ: P&R Publishing, 2000.

Russell, Jeffrey Burton. *A History of Heaven: The Singing Silence*. Princeton, NJ: Princeton University Press, 1997.

Strachan, Owen, and Douglas A. Sweeney. *Jonathan Edwards on Heaven and Hell*. The Essential Edwards Collection. Chicago: Moody, 2010.

Toon, Peter. *Heaven and Hell: A Biblical and Theological Overview*. Nashville: Nelson, 1986.

Venema, Cornelis P. *Christ and the Future*. Carlisle, PA: Banner of Truth, 2008.

Walls, Jerry L. *Heaven: The Logic of Eternal Joy*. Oxford: Oxford University Press, 2002.

Wright, N. T. *Surprised by Hope: Rethinking Heaven, the Resurrection, and the Mission of the Church*. New York: HarperOne, 2008.

Index of Scripture and Other Writings

Genesis
1:1—10, 19–20
1:3—87
1:6–7—87
1:6–8—10
1:7–8—10
1:9—87
1:9–10—10
1:11—87
1:11–12—21
1:14–15—87
1:21—21
1:22—21
1:24—87
1:25—21
1:26—159
1:26–28—88–89, 162
1:27—88, 160–62
1:28—21, 25, 29, 159, 161
1:30—124
2:2–3—55, 58
2:3—125
2:7—21, 22, 124
2:8—57, 58, 125
2:9—125–26
2:11–12—22, 126
2:15—23, 29, 57–59, 126
2:15–17—131
2:15–24—124
2:16–17—128
2:17—23, 91, 114, 129

2:18—23
2:18–20—161
2:18–25—161
2:19–20—127
2:23—2, 161
2:24—23, 162
2:25—127
3:1—90, 104n2
3:4–5—91
3:6—128
3:7—127
3:8—59, 79, 127–28
3:9–13—92
3:10—127
3:14–19—92
3:15—59, 61, 92
3:16—25
3:17—24, 60
3:17–19—60
3:18—26
3:19—26
3:22—129
3:22–24—92
3:23–24—61
3:24—126, 129
4—91
4:12—61
4:13—61
5:28–29—60
6:5—92
6:14—146n8

221

7:15—22
7:22—22
8—148
9:6—165
9:8–17—131
12:1–3—131
12:2–3—167
13:10—124
13:14–17—93
14:17–24—93
14:21—93
14:22–23—94
15:7–21—131
15:13—19
15:13–14—94
15:18—88
17:1–21—131
17:8—186
17:18—33
21:22—135
22:1–19—148
22:17—10
25:29–34—163
26:24—135
28:15—135
47:27—95
48:21—135

Exodus
1—95
2—27n13
3:1–2—148
3:8—63
3:12—130, 135
3:19—95
12:1–9—130
12:33–36—95
14—95
15:1—95
15:11—190

15:13–14—130
15:17—148
15:21—95
19—130
19:1–6—95
19:4—130
19:4–6—96
19:5—147
19:5–6—183
19:6—96
19:12–13—130
20—56
20:3—164
20:8–11—57–58
20:18–19—130
20:19—191
24:9–11—148
24:16–18—148
25:8—131
25:9—150
25:11–13—145
25:24–28—145
25:40—131, 150
26:29—145
26:37—145
27:1—146n8
27:8—131
27:13–16—126
28:15–30—146
28:16—146n8
28:29—147
29:45–46—131
30:1–2—146n8
31:14—56
31:16—56
32:1–6—164
33:14—58, 62
36:15–16—146n8
40:34–35—194
40:34–38—132

Leviticus
11:44—191
19:31—200
20:6—201
25:2—56
26:3–13—131
26:9–12—79
26:11—135
26:11–12—134, 142
26:11–13—131–32
26:12—136
26:14–45—131

Numbers
3:7–8—126
16:30—27n13
18:5–6—126

Deuteronomy
5:12—56
5:15—56
6:3—63
6:5—82, 207
11:16—126
12:10—62
17:18–20—96
18:10–12—201
18:15–22—6, 203
18:21–22—6
25:5–6—44
29:9—63
29:29—8
31:16–20—87
32:4—209

Joshua
1:5—136
1:13—62
1:15—62
4:3—62

4:6–7—62
4:19–24—62
11:23—63
14:15—63
21:44—63
22:5—126

Judges
3:11—63
3:30—63
5:31—63
8:28—63

1 Samuel
8:5—96
8:20—96
9:2—96
15—96
17:25—96
17:26—97
17:33—97
17:34–36—97

2 Samuel
5:2—97
7:1—64
7:8–16—64
7:10–11—66, 76
7:14–16—97
8:11–12—89

1 Kings
4:24—89
5—132
5:2–5—104
5:3—89
6:20—146
7:40–42—146n8
8:10–11—132
8:22–61—132

8:57—132, 135
8:58—132, 135
8:60—135
11:38—136
18:20–40—148
19:8–18—148
21:2—125n4

2 Kings
21:6—201
23:24—201
25:9—132

1 Chronicles
23:32—126

2 Chronicles
3:1—148
6:14—58

Esther
1:5—125

Job
1:6–12—104n2

Psalms
2:8—97
2:9—97
8:5—160, 169, 194
8:5–6—89
8:6—160
8:7—160
10:16—189
16:11—123, 126, 151, 192
19:1—20
23:1–2—97
23:5–6—77
33:11—70
34:21—28

37:1—102
43:3—149
46:10—82
47:7—189
72:12–14—90
92:7—102
93:1–2—92
94:13—63
95—70
103:19—92
106:19–20—164
110:1—97–98
121:4—56
132:8—58
132:14—58
139:7–12—21n5
147:5—206
148:6—87

Proverbs
25:16—163
25:27—163

Ecclesiastes
2:4–5—126
2:8—126
3:13—46

Isaiah
6:3—190, 194
6:5—191
8:19–20—201
11:1–5—97
11:6–11—98
11:9—46
14:24—70
25:6—149
25:8—149
40:9—141
40:28—56

51:3—124, 126
52:1—141, 144
57:20—63
60—48
60:19—172
61:1—99
61:1–2—30
61:10—141
62:3—170, 173
62:5—173
62:6—141
65:17—13, 34
65:19—34
65:20–23—34
65:24–25—104
66:22–23—13, 34

Jeremiah
1:8—136
2:2—141
2:11–13—163
6:16—67
10:10—189
31:3—188

Ezekiel
10:1–22—132
28:13–14—148
31:8—125
31:9—125
34:11–31—98
34:23–24—100
34:27–28—100
36:35—125n2
40:1–2—147
41:21—146n8
43:16–17—146n8
45:2—146n8
48:20—146n8

Daniel
2:35—149
2:45—149
4:35—92, 104n2, 160
7—149
7:22—115
7:26–27—115
11:31—152
12:3—171

Hosea
4:7—164
6:7—131

Joel
2:3—125n2

Habakkuk
2:14—46
2:16–20—164

Haggai
2:4—136
2:9—169

Matthew
1:1—98
5:5—48, 144
5:13–16—167
5:45—29, 165n11
6:21—190
6:24—111
7:21–23—119
10:32—175
11:3—65
11:4–6—65
11:8–10—65
11:28–30—65
11:29—66–67
11:30—66

12:23—100
12:24—100
12:29—100
12:32—199–200
12:38—202
12:39—202
13:21—101
13:22—101
13:24–30—27, 101
13:31–32—101
13:33—101
13:43—171
13:47–50—101
16:18—102
17:1–18—149
17:2—194
18:1—205
19:27—34
19:28—35
19:28–29—34
19:29—35
20:1–16—205
22:30—44, 46, 174
22:37—82, 207
24:36–44—7
25:13—7
25:14–30—176, 179, 206
25:21—176, 179
25:23—47, 179
25:26–27—177
25:34—85, 118, 144, 192
25:41—38
25:46—35, 118, 200
26:41—172
28:9–10—208
28:16–17—208
28:18—138
28:18–20—134
28:20—198

Mark
1:15—100
4:39—27
4:41—27
8:36—50
12:18–27—174n6
14:38—42

Luke
1:28—136
4:16–21—99
4:18–19—30
5:8—191
5:12–13—30
8:19–21—44
9:29—194
11:15—100
11:20—30, 100
13:1–5—27n13
13:22—111
16—201
16:13—111
16:22—202
16:27–31—5, 76
18:15—209
18:30—205
19:12–27—206
20:27–38—174n6
22:69—102
23:43—12, 35, 198
24:16—208
24:31—173
24:31–43—208

John
1:1—132
1:14—132, 163, 191
2:19–22—36
3:16—204

3:18—12
3:29—141
3:36—12
5:28–29—200
5:39–44—180
5:44—182
6:44—29, 176
6:65—29
8:34—193
8:36—47
8:44—91
8:51—98
8:53—98
8:58—98
9:1–7—27n13
10:11—98
10:17—98
10:17–18—36
11:4—202n9
11:15—202n9
11:25—202n9
11:24–25—114
12:31—99, 190
12:32—211
14:1–3—78, 137
14:2—78
14:6—67
14:9—167
14:16–17—133
14:21—175–76
14:23—78, 133, 176
15:5—72
16:11—99
16:13—28
17:3—12, 35
17:21—137
17:22—194
17:22–23—167
17:23—183

20:16—208
20:19—173
20:28—208

Acts
1:6—116
1:7—7
1:9–12—149
2—133
2:23—70
2:32—171n1
2:36—171
3:26—171n1
4:10—171n1
5:30–31—171n1
7:19—209
7:44—150
10:40—171n1
13:6—111
13:30—171n1
13:48—134
15:10—66
17:25—160
17:31—171n1
18:10—135n10

Romans
1:20—20
1:23—21n5
1:25—21n5, 164
2:2–5—209
2:7—180
3:23—164
3:25—177
4:15—115
4:17—87
5:1—115
5:5—176–77
5:8–11—177n9

5:10—171
5:12–21—131n9
5:17—113, 211
5:18—211
5:19—73, 204, 211
6—117
6:4–5—171
6:5—171
6:10—100
6:12–19—28
6:18—100
6:22—100
6:23—204
7:1–2—44
7:15–20—117
7:18—172
8:1—177
8:1–3—100
8:3—133
8:9–11—171
8:11—36, 174
8:14–17—113
8:16–17—73, 118
8:17—205
8:18—9, 35, 194, 204
8:18–23—13
8:19–20—27
8:19–23—35
8:20—23
8:20–21—37
8:20–22—36
8:20–23—80
8:21—35, 36
8:22—27
8:22–23—31, 37
8:23—28, 35, 171, 189
8:26—31
8:28–30—119
8:32—205
8:33–39—151, 178

8:35–39—102
8:37—118, 178
9:33—175
12:1–2—47
12:3—111
13:14—116
15:4—179

1 Corinthians
3:1–9—117
3:13—200
3:13–15—48
3:15—199–200
3:16—133, 191
3:21–23—206
6:2—115
6:3—170
6:19—191
7:31—113, 180
7:39—44
9:25—203–4
12:12–26—205
12:24–26—117, 153
13:9–12—207
13:9–13—167n13
13:10–12—207
13:12—173, 182, 206–7
15:3–8—171
15:12–22—171
15:20—36
15:20–23—171
15:21—113
15:22—131n9, 212
15:23—167, 212
15:23–28—101
15:24–28—44
15:26—107, 113, 189–90
15:28—212
15:35—172
15:36–39—172

15:37—41
15:41–44—174
15:42—41
15:42–44—40
15:42–49—12
15:43—41–42, 171
15:44—42
15:45—131n9
15:51–53—167
15:52–53—40
15:53–54—41
15:54—113
15:54–57—113
15:57—99
15:58—48, 187

2 Corinthians
2:14—99
3:18—165, 167, 180, 194
4:4—165
4:6—165
4:16–18—170
4:17—35, 179, 194
5:1–9—78
5:6–9—114
5:8—12, 35, 186
5:21—73, 115
6:16—134, 152
9:15—152
10:3–6—28
11:3—109, 190
12:2—11
12:1–5—202

Galatians
2:20—189
3:28—174n6
4:4–7—100
4:5–7—118
4:7—73

3:13—74
3:13–14—177n9
5:5—204
5:19–21—201
5:22–23—72
5:26—182
6:3—111

Ephesians
1:3–8—177n9
1:4–5—209
1:4–6—188
1:7—191, 209
1:10—212
1:13–14—171, 209
1:20—102
2:4–6—115
2:4–7—176
2:10—70
2:14–16—117
2:18–22—133
2:19—77
4:1–6—133
4:4–5—166
4:24—112
5:27—113
5:31–32—44
6:10–18—116
6:11—118
6:12—28, 117, 189
6:13—118
6:14—118

Philippians
1:20–23—35
1:21–23—114
1:23—12, 190, 198
2:9–11—212
2:13—72
3:14—119

3:20–21—12, 41
3:21—115, 167n11, 171

Colossians
1:13–14—99
1:15—163, 165, 167
1:16—11, 164
1:18—165
1:20—211
1:27—165, 180
1:29—29, 177
2:6—116
2:8—111
2:8–15—177n9
2:13–15—100
2:14—74
2:17—44
3:1—170
3:1–2—9
3:1–3—116
3:2–4—177n9
3:3—167n11, 178
3:3–4—170
3:4—171, 195
3:5–17—28
3:10—165
3:23–4—73
3:24—73
3:24–25—72

1 Thessalonians
1:1—204
2:19—203–4
2:19–20—204
4:13–17—114
4:14—199n2
4:16–17—13
5:6—14, 111
5:8—111

5:23—200
5:23–24—115, 174

2 Thessalonians
1:5–9—38
2:14—195, 204

1 Timothy
2:1–2—211
2:3–4—211
2:4—211
4:8—49, 74
4:1–3—203
4:10—211

2 Timothy
2:12—115
2:13—72
4:8—203–4

Titus
2:11–14—177n9
2:13—192
3:5—34
3:5–7—177n9

Hebrews
1:2–3—166
1:3—163, 191
1:13—169
2:5–8—101
2:5–10—166
2:9—194
2:9–11—177n9
2:10—166
2:10–18—119
2:11–12—44
2:14–15—26, 99
3:7–4:16—67

4:2–3—71
4:9—71
4:9–10—70
4:13—206
4:14—71, 191
4:16—191
6:1–2—171
6:9–12—190
6:10—71
6:10–12—119
6:11–12—71
6:13–14—186
7:24—191
7:25—191
8:1–2—150
8:5—44
9:11–24—133
9:23–27—133
9:24—150
9:27—202
10:1—44
10:10—200
10:35–36—71
11:3—20, 87, 164
11:6—71, 179
11:10—186
11:13—72, 76, 186
11:16—72
11:23–26—119
12:2—102, 119
12:3—119
12:23—42, 82, 173, 199, 202
13:8—70
13:12—200
13:20–21—101

James
1:11—180
1:12—203–4

1:14—108
2:10—181
2:14–26—72
3:9—29, 165
4:3—167
4:4—111
4:7—81

1 Peter
1:3—11
1:3–4—180
1:3–5—166
1:3–7—180
1:3–9—177n9
1:4—182
1:4–5—73
1:13—111, 190
1:16—191
1:18–19—100
1:18–25—180
2:2—209
2:5—133–34
2:9—183
2:24—178
2:25—101
3:9—180
5:1—195
5:1–5—180
5:2–4—180
5:4—203–5
5:8—75, 101
5:9–10—81
5:10—195

2 Peter
1:3—8, 197
1:17–18—149
2:1—111
3:6—37

231

3:7—13, 36–38
3:9—209, 211
3:10—37, 38
3:10–12—36
3:10–13—13, 36
3:12—37, 38
3:12–13—38
3:13—38, 104, 115, 144, 175

1 John
1:1–2—189
1:3—192
2:15–17—73, 110
2:16—111
2:17—180
3:1—176
3:2—41, 167, 174
3:2–3—14, 115, 167n11, 193
3:2–5—175
3:5—175
3:7—111
4:1—111
4:1–3—203
4:3–6—203
4:9—188
4:9–12—176
4:10—188
4:17–18—181
4:19—181
5:4—178
5:4–5—118

Jude
5–7—104n2
9—118
24—175

Revelation
1:3—138
1:5–6—190

1:6—178, 183
1:11—139
1:12–16—140
1:13—141
1:14—175
1:17—191
1:17–20—140
1:19—139
1:20—140
2–3—178
2:7—178
2:11—178
2:13—104
3:5—112
3:10—110n9
3:21—105, 170, 189
4:2–5:1—105
4:5—140n5
4:10–11—203
5:4—138
5:5–6—189
5:6—140n5
5:8—140n5
5:9–10—115, 137
6:9–11—210
6:10—102, 109
6:11—112
6:15–16—39
7:1–17—149
7:9—112
7:13–14—112, 140n5
7:14—112
7:17—101
8:13—110n9
10:5–7—106
11:4—140n5
11:8—140n5
11:10—110n9
11:15–18—107
12—28

12:1–17—107
12:2—101
12:3—104n3
12:9—91, 105, 112
12:10–11—112
12:12—110n9
13:1—39
13:1–3—104n3
13:1–10—107
13:2—104
13:4—107, 112
13:8—110n9
13:9–10—111
13:11–17—104n2
13:12–14a—110
13:14—110n9
13:18—111
14:1—149
14:6—110n9
14:8—107
14:10–11—76
14:13—70, 72, 74, 76, 139
15:1–22:5—106
15:2—39
15:4—191
16:10—104
16:13—110
16:13–14—140n5
17:1–14—107
17:3—107
17:4–5—108
17:9—140n5
17:12—140n5
17:14—102
17:15—140n5
17:18—140n5
18:3—108
18:4–5—117
18:20—210
18:21–23—109

18:24—108
19:1–2—210
19:6—189
19:6–8—112
19:6–10—148
19:7–8—141
19:8—112, 140n5
19:11–21—144
19:20—106, 110, 112
20:2—91, 140n5, 189
20:4—115
20:10—106, 112, 190
20:10–15—38
20:11—38–39
20:13–15—113
20:14—107
20:14–15—178
21—13, 138, 142
21:1—38, –40, 113, 142, 144
21:1–2—142–43
21:1–3—79
21:2—141–42
21:3—142–43, 192
21:3–4—75
21:3–8—142–43
21:4—107, 113, 171, 190, 192, 210
21:4–5—144
21:5—38, 139, 142
21:5–7—80
21:6—46
21:7—118, 144
21:7–8—200
21:8—140n5, 201
21:9–10—143
21:9–11—142
21:9–27—142, 145
21:10—147, 187
21:10–11—145
21:11—172
21:11–27—143

21:14—146
21:16—146
21:18—145
21:19–20—146
21:21—145
21:22—150
21:23—172, 194
21:24—48
21:25—144
21:27—115, 144
22:1—105

22:3—37, 47, 75, 144
22:3–5—115
22:14—192
22:16—76, 105
22:20—76

EXTRABIBLICAL SOURCES

2 Maccabees
12:42–45—199–200

Index of Subjects and Names

Abelard, Peter, 54

Abraham, 3, 5, 10, 33, 93–94, 98, 130–31, 135, 148, 186

acceptance by God, 133–34, 177, 182

Adam, 21–26, 57–61, 66, 77, 90–92, 111, 115, 123–31, 161–62, 194, 211

Alcorn, Randy, 219

angels, 3, 44, 76, 82, 106, 115, 118, 148, 164, 166, 169–70, 174

Augustine of Hippo, 173, 219

babies who die, 25, 41, 208–9

Bavinck, Herman, 22, 219

Baxter, Richard, 85–86

Beale, G. K., 91, 110, 116, 125–26, 140, 219

Blomberg, Craig, 177

Bock, Darrell L., 105,

bodies, our,
  in heaven, 12, 35–37, 40–43, 47, 113, 170–75, 186–87, 195–96, 207–8
  on earth, 11, 21–23, 28, 31, 49, 159, 182, 195–96, 202–3

bride of Christ, the church, 141–42, 150, 173

Burpo, Colton, 3

Burpo, Todd, 3

Camping, Harold, 7

Christ,
  death of, 14, 26, 67–69, 73–74, 76, 98–101, 113, 115, 117, 171, 176–78, 188–89, 194–95, 200, 211
  incarnation of, 26, 31, 132, 191
  resurrection of, 14, 76, 101, 113, 171, 176, 188–89, 195
  return of, 8, 46, 49, 85, 101, 116, 171, 175, 180, 200

church, 31, 44, 102, 111, 113, 117–18, 133–34, 139–41, 150–53, 191–92

Clines, David J. A., 22–23, 88–89, 159, 165

Clouse, Robert. G., 105

Collins, C. John, 18, 129, 161,

comfort, 28, 67, 140, 152,

community, 152–53, 163

creation, 17–24, 53–59, 86–90, 124–28, 159–63

crowns, 89, 160, 170, 180, 203–5

curse, 24–26, 36–37, 46–47, 59–61, 74–75, 92, 114–15, 131–32

Dante, 205–6

date–setting for the second coming, 5–8

David, 64–66, 70, 76–78,
    89–90, 96–101, 105–6
death, 1–2, 41, 44, 100–101,
    107, 113–14, 129, 144,
    186–91, 198–200, 202–10
deception, 91, 107–11, 189–90
delight in God. *See* joy
devil, 26–28, 75, 81–82, 90–91,
    99, 101, 104–12, 118–19, 189
disembodied souls, 186, 202
dominion, 29, 35, 88–89,
    159–62, 166
Donne, John, 113–14
dreams, 3–4, 188, 201
dwelling place of God, the
    heavenly, 10–11, 77–80,
    137, 142–50, 192

ecology, 48–50
Eden, the garden of, 21–25,
    47, 57–61, 91–92, 113–15,
    123–31, 148, 169, 191
Edwards, Jonathan, 78–79,
    123, 173, 220
enjoying God. *See* joy
environment, 48–50
eternal state, 12–13, 43–44, 67,
    72, 76, 186–88, 194, 204–5
Eve, 14, 18, 22–26, 58–59, 61,
    77, 90–92, 111, 124–30,
    148, 161–62, 194

fall (into sin), 24–26, 29, 41–43,
    47, 59–60, 69–70, 111,
    128–29, 136, 163–65, 194
family, 23, 43–44, 81, 92, 183
Ferguson, Sinclair, 9, 185,
    208, 210, 220
final state. *See* eternal state
Foh, Susan T., 25n

Gadsby, William, 26
George, Timothy, 171
Gerstner, John H., 173
glorification, 167, 206
glorifying God, 21, 73, 137,
    162, 175, 194–96
Goliath, 96–97
groaning, 26–28, 31, 35
Gurnall, William, 116

Hamilton, Victor P., 59
Hauerwas, Stanley, 44
heaven, meanings of the
    word, 10–13
hell, 38, 46, 51, 72, 76, 102, 106,
    112, 190, 200, 205, 209–12
Hendriksen, William, 102
hermeneutics, 7, 138–43
Hoekema, Anthony A., 40,
    159–60, 187, 219
Holy of Holies, 145–47, 150, 152
hope, 9–13, 35, 74, 79, 110–11,
    114, 132, 171, 175, 177,
    179–81, 187, 192–93, 204

image of God, 21–22, 25, 29,
    45, 57, 88–90, 119, 124–25,
    159–67, 172, 180–83
intermediate state, 11–13, 186
interpretation, biblical.
    See hermeneutics

Jehovah's Witnesses, 6
joy, 24, 34, 47, 56, 58, 60,
    119, 123, 126, 129, 151,
    176–79, 192, 195, 204

Kidner, Derek, 159
Kittel, Gerhard, 138

knowing God, 12, 35, 82, 131,
133, 186–88, 198, 206–7
knowledge, in heaven,
42–43, 46, 206–8
Köstenberger, Andreas J., 98

Lane, William L., 166
Lawrence, Brother, 151
levels in heaven, 205–6
Lewis, C. S., 43, 45, 109,
157–58, 219
Lot, 93–94, 124
love of God, 22, 78, 82, 98, 102,
133, 153, 158, 167, 175–79,
181, 183, 188, 196, 209
Lutzer, Erwin W., 176

marriage in heaven,
43–46, 174, 208
McGrath, Alister E., 9, 123, 219
Medley, Samuel, 26
Michaels, J. Ramsey, 110, 180
Miller, William, 5–6
mission, God's, 29, 31, 49–50, 92
Moo, Douglas J., 36, 74
Morris, Leon, 105, 110, 112–13
Moses, 3, 5, 19, 62, 94–96, 110,
118, 125–28, 130, 135–36,
148, 150, 191, 194
Mounce, Robert H., 72, 108
Mouw, Richard J., 48

near-death experiences (NDEs),
3, 188, 196, 202–3
new creation. See new heaven
and new earth
new heaven and new earth,
2, 33–40, 79, 114, 142,
159, 183, 186–87, 194

New Jerusalem, 44, 48, 79–80,
115, 141–50, 172, 187

O'Brien, Peter. T., 74
Oliphint, K. Scott, 9, 185,
208, 210, 220
Overstreet, R. Larry, 159

Page, Sydney H. T., 104
perseverance, 119, 190
Piper, Don, 3–4
present state, 11–12, 41, 207
purgatory, 199–200, 205

Ramsay, William Mitchell, 139n2
Ramsey, George W., 128
rapture, 7
recognizing others in
heaven, 207–8
Reichenbach, Bruce R., 88
rest, 53–82, 197–99
resurrection of believers'
bodies, 40–46, 113–16,
170–74, 182, 186–87
Revelation, the book of, interpretation of, 138–41
rewards, 47, 71–74, 176–79, 205–6
Rhodes, Ron, 6
rich man and Lazarus, 5, 76, 201
Richter, Sandra L., 18, 23–24
righteousness, 23–48, 73, 82,
98, 112–13, 115, 143–44,
174–74, 193, 203–4, 211
Roman Catholicism, 199–200
Ryken, Leland, 149

Sabbath rest for the people of
God, 54–57, 69–75, 187–89
Satan. See devil
satisfaction in heaven, 45, 205

Scripture, 4–11, 50, 57, 169, 179, 182, 186–89, 197–201
seduction, 91, 107–10, 189–90, 193
seeing God, 14, 149, 151, 175, 191, 206
serving God, 42, 46–47, 73, 111, 124–8, 176–79, 189–90, 206
sex in heaven, 45–46
sky, 10, 20, 39
sola Scriptura, 4–5, 196
sorcery, 201
sorrow in heaven, 149, 209–10
speculation, 5–8
stars, abode of, 10
Stott, John, 10–11
struggling, 27–29, 35, 73, 76, 82, 113, 117, 173, 192
Stuart, Douglas K., 95
suffering, 9, 75, 81, 114, 117, 153, 188, 194–95, 200

tabernacle, 58, 126, 128–34, 140, 145–46, 150, 191, 194
talking to the dead, 200–201
Taylor, David, 3
temple, 58, 80, 89, 104, 124–28, 130–35, 140, 143–50, 152, 164, 191
Trinity, 72–73, 104–5, 186, 205

trips to heaven, 2–5, 188
Twelftree, Graham, 30–31

union with Christ, 44, 103, 115–18, 118, 141, 152, 176, 178

Vasholz, Robert I., 25
victory, 60, 92–104, 106–18, 178, 189–90
visions, 3–4, 38–39, 76, 79, 104–06, 110, 112, 137–45, 147–50, 188
Von Rad, Gerhard, 128

Waddell, Helen, 55
Walters, Barbara, 2
Waltke, Bruce K., 159, 161
Walton, Izaak, 8–9
wandering, 61–62, 67, 77–80
war, 59–60, 65–66, 75–76, 89–97, 101–4
Wenham, Gordon J., 19, 56, 87, 90, 127
Whisenant, Edward, 7
work, 23–26, 46–50, 55–57, 59–61, 63, 66–67, 69–74, 80–81, 126, 187
Wright, N. T., 44, 171, 220